IMAGES
of America

WESTCHESTER TOWNSHIP

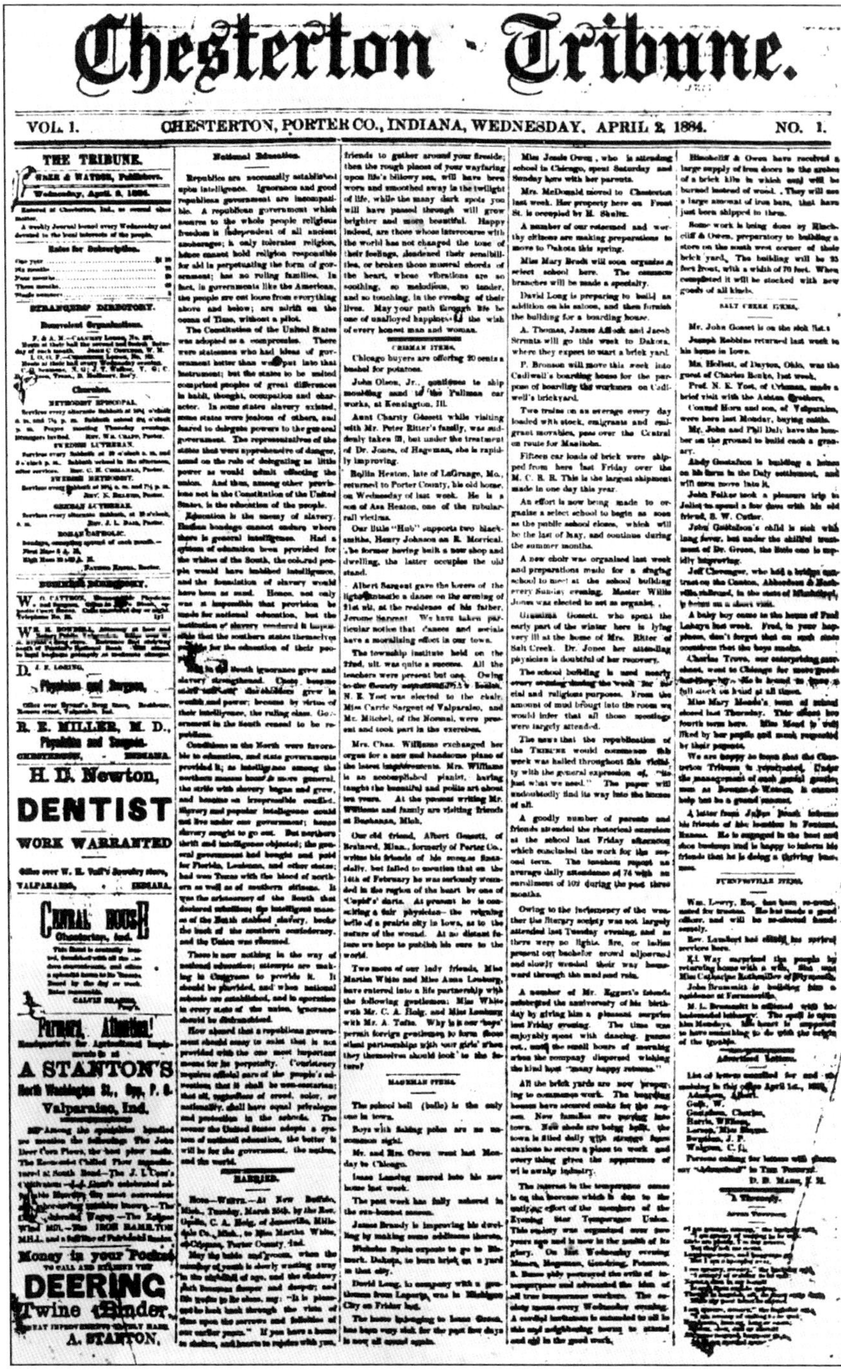

Chesterton Tribune.

VOL. 1. CHESTERTON, PORTER CO., INDIANA, WEDNESDAY, APRIL 2, 1884. NO. 1.

THE TRIBUNE.

H. D. Newton,

DENTIST

WORK WARRANTED

R. E. MILLER, M. D.,

Physician and Surgeon.

A STANTON'S

Valparaiso, Ind.

Money in your Pocket

DEERING

Twine Binder

A. STANTON.

The Chesterton Tribune. Arthur Bowser, a 21-year-old reporter for the *Valparaiso Vidette*, founded the *Chesterton Tribune* in 1884 and printed the first issue, seen above, on April 2 of that year. Northwest Indiana's oldest continuously published independent newspaper, the *Chesterton Tribune* continues to serve Westchester Township and neighboring Liberty, Jackson, and Pine Townships, publishing Monday through Friday, with a daily circulation of 5,261 in 1999.

IMAGES
of America

WESTCHESTER TOWNSHIP

Westchester Public Library

ARCADIA
PUBLISHING

ISBN 978-0-7385-9031-8

Published by Arcadia Publishing
Charleston, South Carolina

Printed in the United States of America

Library of Congress Catalog Card Number: 99-62620

For all general information contact Arcadia Publishing at:
Telephone 843-853-2070
Fax 843-853-0044
E-mail sales@arcadiapublishing.com
For customer service and orders:
Toll-Free 1-888-313-2665

Visit us on the Internet at www.arcadiapublishing.com

Dedicated to the memory of

William Murray "Bill" Bailey

Historian, volunteer, esteemed friend, and computer wizard.

(1923–1999)

WESTCHESTER PUBLIC LIBRARY
200 W. Indiana Avenue
Chesterton, IN 46304

Phil Baugher, DIRECTOR

ARCADIA BOOK PROJECT:
Jane Walsh-Brown, **EDITOR;** Sandra Trezzo, **ASSISTANT EDITOR**; Nancy Vaillancourt, **RESEARCHER**; Dan Bruhn, **PHOTOGRAPHER;** and Howard Johnson, **HISTORICAL CONSULTANT**

COMMITTEE: Jessie Affelder, Lucille Basista, Carol Cherepko, Sue Enamorado, Eva Hopkins, Lynne McGrath, Tama McGuire, and Arlene Prescott

Contents

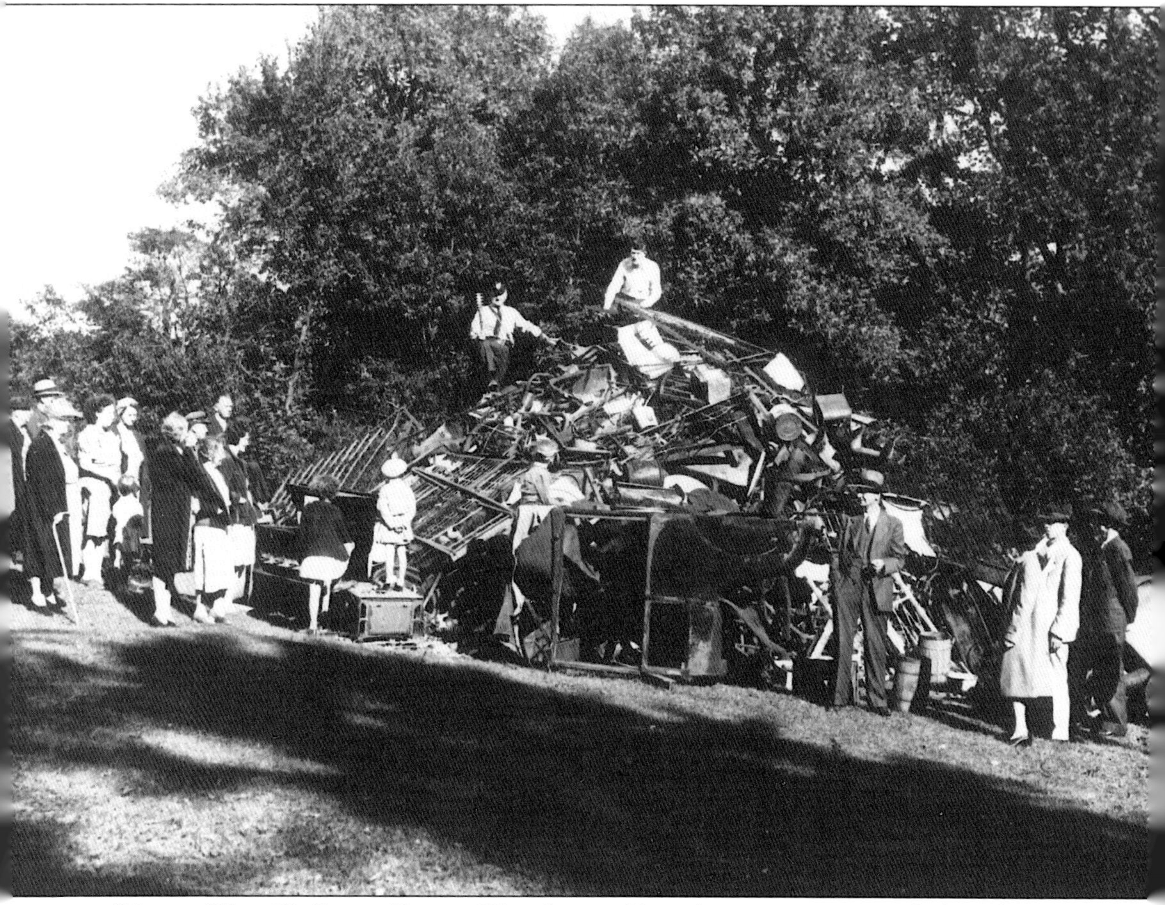

World War II Scrap Drive. Westchester Township citizens scoured their basements and garages in September of 1942 to salvage scrap metal in aid of the war effort. Chesterton Town Marshall Joe LaRoche, on the pile wearing a black tie and hat, is shown supervising the growing mountain of metal that arose in Railroad Park (now Thomas Centennial Park) in downtown Chesterton.

ACKNOWLEDGMENTS

We would like to thank all those who provided information and photographs for this book. Please note that photograph credits for institutions are included in the text. Individuals are credited in the Contributors list at the end of the book.

Foremost among those whom we wish to thank are the publisher and editor of the *Chesterton Tribune*, Warren Canright and David Canright, as well as all those who have worked as photographers for the paper. Their generous gift of the *Tribune's* photograph morgue forms the core of Westchester Public Library's Historic Photograph Collection, from which many of the photographs for this book were drawn. The microfilm copies of the full span of the paper served as our prime resource for our text. We would also like to thank those *Tribune* staff members who have researched and written numerous local history articles for the paper over its 115 year history.

Our special thanks also go to the many local professional photographers who have worked so diligently over the years to record the land and lives of Westchester Township and to preserve local historic photographs. In particular, we would like to acknowledge the contributions made to this book by Arthur Anderson, Dan Bruhn, Damon Dietrich, Reggie Pomeroy, John Saidla, and Don Swoverland.

We would also like to express our gratitude for the assistance provided by the following area residents who have graciously answered our many questions: Margaret Doyle, Martha Miller, Robert Griffin, Adeline Janowski, Margaret Larson, Steve McIntire, James Newman, James Ruge, Adelyne Ruoff, A. Henry Studebaker and I. Jo. Summers. In addition we acknowledge the contributions of the current and past members of the Duneland Historical Society whose public programs and research papers have done so much to preserve the history of Westchester Township.

We also owe a great debt to the generous help provided to us by our colleagues: Dorri Partsch, Janice Slupsky, and Jude Rakowski of the Indiana Dunes National Lakeshore; Steve McShane of the Calumet Regional Archives at Indiana University Northwest; Larry Clark and staff of the Genealogy Dept. of the Porter County Public Library; Al Loomis and Bonnie Cusson of the Historical Society of Porter County; Wendy Smith of the Indiana Dunes State Park; Dick Spurgin of the Prairie Club, and Amanda Holmes of the Historic American Buildings Survey.

Finally, we wish to express our thanks to the Duneland Millennium Celebration Committee for choosing to designate this book as one of the community's official Millennium projects. All proceeds from the book will benefit the Westchester Township Historical Museum, an educational service of Westchester Public Library.

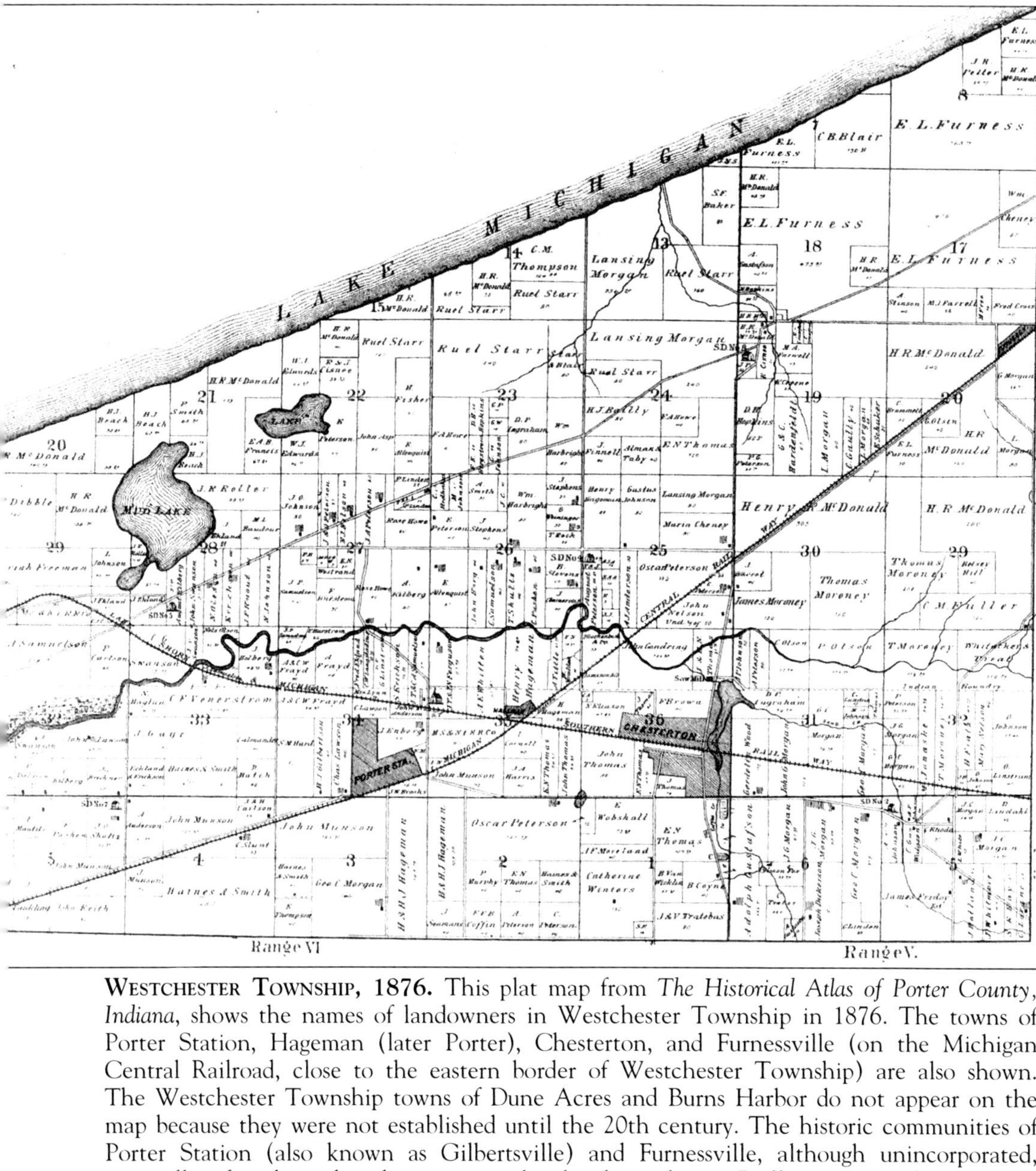

WESTCHESTER TOWNSHIP, 1876. This plat map from *The Historical Atlas of Porter County, Indiana*, shows the names of landowners in Westchester Township in 1876. The towns of Porter Station, Hageman (later Porter), Chesterton, and Furnessville (on the Michigan Central Railroad, close to the eastern border of Westchester Township) are also shown. The Westchester Township towns of Dune Acres and Burns Harbor do not appear on the map because they were not established until the 20th century. The historic communities of Porter Station (also known as Gilbertsville) and Furnessville, although unincorporated, are still referred to by these names by local residents. Baillytown, another historic community, was centered north of what is now Route 12, between Route 149 and the east gate of Bethlehem Steel.

A Brief History of Westchester Township

Location: Westchester Township, Porter County, Indiana, is located on the southern shore of Lake Michigan, about 50 miles southeast of Chicago. It stretches from the famous Indiana Dunes on its northern border, south to the Valparaiso Moraine, a ridge of rolling hills left by the last glacier to pass through the area.

First People: Part of a great continental crossroads, the land of Westchester Township was for thousands of years the home to a succession of early people attracted by its rich animal and plant life. The Miami and Potawatomi of the Great Lakes Woodland Culture were the last of the Native-American cultures to hunt and farm the township's densely forested land. Contact with the French fur traders known as *voyageurs* began about 1650. The resulting fur trade was initially beneficial to both cultures, but ultimately disastrous for the Potawatomi who, after selling their land to the U.S. government, were forcibly removed from Indiana in 1838.

Wars and Conquest: Control of the Great Lakes region passed to the British in 1763 with their victory over the French in the French and Indian War, and to the new nation of the United States at the conclusion of the American Revolution in 1783. What would later become Westchester Township formed part of the Northwest Territory, until the creation of the Indiana Territory in 1800. Following the federal government's purchase of land in northwestern Indiana from the Potawatomi in the treaties of 1826 and 1832, the area was added to the new state of Indiana, which had been created in 1816.

Founding Families: In 1822 Joseph Bailly, a French fur trader, moved with his wife Marie and their family to land that would become part of Westchester Township. He established a trading post on the Little Calumet River, the primary waterway in the township. The Bailly Homestead is now one of two historic homes included within the Indiana Dunes National Lakeshore. In 1833 Jesse and Jane Morgan and their seven children settled in the area southeast of the present town of Chesterton. They established a stage house on the Detroit to Fort Dearborn (now Chicago) stagecoach road, cleared their land, and began farming. They were followed the next year by the Thomas family, founders of Chesterton, and shortly thereafter by an influx of pioneers from the East Coast and southern states.

Founding of Towns: Porter County was organized in 1836 as were its townships, including Westchester, in the same year. The towns of Waverly and City West, two of the township's first three communities, were founded in the mid-1830s, but failed to thrive and are now just footnotes to history. The community of Coffee Creek fared better. Named after a nearby stream, it was settled in 1834 by the Thomas family, who platted it as the town of Calumet in 1852. The coming of the railroads to the area later the same year brought many changes to the community, including the change of the town's name to Chesterton.

Railroads, Immigration, and Growth of Industry: The building of the Lakeshore and Michigan Southern and the Michigan Central Railroads through the township in 1852 transformed the dusty little village from a strictly agricultural community to a thriving rail center offering far more than just agricultural products. Immigrants from Ireland, Germany, Sweden, and other countries were attracted to the area to help build and maintain the railroads and later to work in the organ, china, and brick factories that were established here. In addition to new industries, the steam railroads also spurred the growth of new towns such as Porter Station, Hageman (now Porter), Furnessville, and Baillytown.

POPULATION AND CULTURAL GROWTH: Between 1850 and 1910, the population of Westchester Township grew from 360 to 2,953 residents. During that time, numerous churches were established throughout the township and one-room schoolhouses were replaced by centralized schools in Chesterton and Porter. A great variety of civic and social groups were founded during the same 60-year period and both Chesterton (1869 and 1899) and Porter (1908) were incorporated.

DEPRESSION AND WORLD WARS: The period from 1910 to 1945 was one of great hardship but also wonderful new opportunities for area residents. While many local men and some women served in the military during the two world wars, citizens on the local home front contributed in efforts to increase farm production and worked in area factories and steel mills to produce parts for the military. In the 1920s women gained the right to vote (August 26, 1920), the town of Dune Acres was incorporated (1923), and township residents for the first time enjoyed such features of modern life as the automobile, electricity, and telephone service. The 1920s also saw the opening of the Indiana Dunes State Park and of the newly constructed Dunes Highway (Rt. 12), the first paved east-west road through Westchester Township. Although the Great Depression of 1929–1934 caused hardship for many of the residents of the township, vital businesses such as the *Chesterton Tribune* and Chesterton Bank survived the Depression, and New Deal programs such as the WPA and the CCC brought relief to those who were most in need.

1945–1998: Following World War II, Westchester Township experienced tremendous population growth as new residents flooded into the area to take advantage of new industrial jobs. Interstate Rt. 94 and the Indiana Tollroad Rt. 80/90 were built across the township, tying it closer both to Chicago and to the Eastern states. The town of Burns Harbor was incorporated in 1967 after it became the home of the county's largest employer, Bethlehem Steel. To meet the needs of the expanding population, new schools and libraries were built, a YMCA was founded, new businesses opened, and many new housing developments were constructed throughout the township. Citizens debated the Equal Rights Amendment, the Vietnam War, civil rights, and the environmental movement, but generally supported the successful campaign to prevent the construction of the Bailly Nuclear Plant on the shore of Lake Michigan, just west of Dune Acres. The creation of the Indiana Dunes National Lakeshore in 1966, although criticized by a small minority of local citizens, was applauded by most as means to safeguard and preserve the unique beauty of the Indiana Dunes.

THE PRESENT AND BEYOND 2000: As we stand on the brink of the new century, Westchester Township is a study in contrasts. Blessed with a vigorous economy and a diverse and energetic population of just over 17,000, the township is also home to the Indiana Dunes, one of the most beautiful and unusual natural areas in the Midwest. Our ability to maintain and protect this tenuous balance of opposites will be our legacy to the township residents of the new millennium.

To learn more about the history of Westchester Township, please visit Westchester Public Library's local history museum:

WESTCHESTER TOWNSHIP HISTORICAL MUSEUM, Jane Walsh-Brown, Curator
100 W. Indiana Avenue, Chesterton, IN 46304, (219) 921-0963
e-mail: museum@wpl.lib.in.us, website: http://wpl.lib.in.us/museum

One

LOCAL FACES

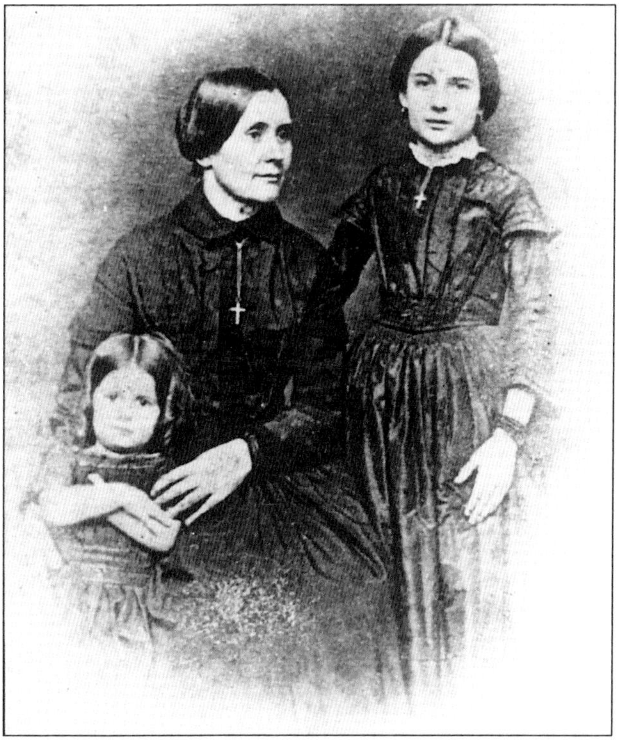

BAILLY FAMILY. Rose Bailly Howe, daughter of the first settler of Westchester Township, Joseph Bailly, is seen above in the early 1850s with her daughters. Her younger daughter Frances Rose is pictured on the left, and her elder daughter Rose Frances stands to the right. In 1907 Frances Howe published *The Story of a French Homestead in the Old Northwest*, an account of the history of her family. Her sister, Rose Frances Howe, an artist, lived on the Bailly Homestead until her death at about age 40. Frances died in 1917 while on a trip to Los Angeles. (Courtesy Indiana Dunes National Lakeshore, NPS.)

The history of Westchester Township is not so much the story of a place, as it is the story of the people who have made their homes within its boundaries. We begin this volume with images of some of those who have contributed to the diversity, economic growth, and rich culture of Westchester Township.

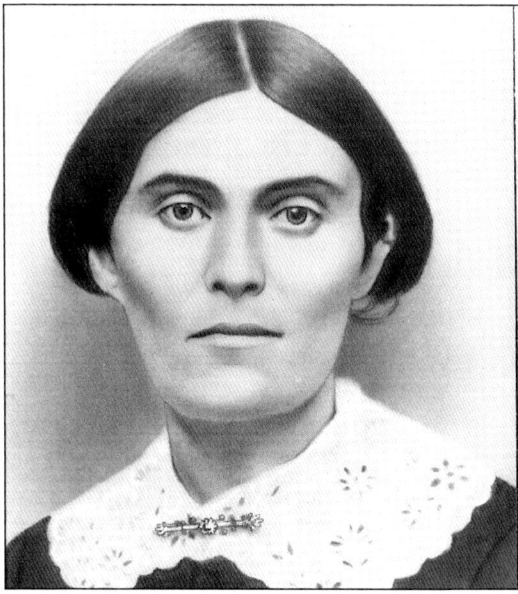
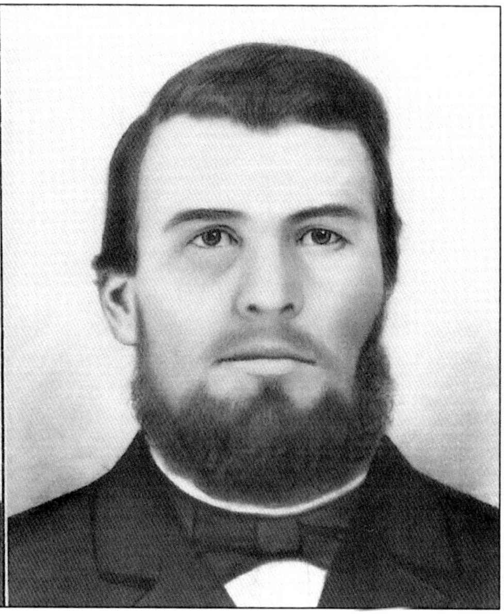

WILLIAM THOMAS II (1818–1865) AND ANN MORGAN THOMAS (1822–1865), FOUNDERS OF CHESTERTON. William, son of early landowner William Thomas Sr., married Ann, eldest daughter of first settlers Jesse and Jane Morgan, in 1845. William ran a local saw mill and operated a store. In 1852 he platted the town of Calumet (later Chesterton) and helped ensure the growth of the community by offering land for a right-of-way and a wood lot (now Thomas Park) to the Lake Shore and Michigan Southern Railroad. Of their 13 children only two, Elena and Elias, survived to adulthood.

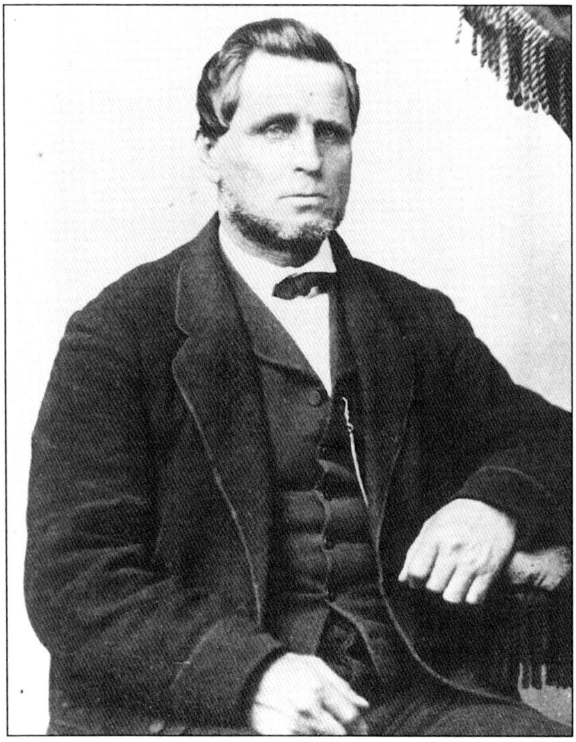

DAVID HOPKINS, EARLY BUSINESSMAN (1820–1870). One of the area's earliest and most successful businessmen, Hopkins settled in Chesterton in 1850. A major landowner, he operated a general merchandise store and a cooperage for making barrels. He also served as postmaster and Township Trustee.

JOHN G. MORGAN, FARMER (1832–1919). The youngest son of Jesse and Jane Morgan was active in civic affairs and was one of the most successful farmers in the area. He and his wife, Mary Ann Holland, (1838–1909), a former schoolteacher whom he married in 1860, raised three children. In 1867, when the Morgan homestead was divided, they built a home, which still stands at 168 E. Porter Avenue (1200 N.) and operated a farm of nearly 400 acres.

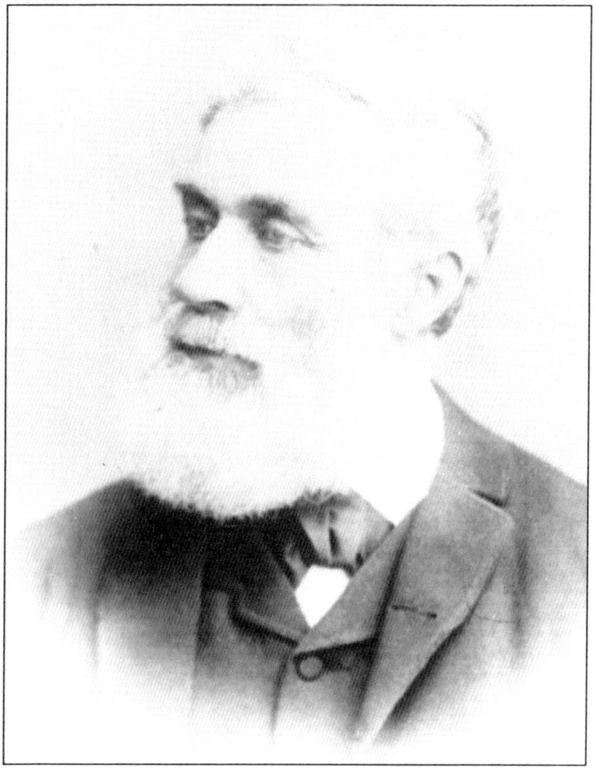

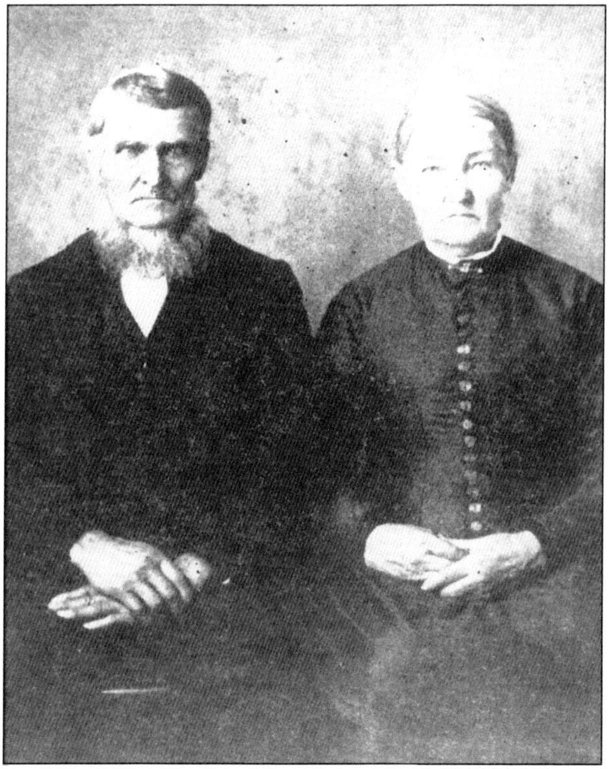

HENRY AND HANNAH HAGEMAN, FOUNDERS OF HAGEMAN (PORTER). In 1841 Henry (1816–1899) came to Porter County in 1833 and married Hannah Gossett (1820–1891), daughter of landowner and early settler William Gossett. Together they had 13 children, seven of whom lived to maturity. Henry platted the town of Hageman (later Porter), in 1871 and sold land to workers attracted to the area by local industries such as the brickyards. Mr. Hageman was also active in civic affairs, serving as Westchester Township Trustee and Assessor.

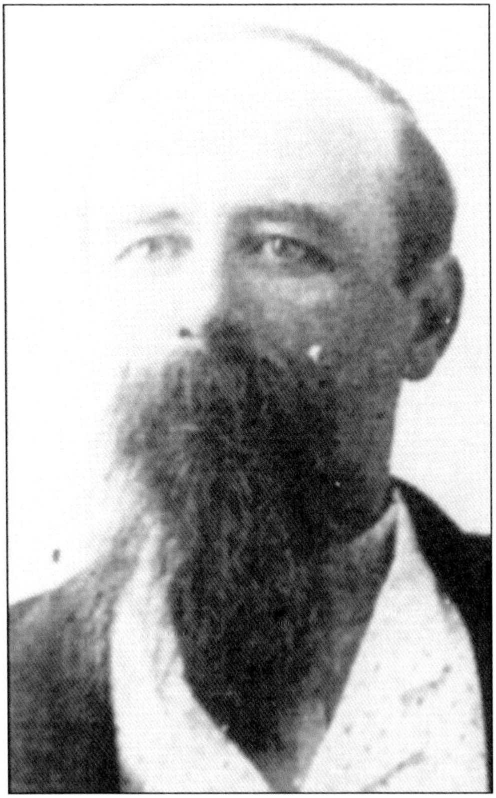

JOHN B. LUNDBERG, FIRST CHESTERTON TOWN BOARD PRESIDENT (1840–1909). A native of Sweden who settled here in 1866, Lundberg was a well-regarded, successful businessman and civic leader. He established a cabinet-making and wood-turning venture and was involved in the lumber business for a time. In 1875 he sold his other interests to concentrate on his furniture store and undertaking business. He served as Township Trustee, Township Assessor, County Commissioner, and as first President of the Chesterton Town Board.

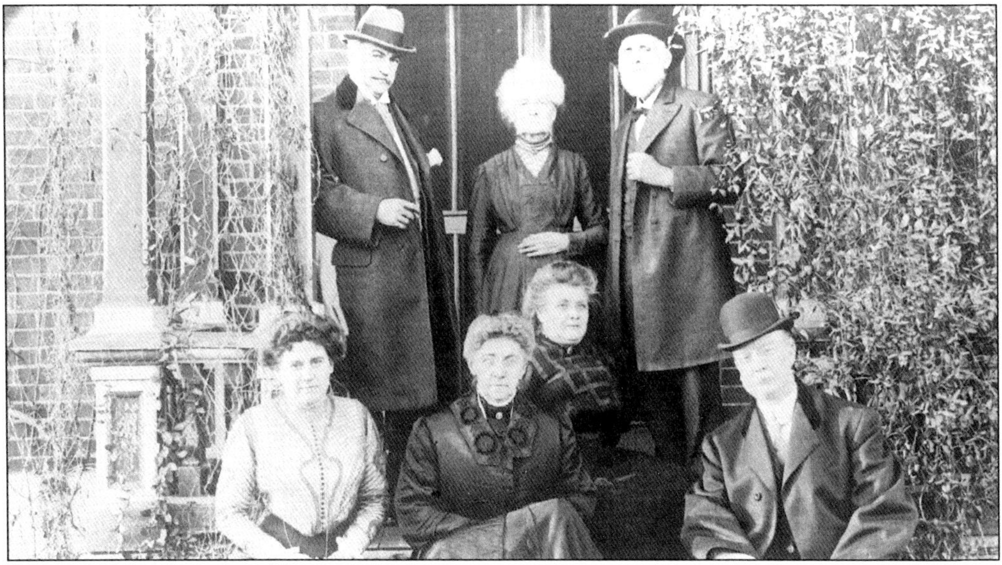

FURNESS FAMILY, FOUNDERS OF FURNESSVILLE. This picture was taken during a visit by the Furness's daughter and son-in-law and his parents from Chicago. Pictured in front of the Furness home are (front row, left to right): Mrs. Wymer, Mr. Leigh's secretary, Mrs. E.B. Leigh, Clara Furness Leigh and Dr. E.B. Leigh. On the back row are E.B. Leigh, president of the Chicago Railway Equipment Company, Louise Furness, and her husband E.L. Furness, the founder of Furnessville.

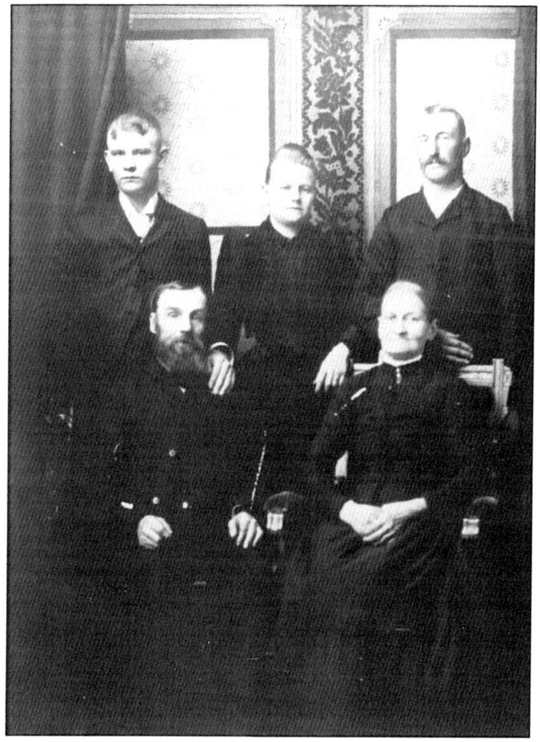

CHELLBERG FAMILY, SWEDISH SETTLERS. This formal family portrait shows Anders Ludwig Kjellberg and his wife Johanna, who emigrated from Sweden to Baillytown in 1863. Their daughter, Emily, stands behind them. The man to the left is identified as Simon Larson, and to the right is Carl (C.L.). The family later changed their surname to "Chellberg."(Courtesy Indiana Dunes National Lakeshore, NPS.)

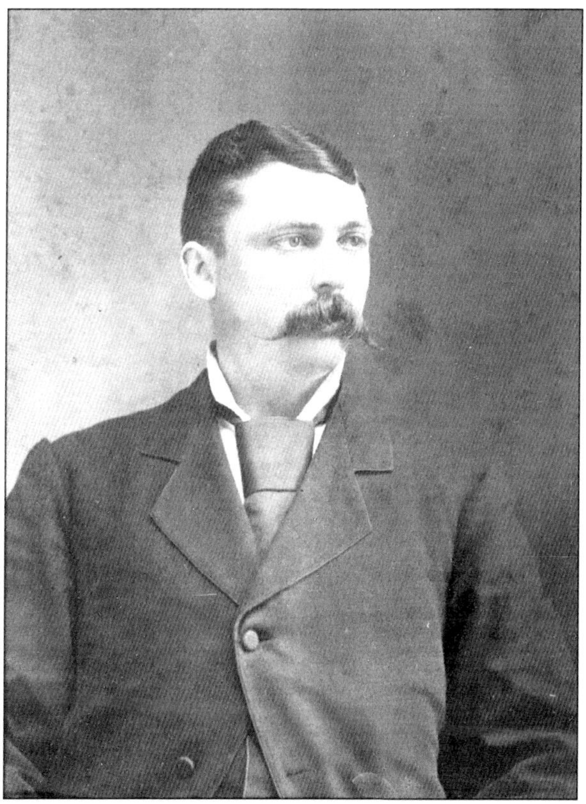

ELIAS THOMAS, BUSINESSMAN (1849–1927). The only surviving son of William II and Ann Thomas was orphaned at an early age and sent to Valparaiso to live with a guardian. Returning to Chesterton as a successful businessman, he built the Thomas block in 1888; it still stands at the southeast corner of Broadway and Calumet. He served as Sheriff of Porter County from 1884 to 1888. Following personal and financial difficulties, he found work as a rural mail carrier, and later as Westchester Township Assessor.

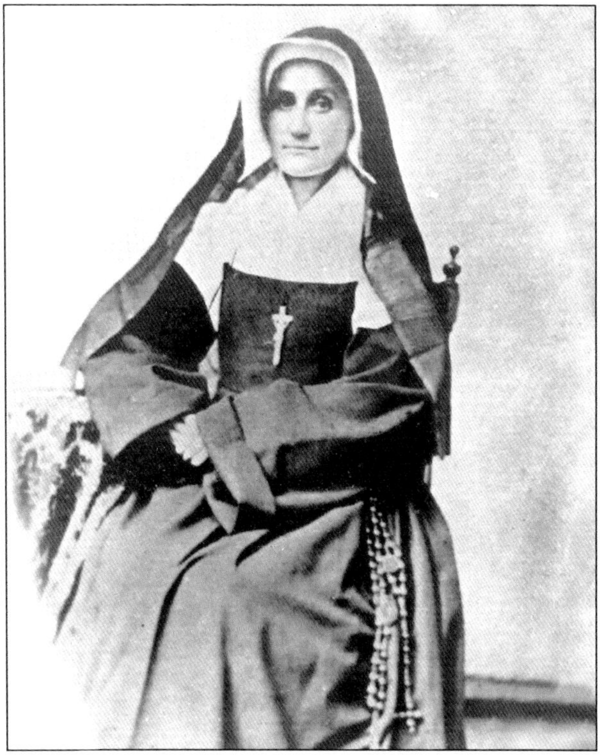

Eleanor Bailly, Mother Mary Cecilia (1815–1898). The well-educated, cultured daughter of Joseph and Marie Bailly devoted her life to the Catholic Church. In 1841 she joined a group of French nuns who had organized the Order of Sisters of Providence in America in Terre Haute. She remained there and rose to the position of Superior General of St. Mary-of-the-Woods Academy in 1856. Her nieces, Rose and Frances Howe, both attended the Academy, now known as St. Mary-of-the-Woods College. (Courtesy St. Mary-of-the-Woods College.)

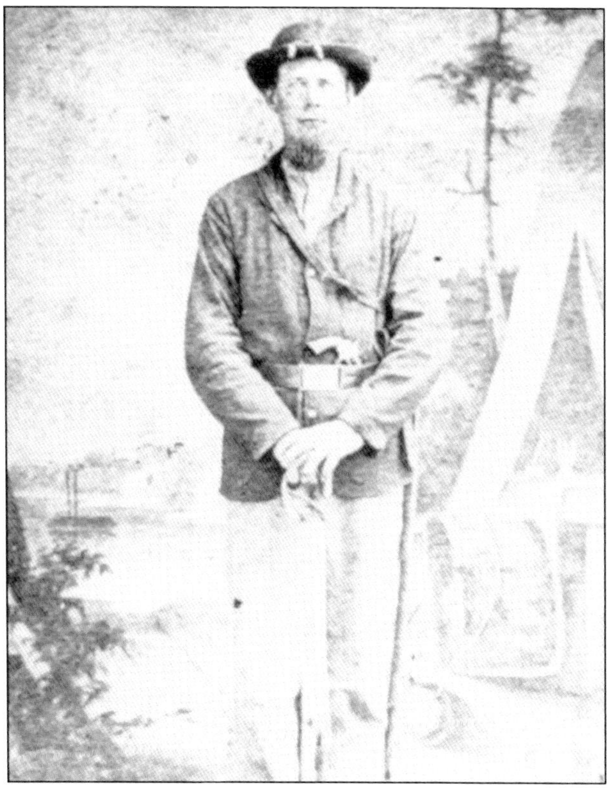

James Bradley, Civil War Veteran (1827–1889). This photograph was taken in 1865, when Bradley was mustered out of the Union Army at Vicksburg after serving with the 12th Indiana Cavalry. A native of Ohio and a carpenter by trade, Bradley farmed in Liberty Township from 1856 to 1863. Following the war, he returned to his farm for a number of years. He and his second wife, Lavina, moved to Chesterton in 1881 and he opened a cabinet/wood shop at 115 S. Fourth Street with his son, Charles.

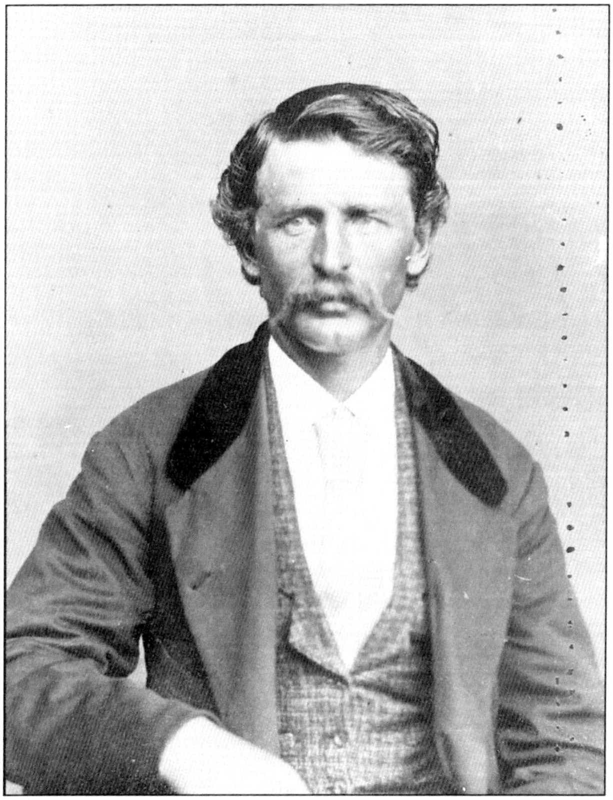

Peter Conrad Wistrand, Postmaster (1843–1935). A native of Sweden, Peter Wistrand moved to Baillytown in 1864. A carpenter by trade, Peter was appointed Postmaster of Hageman in 1889 and of Porter in 1892. The post office was located in the Union Block Department Store owned by Wistrand and John Busse, at the northwest corner of Lincoln and Sherman in Porter.

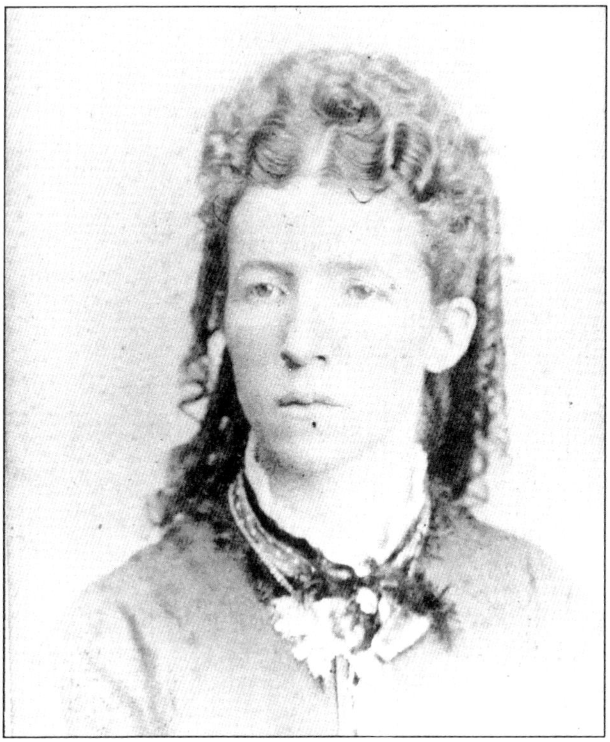

Louisa Buck Wistrand, Teacher (1847–1940). A hard-working and devoutly religious young woman, Louisa Buck learned Swedish in order to teach at the school in Baillytown (now known as the Burstrom Chapel). Following her marriage to Peter Wistrand in 1881, she had six children and ran the Wistrand store in her husband's absence.

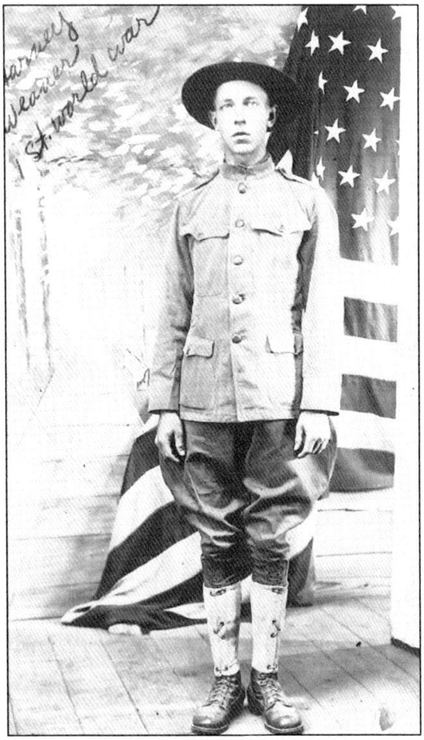

HARVEY WEAVER, WORLD WAR I VETERAN. Local resident Weaver was attached to the Rainbow division during WW I. While loading a cannon on board a ship, his leg was broken when the cannon slipped. As a result, he was not with his division when it entered battle and was wiped out, leaving him as the only survivor of the division.

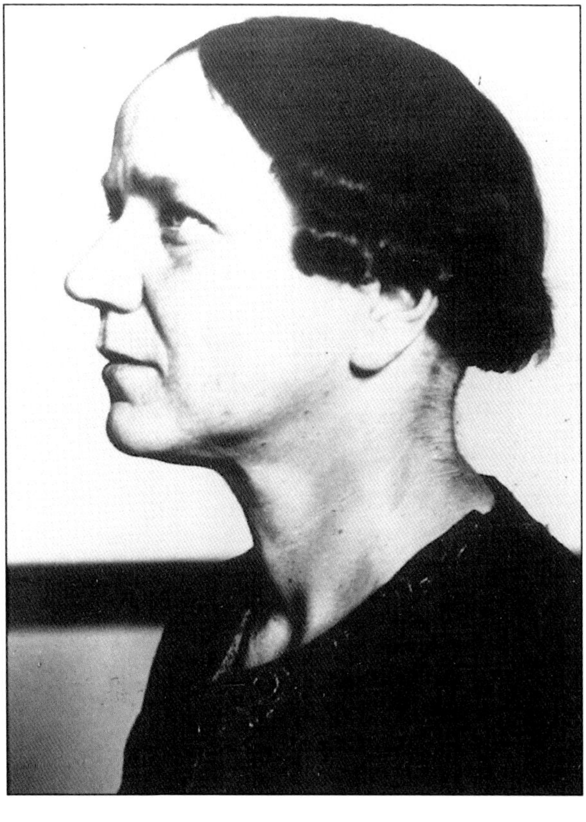

ALICE GRAY, "DIANA OF THE DUNES" (1881–1925). The enigmatic and misunderstood woman who was memorialized as "Diana of the Dunes" posed for this portrait in 1917. A brilliant graduate of the University of Chicago who had become disenchanted with city life and the limited opportunities for educated women, she came to this area in 1915 to write and live a simple life in the unspoiled dune country east of Gary. (Courtesy Chicago Historical Society, DN-067767.)

William and Flora Richardson, Naturalists. The Richardsons, Chicago residents and original members of the Prairie Club, built a shelter in 1910 and, later, a cottage in the area that is now Dune Acres. The couple shared a love of nature, the arts, and particularly the Indiana Dunes. An industrial chemist by profession, William Richardson was also an avid ornithologist and accomplished photographer who chronicled life in the dunes through photographs of the landscape, flowers, and birds. Following her husband's death in 1936, Mrs. Richardson built a year-round home in Dune Acres and continued her interest in the environment of the dunes. In 1958, she established the Richardson Wildlife Sanctuary, which houses the Richardsons' extensive library and photograph archives and provides free educational materials to schools and other groups. (Courtesy Richardson Wildlife Sanctuary.)

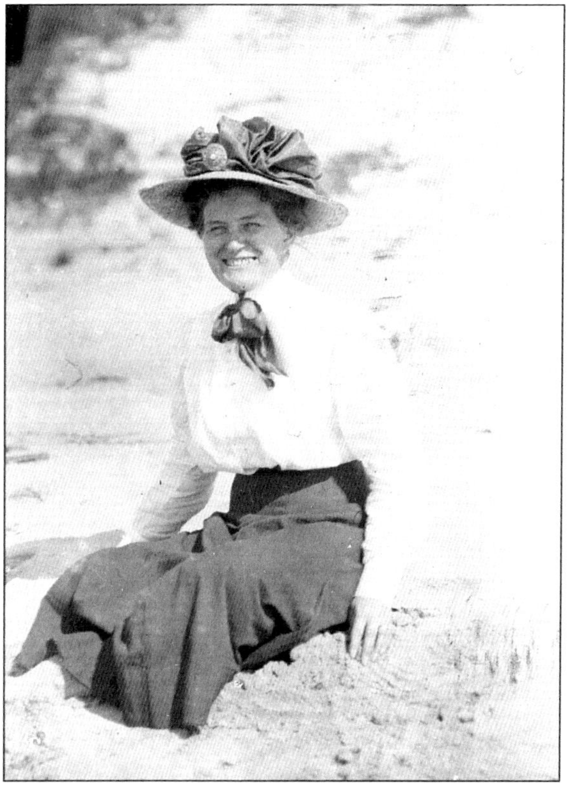

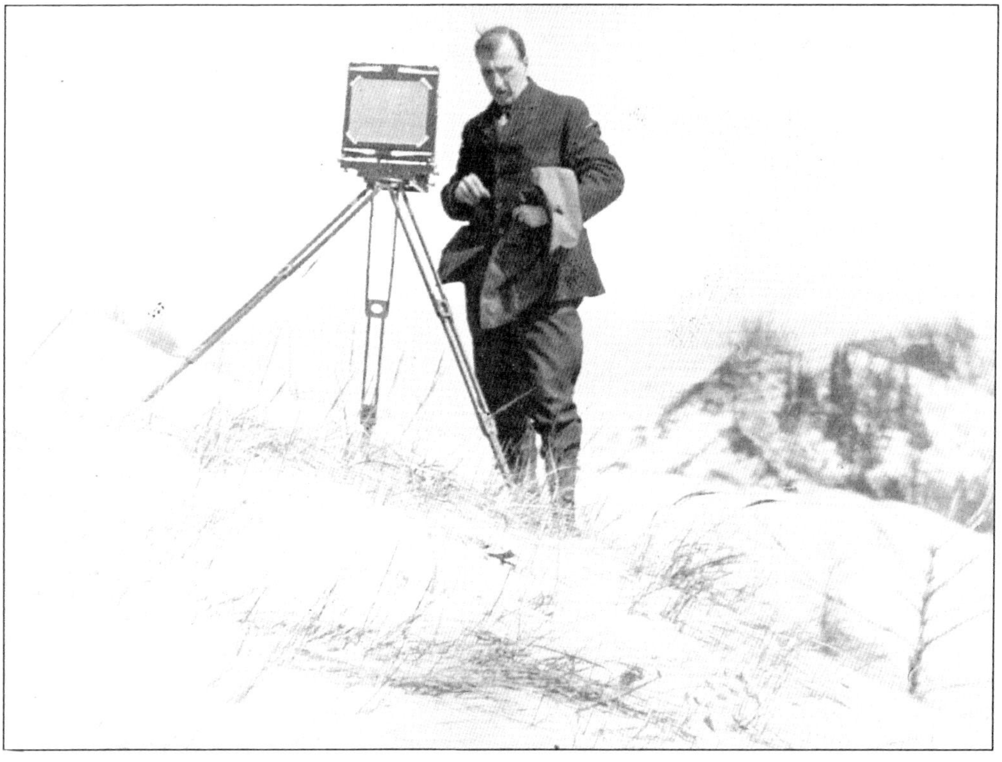

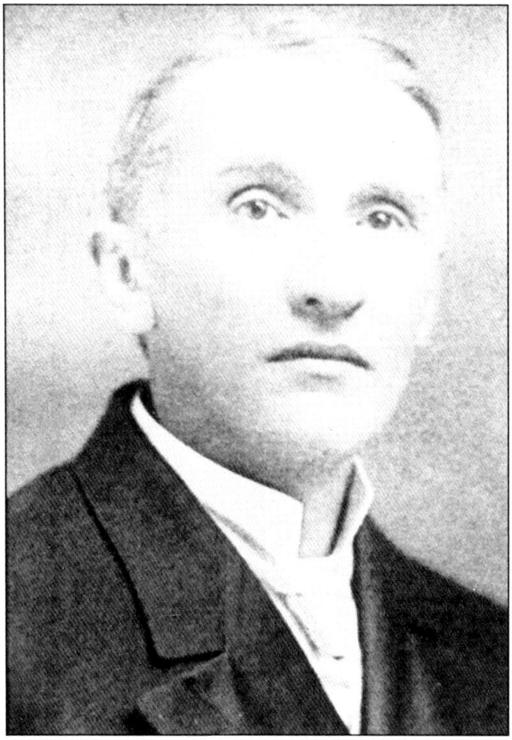

Arthur J. Bowser, Founder of *Chesterton Tribune* (1862–1935). A Valparaiso native, Bowser founded the *Chesterton Tribune* in 1884. A tireless promoter of the communities of Chesterton and Porter, he advocated civic improvement and industrial growth throughout his almost 40-year tenure as editor and owner of the newspaper. Bowser was also active in real estate and politics. He served on the Porter County Council and in the Indiana Senate from 1907 to 1911, where he authored the Reclamation bill that enabled U.S. Steel to build in Gary.

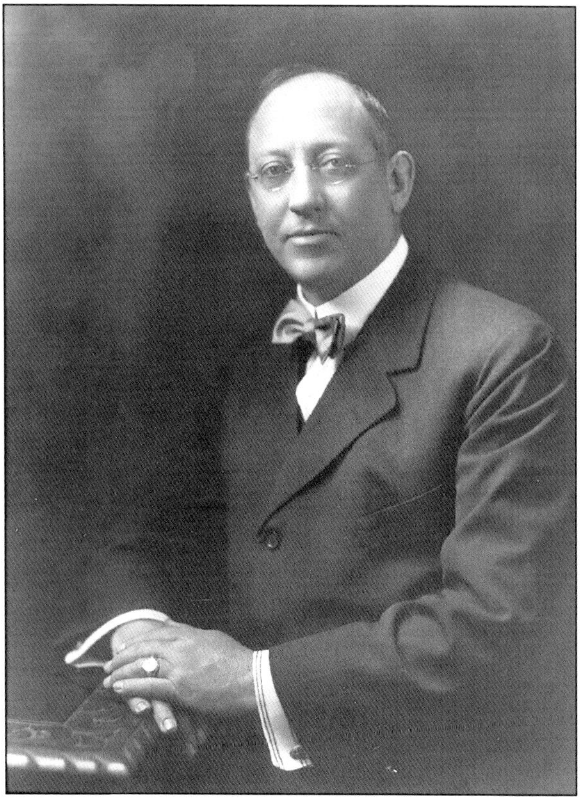

Charles L. Jeffrey, Banker (1869–1933). A well-regarded member of the local business community, Mr. Jeffrey came to Chesterton in 1890. Associated with Chesterton State Bank since its inception that year, Mr. Jeffrey first served as cashier and later acquired George C. Morgan and Joseph Gardner's interests in the bank. In 1901 he entered into an equal partnership with Edward L. Morgan, grandson of Jesse Morgan, and served as president of the bank until his death.

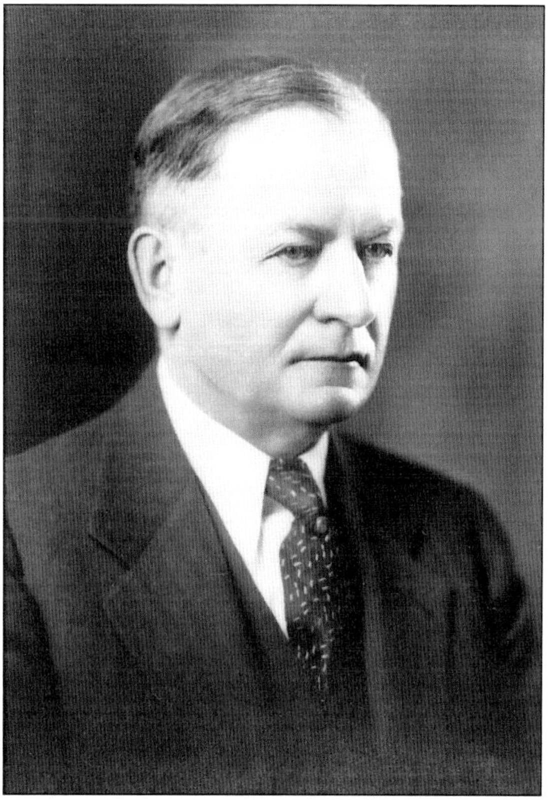

WILLIAM WIRT, DUNE ACRES FOUNDER. The innovative superintendent of the Gary Public Schools was also president of Dune Acres, Incorporated, the company responsible for the planned lakeside community of Dune Acres, which was formed in September 1923, as Westchester Township's third incorporated town. Developer of the nationally renowned "Gary System" of school administration, Wirt was also actively involved in a number of business and real estate ventures. (Courtesy Calumet Regional Archives, Indiana University Northwest.)

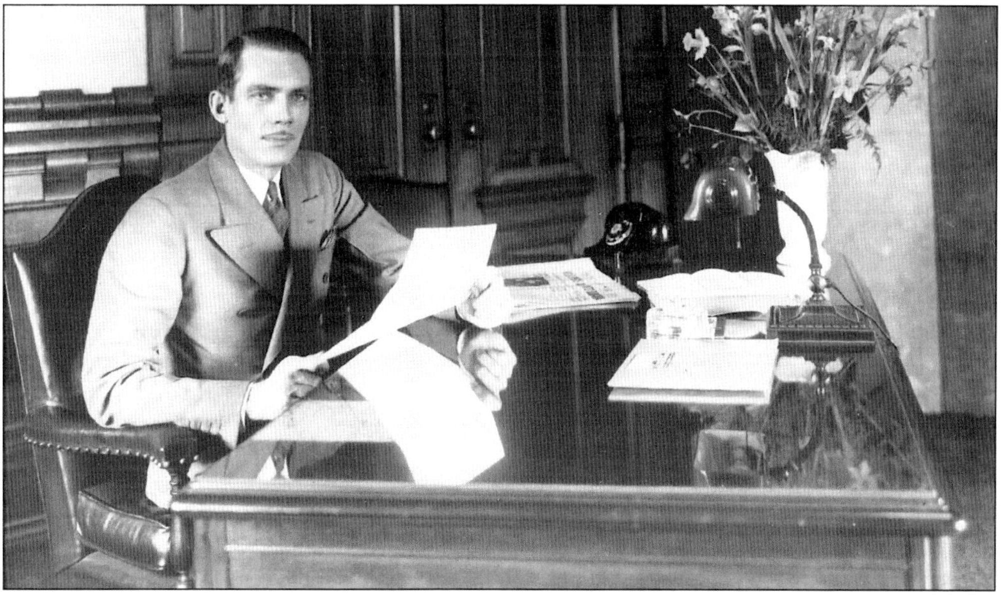

JAMES M. GIVENS, TREASURER OF THE STATE OF INDIANA. Local son Givens is shown in his Indianapolis office on March 20, 1941. Givens was honored by a parade through Chesterton and Porter after his election to state office in 1940. He was also cashier and later Chief Executive Officer of the First State Bank of Porter and served as president of the Porter Chamber of Commerce in the early 1930s.

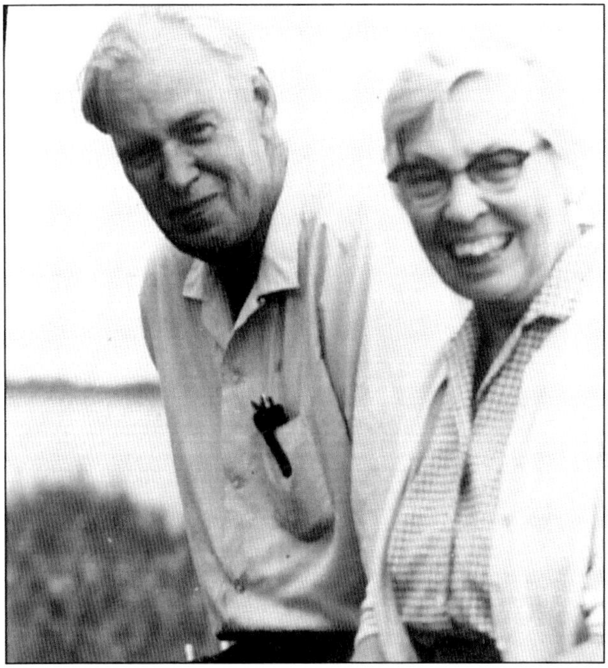

Austin and Rheua Rand, Naturalists. The Rands, both ornithologists, moved to Chesterton in 1947 after Austin was appointed Curator of Ornithology at the Field Museum. They were actively involved in the local community, writing a weekly column "Country Diary" in the *Chesterton Tribune*, participating in local art shows, and leading nature-study field trips. Austin Rand wrote numerous books on birds and the couple collaborated on the work *Midwestern Almanac*.

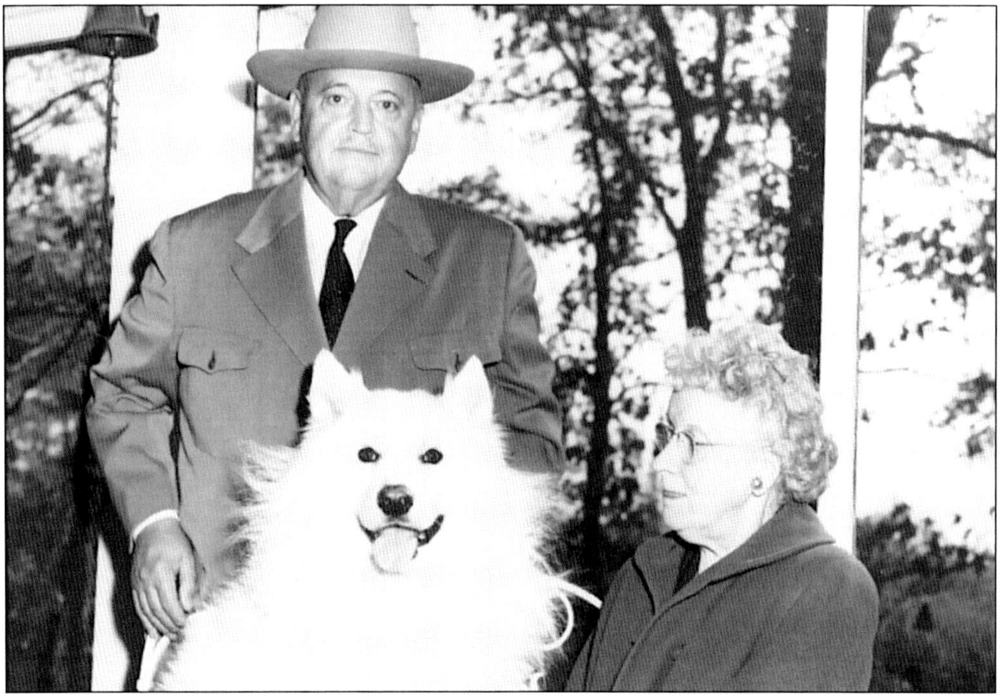

Col. Edward Wentworth, Historian. Colonel Wentworth, a well-regarded expert in the field of animal husbandry, is pictured above with his wife, Alma, and dog, Ditko. Colonel Wentworth retired as director of Armour & Company's livestock bureau in 1954 and moved to the Baillytown area. A longtime member of the Duneland Historical Society, he took particular interest in the history of Le Petit Fort and was one of the first local residents to urge the preservation of the Bailly Homestead and Cemetery.

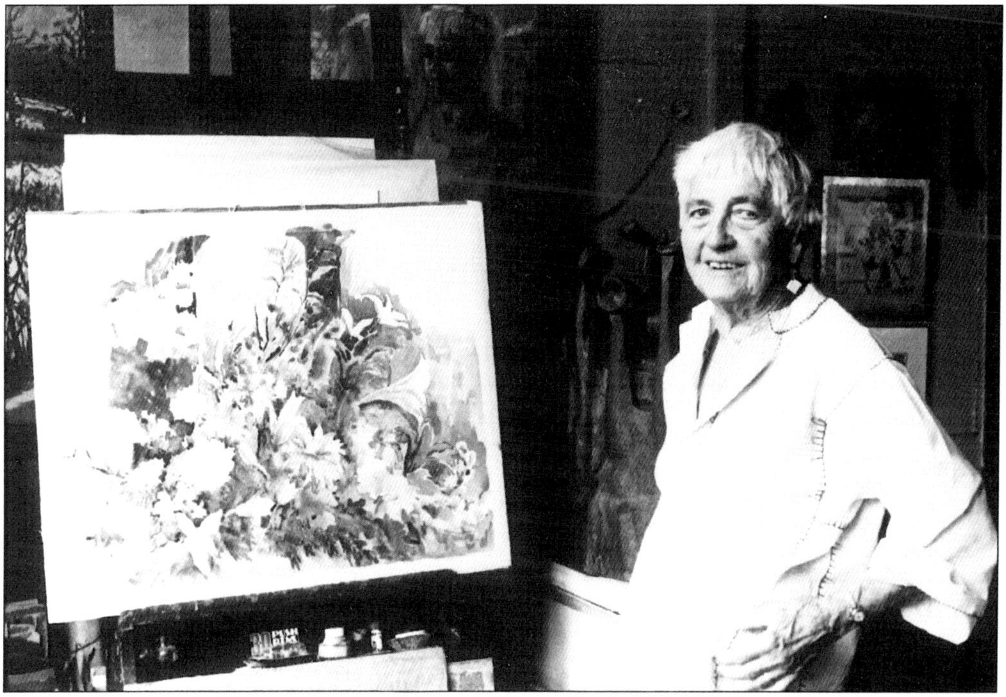

HAZEL AND VIN HANNELL, ARTISTS. The Hannells came to the Furnessville area from Chicago during the Depression and were founding members of the artists' community that flourished there. V.M.S., "Vin" Hannell, pictured to the right, was a painter and a wood sculptor who exhibited nationally and garnered many awards for his work. The Hannells built a studio and kiln near their home and used the native red clay to produce highly prized pottery. The Hannells were founding members of the Association of Artists and Craftsmen of Porter County, and were instrumental in organizing the long-running annual Chesterton Art Fair. Following her husband's death in 1964, Hazel Hannell, seen above, continued to operate the Hannell Pottery until the late 1980s. A charter member of the Save the Dunes Council, Hazel worked to preserve the natural beauty of the dunes landscape and flora, which she captured in her watercolors. In 1988, she sold her Furnessville property and moved to Oregon.

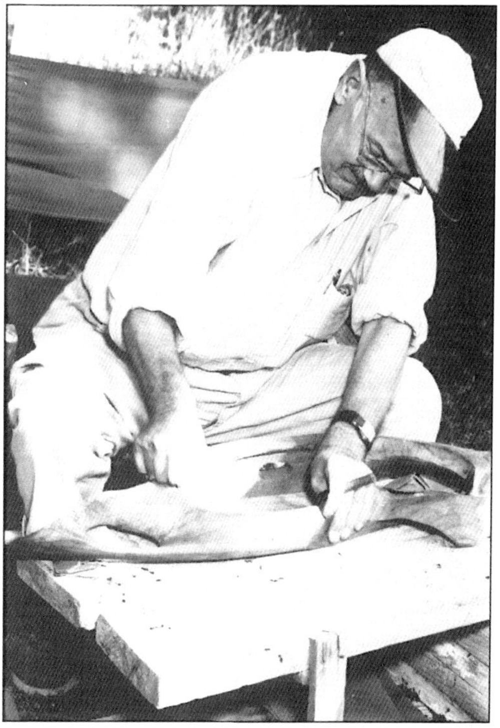

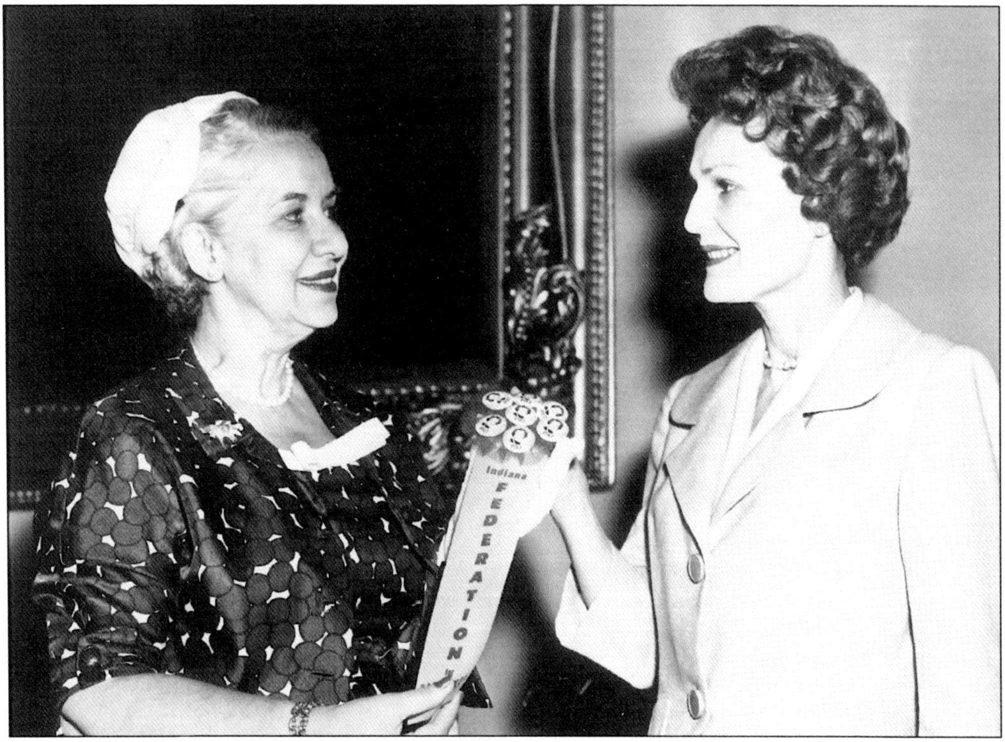

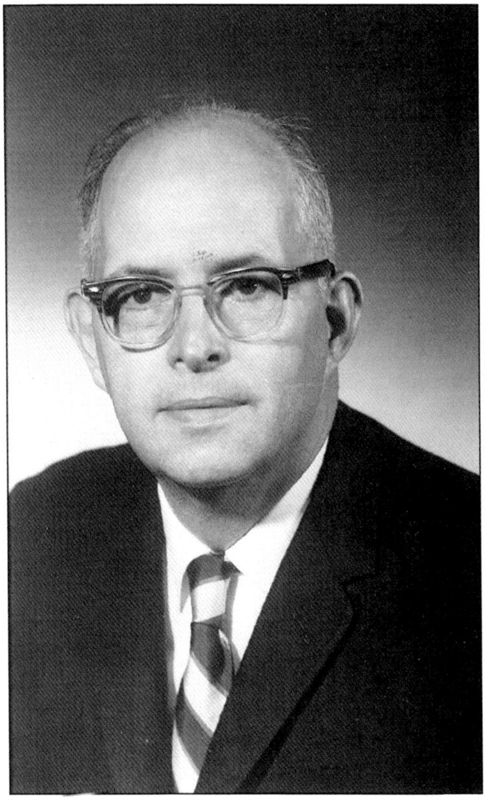

Ione Flynn Harrington, Politician. Pat Nixon poses with Ione Harrington at a meeting of the National Federation of Republican Women in the late 1960s. Mrs. Harrington was actively involved in the Republican Party at the local and national level for many years, serving as a member of the Republican National Committee and as vice-chairman of the Citizens for Goldwater committee. Honored as a Sagamore of the Wabash for her contributions, Mrs. Harrington was the granddaughter of furniture retailer John Lundberg.

Norris Coambs, Local Historian. Coambs, the long-term President of the Duneland Historical Society, had a keen interest and extensive knowledge of local history that he employed in writing the *Duneland Notes*. He was appointed Porter County Historian in 1984 and honored as a Sagamore of the Wabash in 1985. For more than 40 years, Norris Coambs owned and occupied the all-steel Lustron home at 411 Bowser Avenue, which is on the National Register of Historic Places. He died in 1988.

Two

AGRICULTURE

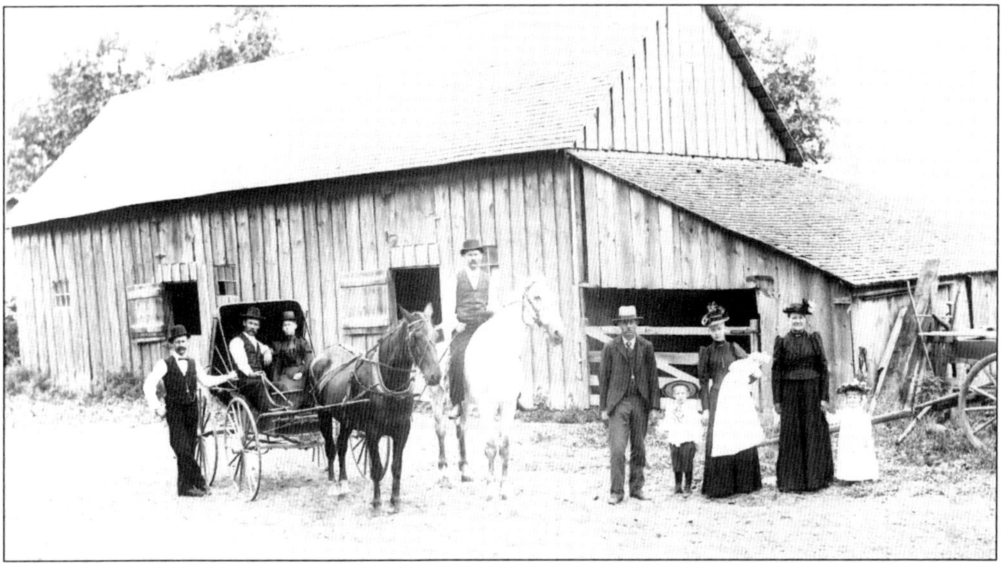

CHARLSON FARM, PORTER. Swedish immigrants and Swedish Americans such as Gust and Amanda Charlson began settling in Baillytown in northwestern Westchester Township about 1850. The Charlsons are shown here on the right with their young son Harry and baby Raymond in front of their barn. Their daughter, Alice, stands beside her grandmother. The others in the photograph are members of the Ecklund family, related to the Charlsons by marriage.

Jesse Morgan and his family established the township's first farm in 1833. The original Morgan farm was located on East Porter Avenue, where the Sand Creek Country Club is now located. Americans from the East Coast and immigrants from Ireland, Germany, and particularly Sweden arrived in the area in the 1840s to farm, and in the 1850s to work on the railroad, when it was laid through the township.

The railroads brought increased prosperity to area farmers who began to ship grain, produce, and milk via train to Chicago. Drainage of wetlands c. 1900 produced more farmland and mechanization after WW I increased the productivity of area farms.

Photographs of early farms in the neighboring townships of Liberty, Jackson, and Pine are also included to illustrate the fact that the four communities have long shared a close and interdependent relationship.

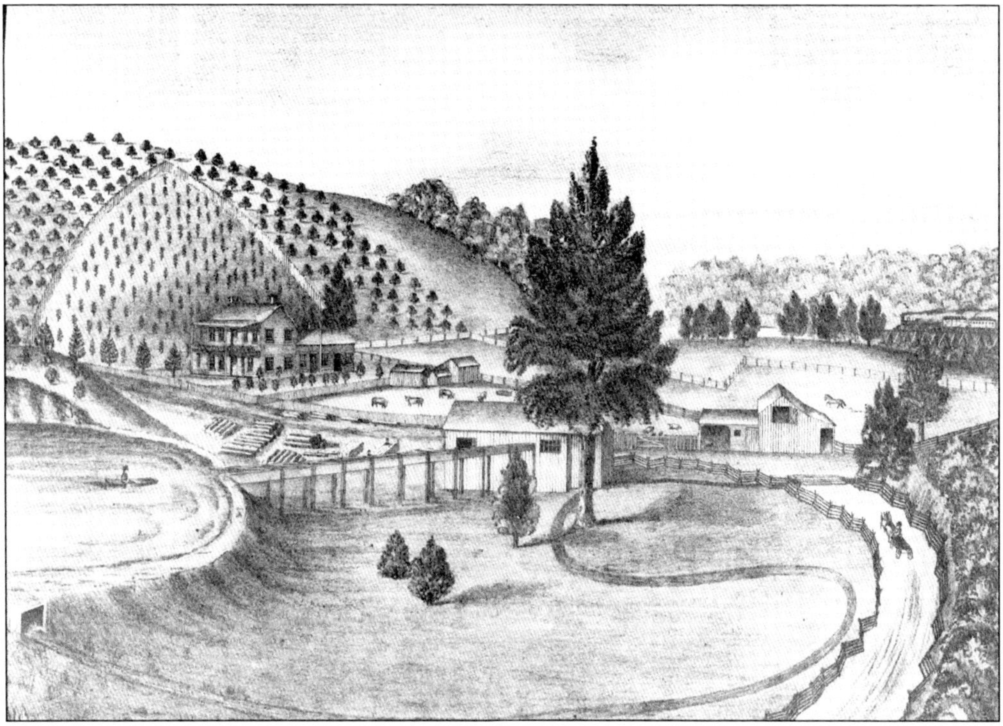

SUMAN FARM AND MILL, JACKSON TOWNSHIP. In 1865 Col. Isaac C.B. Suman returned to the area after a distinguished career in the Civil War. He and his wife, Kate, purchased the above property in Section 28 of Jackson Township adjacent to the Baltimore and Ohio Railroad, seen to the right. Colonel Suman raised high-grade livestock and operated a sawmill. In 1881 he moved to Valparaiso, where he was appointed postmaster and later elected mayor. (*Historical Atlas of Porter County*, 1876.)

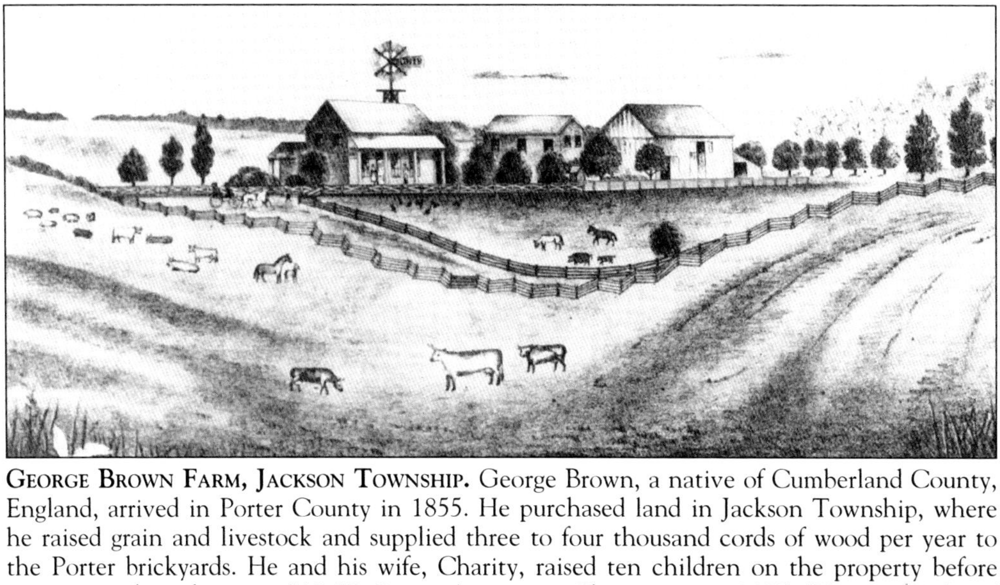

GEORGE BROWN FARM, JACKSON TOWNSHIP. George Brown, a native of Cumberland County, England, arrived in Porter County in 1855. He purchased land in Jackson Township, where he raised grain and livestock and supplied three to four thousand cords of wood per year to the Porter brickyards. He and his wife, Charity, raised ten children on the property before retiringto a large home at 700 W. Porter Avenue in Chesterton, in 1885. (*Historical Atlas of Porter County*, 1876.)

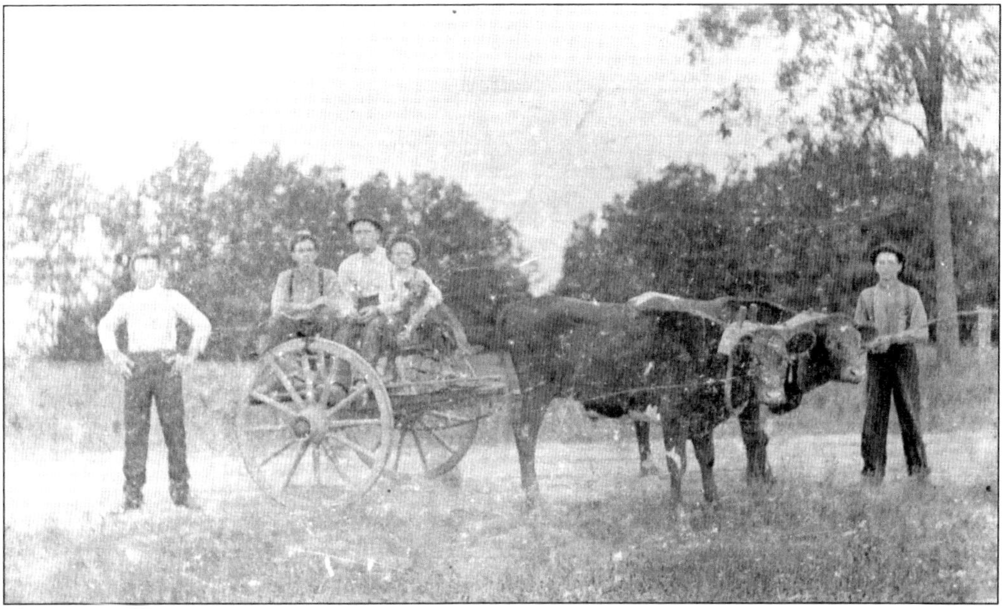

WARREN L. DILLINGHAM FARM, LIBERTY TOWNSHIP. Oxen were frequently used in the area to pull farm equipment before the widespread use of horses. The above photograph was taken on the Warren Dillingham farm on old State Road 49 in Liberty Township. Warren Dillingham was the son of Isaac Dillingham, a prosperous farmer who owned extensive property in Liberty Township, and the grandson of Olcott Dillingham, an early pioneer who moved to the county in 1837.

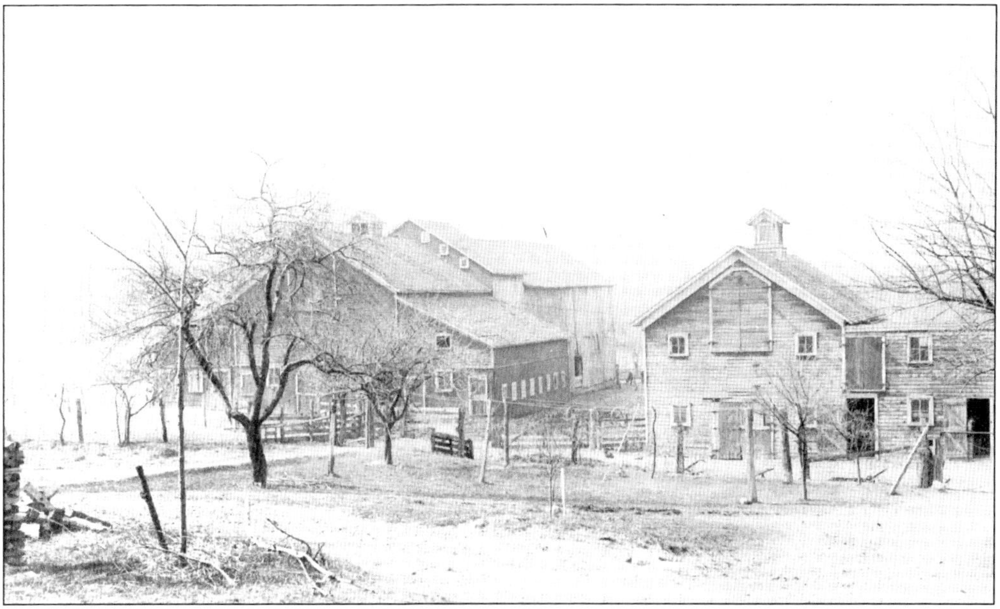

E.L FURNESS BARNS, FURNESSVILLE. E.L. Furness and his wife, Louise, settled in eastern Westchester Township in 1856. By 1890 they had built the barns seen above north of their Furnessville home for their large dairy business. In addition to milk, they and other area farmers shipped strawberries and other farm produce to Chicago via the Michigan Central Railroad, which stopped at the Furnessville Station, in front of their farmstead.

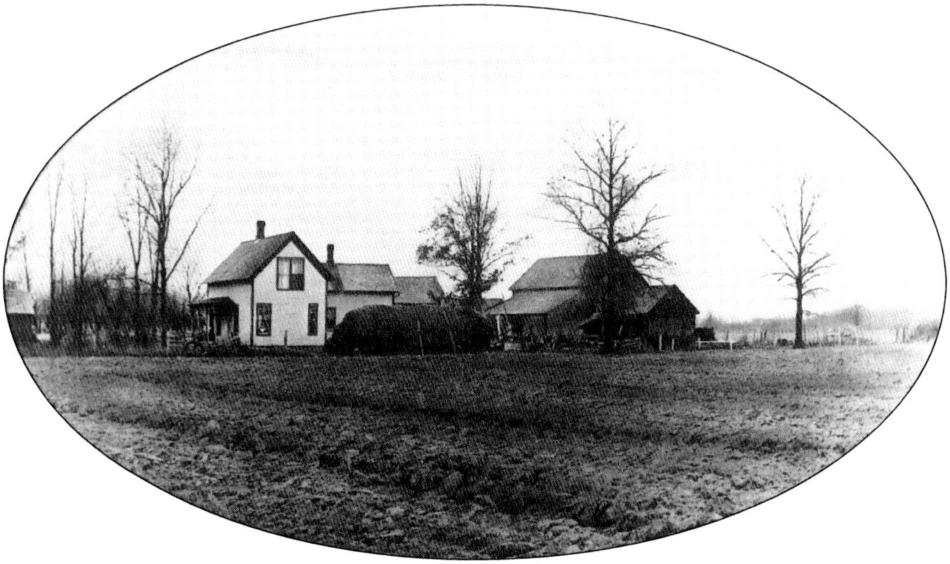

Hickory Grove Dairy Farm, Burns Harbor. Otto Peterson and his wife, Ida, operated the Hickory Grove Dairy Farm from the 1880s into the 1900s. The large hay pile to the side of the house protected it from the cold north winds off Lake Michigan. Extensively expanded and remodeled over the years, the house still stands at 1136 State Road 149, in what is now Burns Harbor, surrounded by many of the original shagbark hickories for which the farm was named.

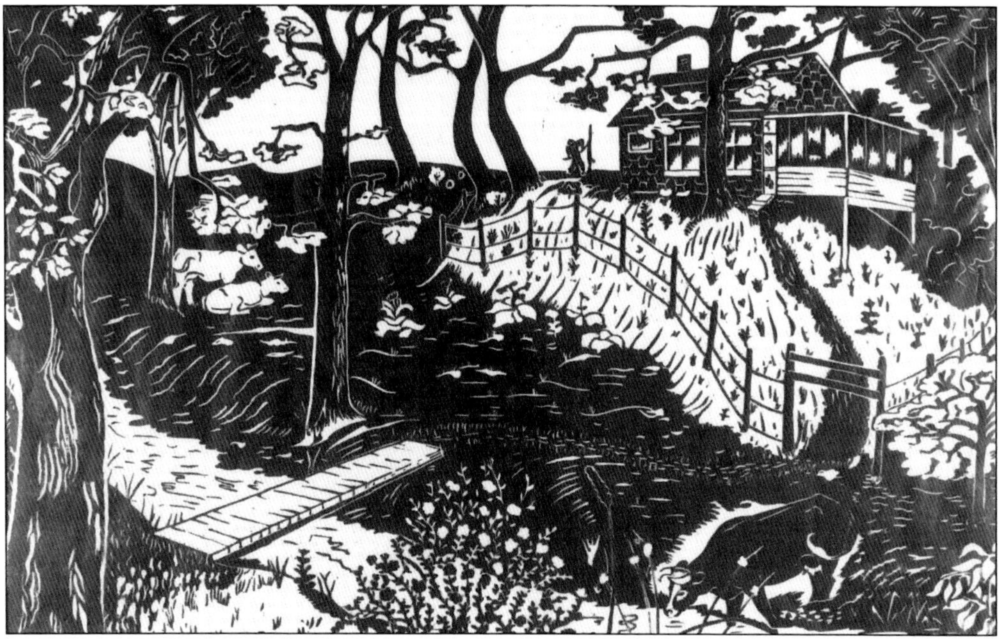

Brummitt's Calumet Stock Farm, Pine Township. The above linoleum block print by Lillian Hall depicts a scene along the Little Calumet River in Pine Township. When Marion Brummitt, proprietor of the Calumet Stock Farm, sold land to Chicago journalist John Drury about 1935, Brummitt required that Drury provide access to the river for his livestock, causing the latter to construct a fence with a cow gate around his property. Brummitt Elementary School was named in honor of Mr. Brummitt in 1969.

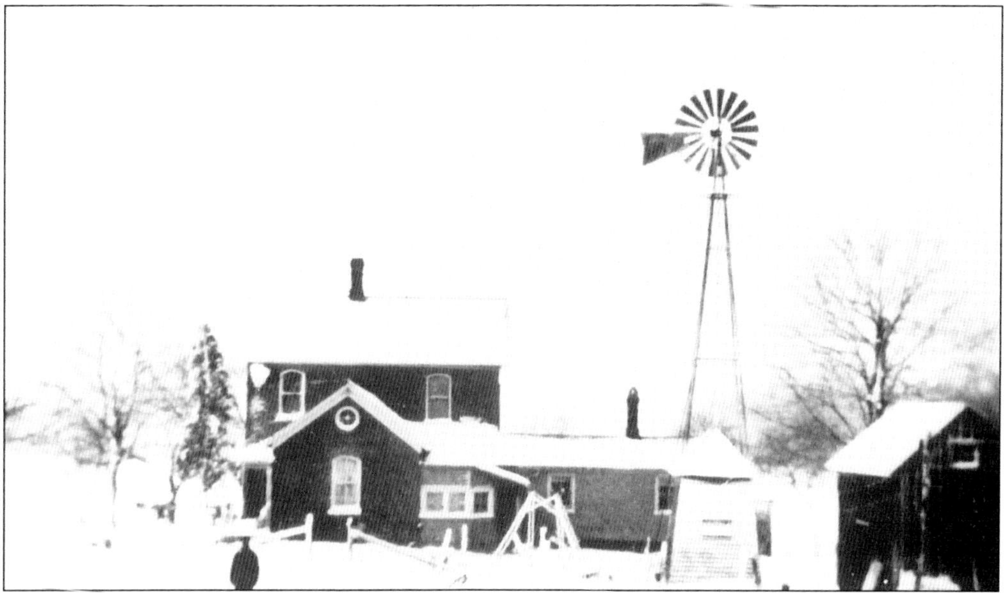

CHELLBERG FARM, PORTER. Anders and Johanna Chellberg bought land in Baillytown in 1869 from Joel Wicker, Joseph Bailly's son-in-law. Their first house burned in 1884 and was replaced with a structure made of Porter brick, seen in this *c.* 1922 photograph. Other farm buildings included a granary, corncrib, chicken house, woodshed, outhouse, smokehouse, and pump house with windmill. The farm is now part of the Indiana Dunes National Lakeshore. (Courtesy Indiana Dunes National Lakeshore, NPS.)

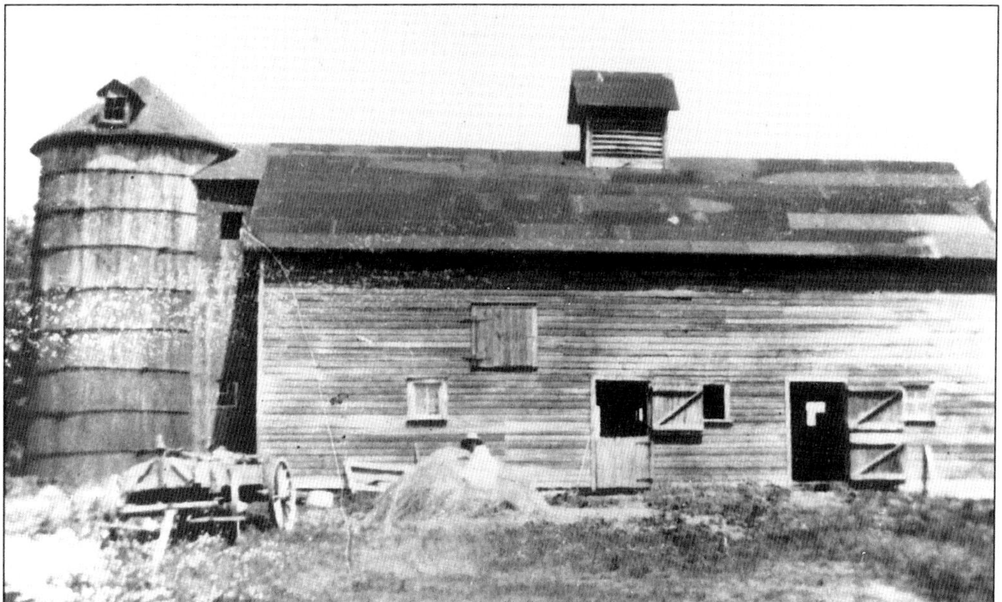

CHELLBERG BARN. According to family tradition, the Chellbergs' timber-framed, two-story barn was completed between 1880 and 1890. The family grew a variety of grains, including rye, wheat, corn and oats, and added dairy cows after the South Shore Railroad was built in 1908. A railroad stop close to the farm enabled the family to make daily shipments of milk to Chicago. (Courtesy Indiana Dunes National Lakeshore, NPS.)

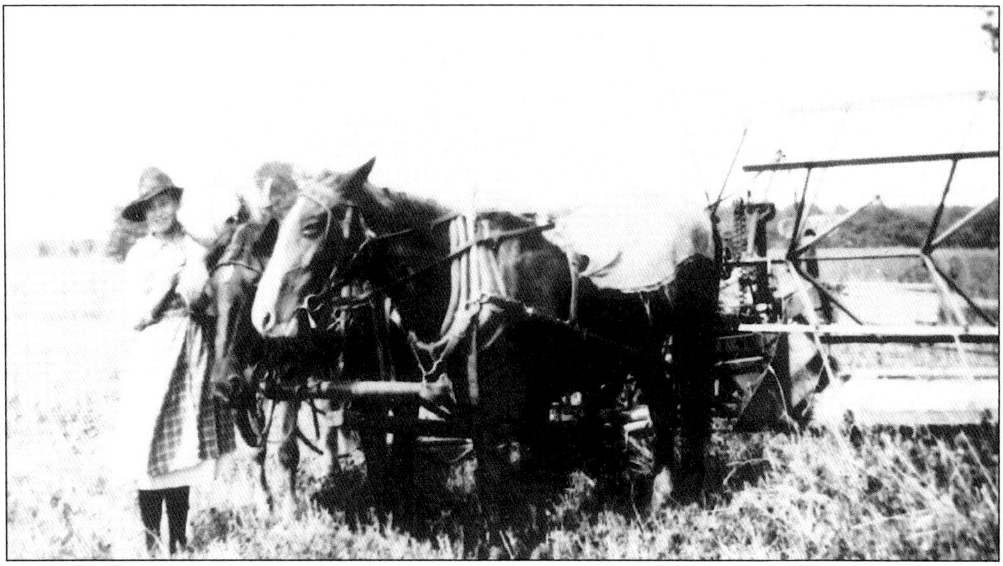

Ruth Chellberg with Binder. In 1887 C.L. Chellberg took over the farm when his parents retired. He and his wife, Mina, had four children: Frank, who died as an infant, Ruth, Naomi (who later married Alden Studebaker), and Carl. The children helped with the farm work, as seen in this photograph of Ruth, who is leading a team of horses attached to a grain binder, in the field northeast of the farmhouse. (Courtesy Indiana Dunes National Lakeshore, NPS.)

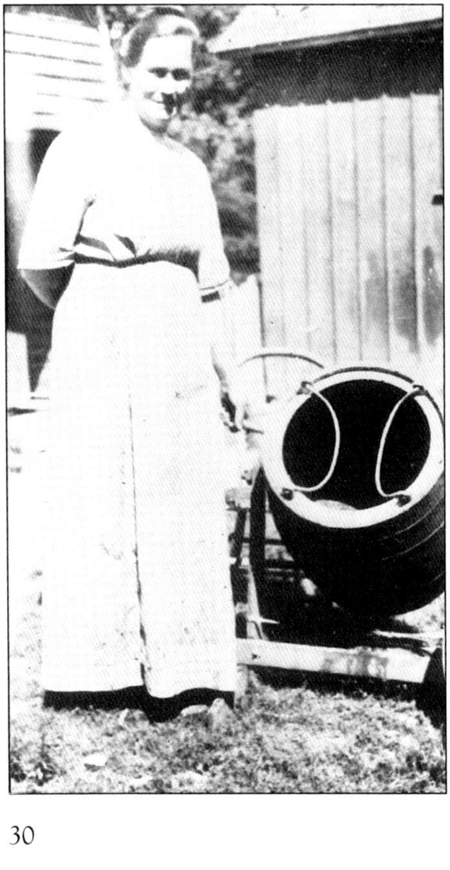

Mina Chellberg with the Butter Churn. Mina Peterson, the daughter of Swedish immigrants who settled in Baillytown, worked as a cook for the Barker family of the Pullman Standard Co. in Michigan City before her marriage to C.L. Chellberg in 1901. She is seen here in 1914, in the yard next to the pump house, with the wooden churn that she used to make butter from milk produced by the family dairy herd. (Courtesy Indiana Dunes National Lakeshore, NPS.)

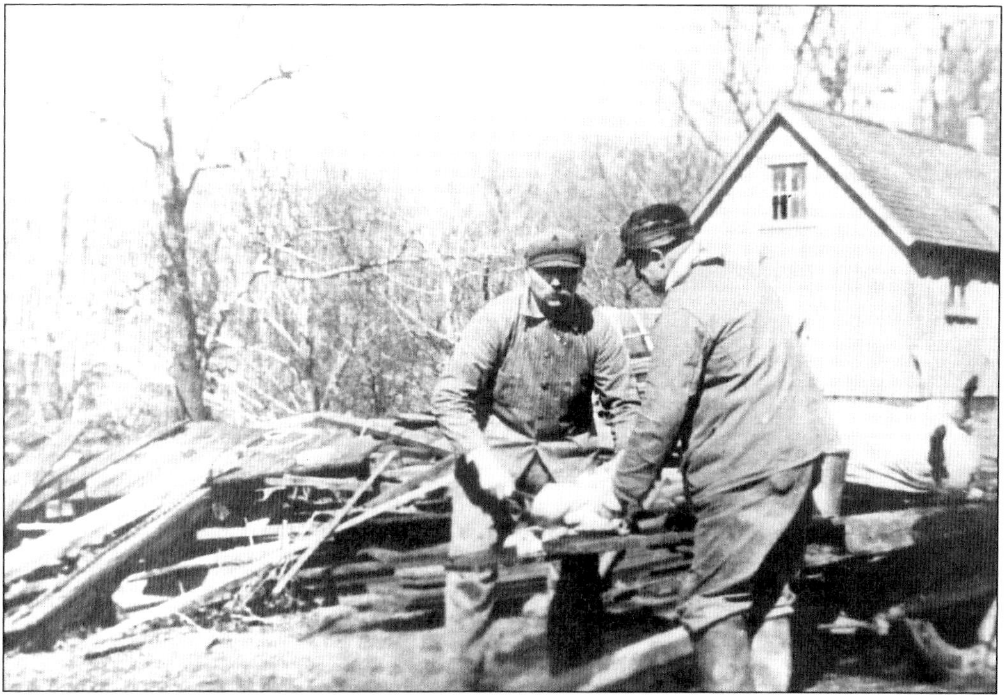

Spring Butchering. Emil Peterson, Mina's brother, is shown helping his brother-in-law, C.L., in this 1921 photograph of hog butchering. The event took place in the farmyard between the Chellberg house and barn. The Chellbergs raised twelve hogs a year, butchered six, and sold the others or used them for new stock. They butchered hogs in the early spring and December then cut each carcass into hams, bacon, and roasts, and rendered the fat for lard. (Courtesy Indiana Dunes National Lakeshore, NPS.)

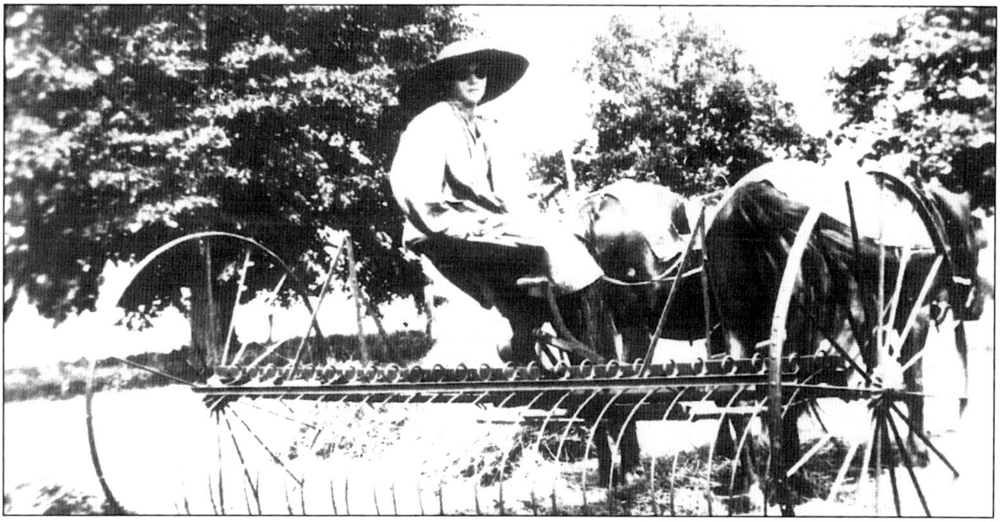

Ruth Riding the Hay Rake. Ruth Chellberg was about 16 when the above photograph was taken of her riding the farm's horse-drawn hay rake. During the summer months, the hay was mowed, raked, and loaded on the hay wagon. At the barn, the hay was raised up into the loft by a fork attached to a horse-powered pulley system. The hay was used to feed the farm animals during the long winter. (Courtesy Indiana Dunes National Lakeshore, NPS.)

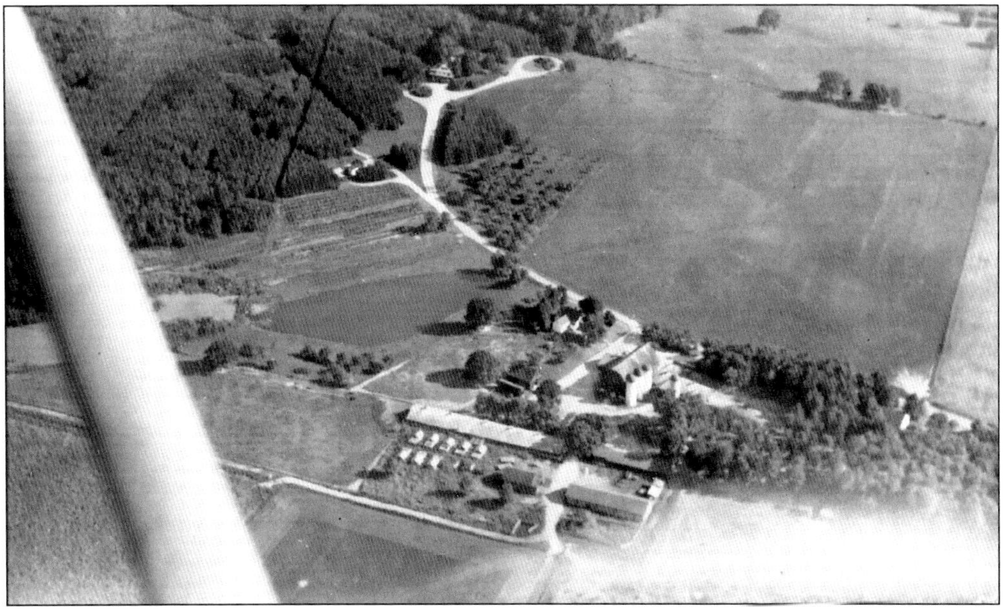

Sunset Hill Farm Park, Liberty Township. In 1934 Chicago businessman Robert Heffron Murray began his farming career with the purchase of 80 acres of land in Liberty Township. The farm seen in the above photograph eventually consisted of 235 acres and included a hillside home, a variety of farm buildings, and four additional residences. When Colonel Murray died in 1972, he left the farm to Porter County. Sunset Hill Farm Park officially opened August 7, 1993, as the first park in the new Porter County Park System. (Courtesy Porter County Parks and Recreation Dept.)

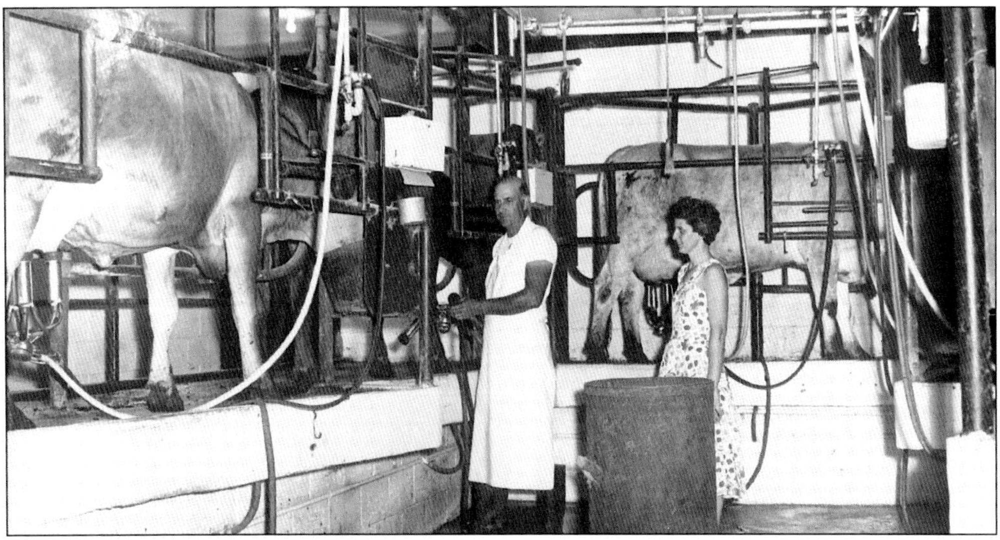

Milking Parlor at Sunset Hill Farm. Farm manager Lloyd Prosser and his wife, Ethel, are shown in the five-station milking parlor at Sunset Hill Farm c. 1954. Milk was sold to the public at the farm from 1939 to 1970 and, after that, in bulk to Dixie Dairy through 1978. Colonel Murray was frequently honored by the dairy industry for his continuing efforts to increase milk production through crossbreeding and improved hay production and curing. (Courtesy Porter County Parks and Recreation Dept.)

Three

Business and Industry

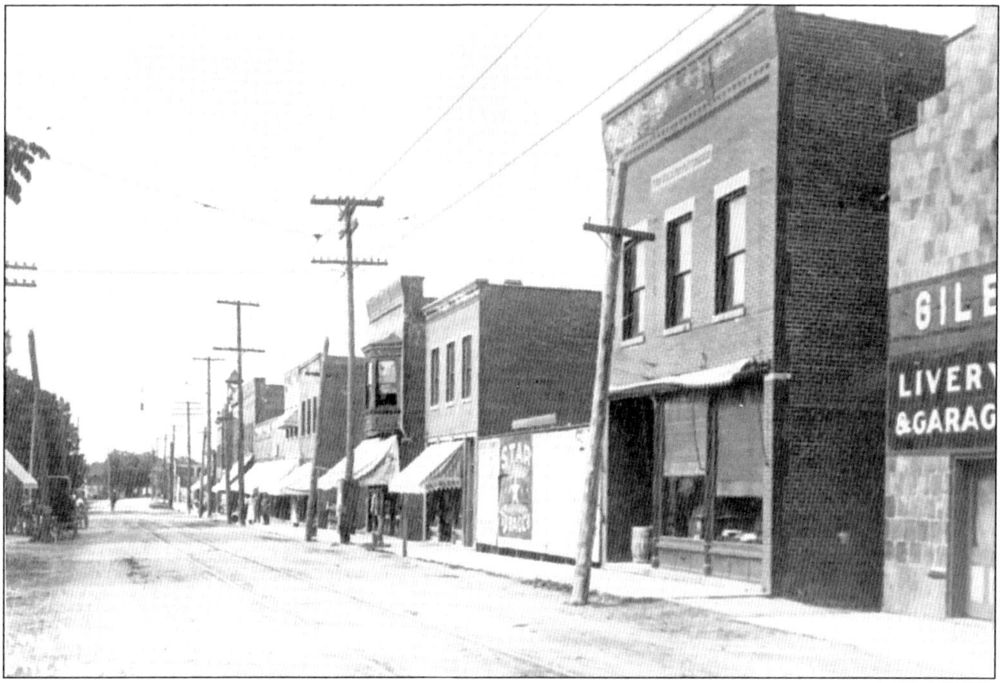

Calumet Road, 1911–1914. This early postcard of downtown Chesterton was taken looking north from the corner of Calumet Road and W. Indiana Avenue. Gile Livery & Garage, to the extreme right in the above photograph, was later demolished and replaced by a series of automobile service stations. The building beside it, built by the *Chesterton Tribune* in 1904, is still occupied by the newspaper. Charles Smith built the Smith Block in the vacant lot to its left in 1914. The arc light, suspended from the intersection of Broadway and Calumet and the inter-urban rail, dates this photograph between 1911 and 1914.

The area's business and industry began with the French and Native-American fur trade, c. 1650–1830. With the settlement of the township, subsistence farming and hunting provided a livelihood for pioneer families. The first entrepreneurs in the area operated the early sawmills and gristmills. General stores and small factories using local sources of raw materials followed. Area farmers gained access to larger markets with the coming of the railroads in 1852, and the economy expanded as better transportation facilitated the establishment and growth of industry in the township.

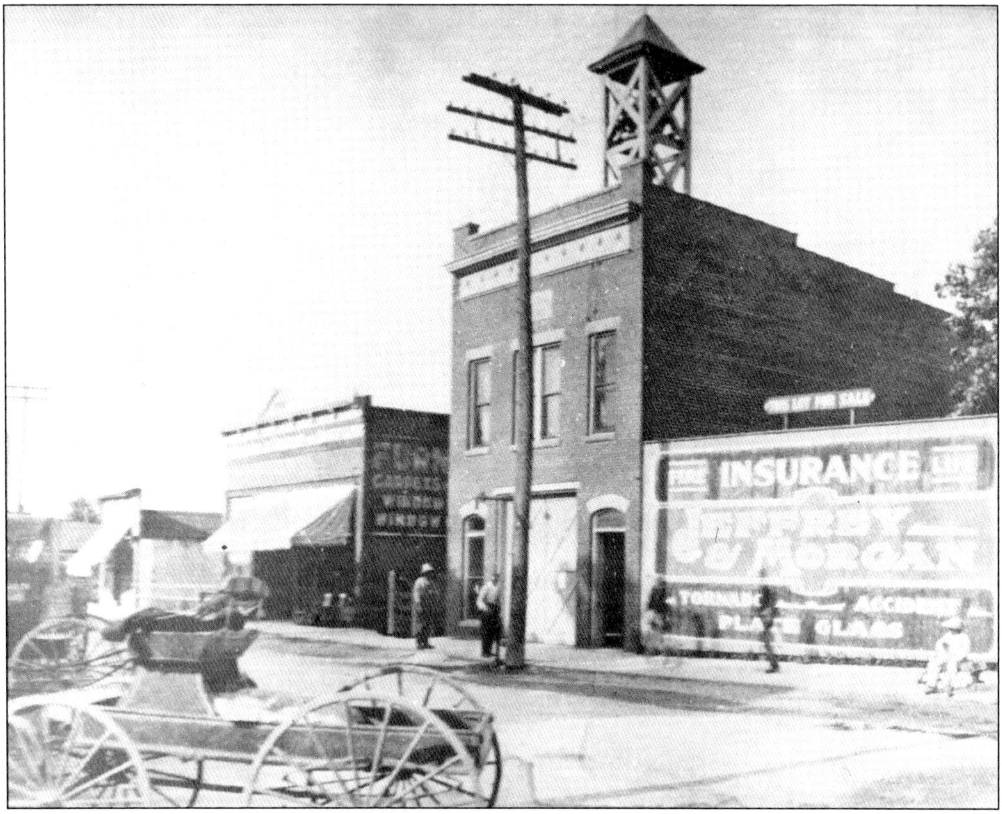

CHESTERTON TOWN HALL AND FIRE STATION. In 1903 Chesterton dedicated its first town hall, seen above in the center of this photograph taken at the intersection of Broadway and Calumet. The basement was used for storage and as a jail. The first floor housed the horse-drawn fire engine, and the second floor contained a meeting room in front and a courtroom in the rear. Now an art gallery, the building stands at 109 Broadway.

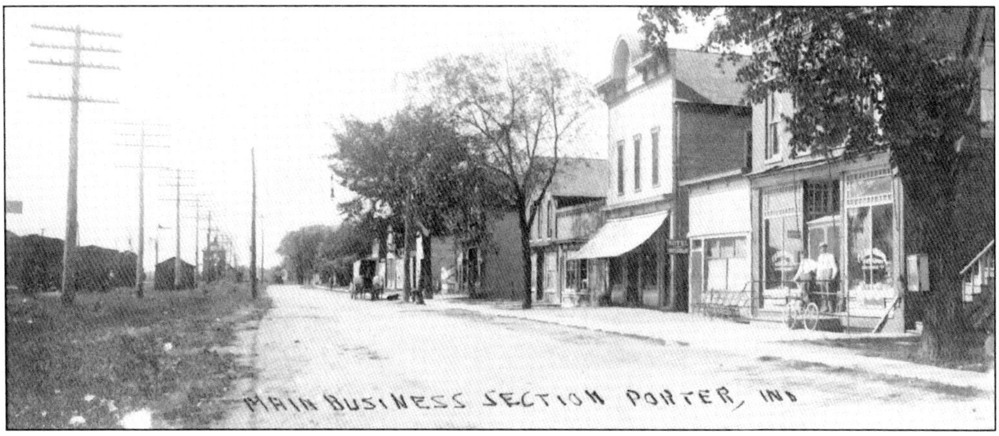

LINCOLN STREET, PORTER. This turn-of-the-century photograph of Porter's main business section features two men standing in front of C.E. Jacobson's Dry Goods and Grocery. To the left of Jacobson's is the Columbia House Hotel and Restaurant run by Fred Sievert and Sievert's saloon with a hall upstairs. Zahrn's Drug Store, which later became Imhof's, can be seen in the center of the photograph.

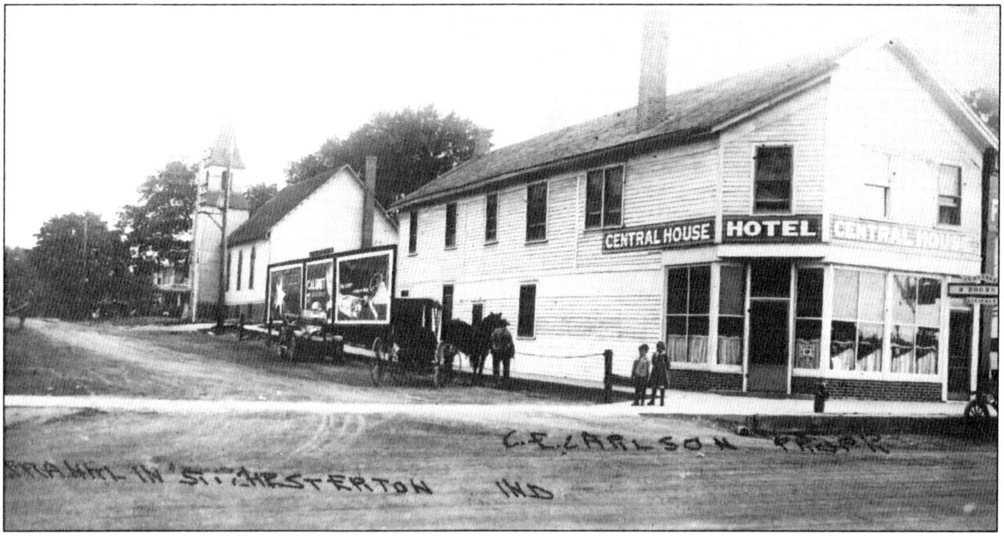

CENTRAL HOUSE HOTEL, CHESTERTON. The above c. 1920 photograph shows the corner of Second Street and Broadway, when it was occupied by the Central House Hotel (part of which may have been moved from City West on rollers to Chesterton). Note the chain-hitching post to the left of the hotel. Later the site of Eschenbach's Restaurant and Youngblood's Country Store, the building was demolished in 1958. The original Methodist Episcopal Church can also be seen at the corner of Second Street and W. Indiana Avenue.

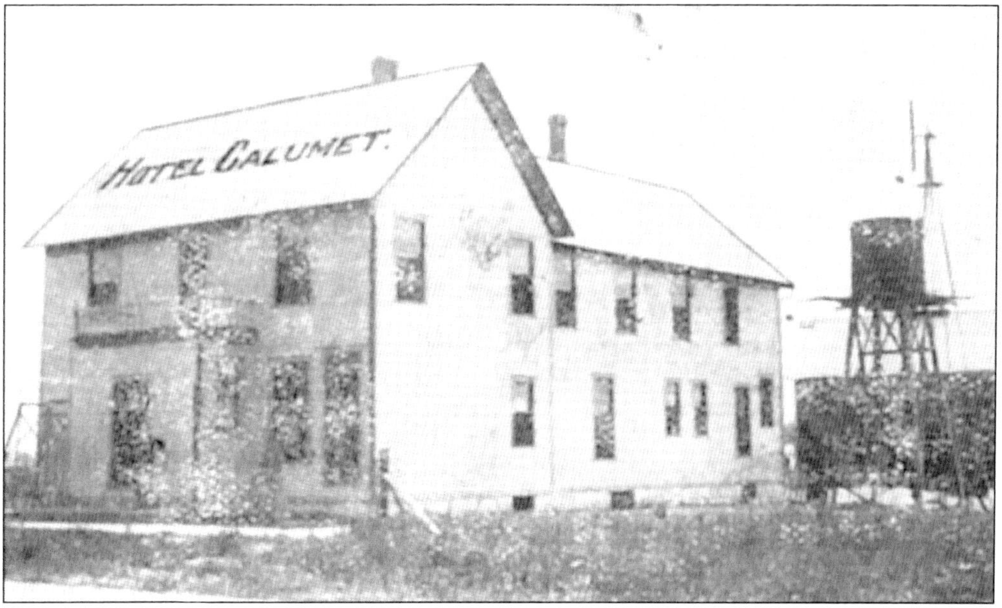

HOTEL CALUMET, CHESTERTON. The building that once housed the Hotel Calumet still stands at 1115 Broadway, across from the china factory building, the site of various industries in the town's past. The hotel, which was first operated by H.J. Friday, was proud to offer "meals at all hours, first-class baths, steam-heated rooms, and a hack to meet all trains" for only $1.25 per day.

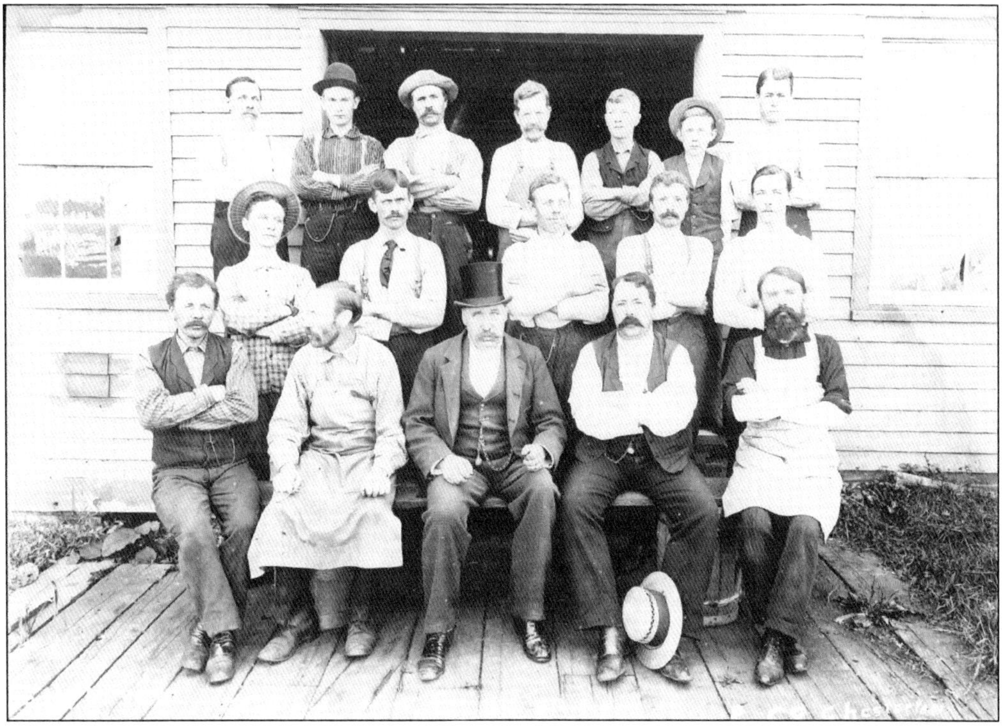

HILLSTROM ORGAN FACTORY WORKERS. C.O. Hillstrom, wearing the top hat in this August 1895 photograph, sits with some of his employees at the Hillstrom Organ Company, located at the northwest corner of Fourth and Broadway in Chesterton. The factory moved from Chicago in 1880 and employed as many as 125 men, most of whom were Swedish, including Hillstrom. The company was sold in 1898 and closed in 1912, due to the growing popularity of the piano.

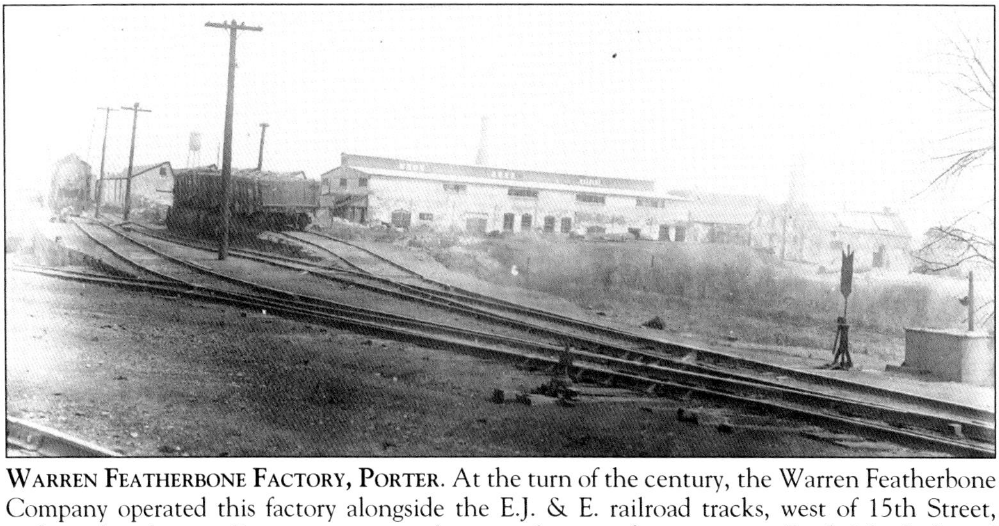

WARREN FEATHERBONE FACTORY, PORTER. At the turn of the century, the Warren Featherbone Company operated this factory alongside the E.J. & E. railroad tracks, west of 15th Street, and employed many Porter women in the manufacture of corset stays. Reid, Murdock and Co. operated a pickle factory just north of the Featherbone Factory from 1902 to 1904. In 1904, Featherbone moved its operations back to Michigan and sold the plant to Sall Mountain Asbestos Manufacturing, which remodeled and substantially enlarged the plant, employing over 100 workers until the mid-1920s.

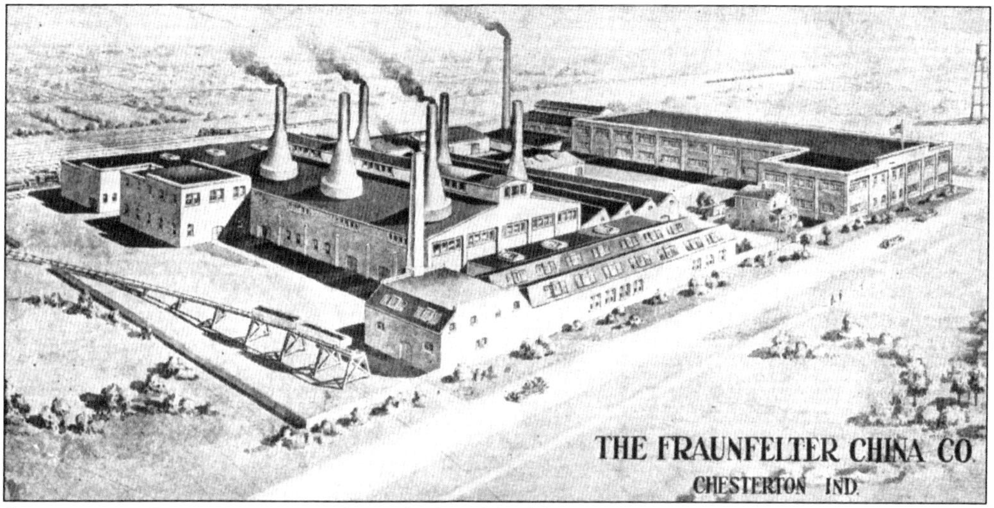

CHESTERTON CHINA FACTORY. The right-hand building of the Chesterton china factory in the above engraving still stands on Broadway between Ninth and Eleventh Streets, and is now occupied by a number of small retail businesses. The American China Co., and later, the Fraunfelter China Co. operated in the former glass factory from 1919 to 1925. Both companies produced heavy porcelain dinnerware for hotels, restaurants, and railroads.

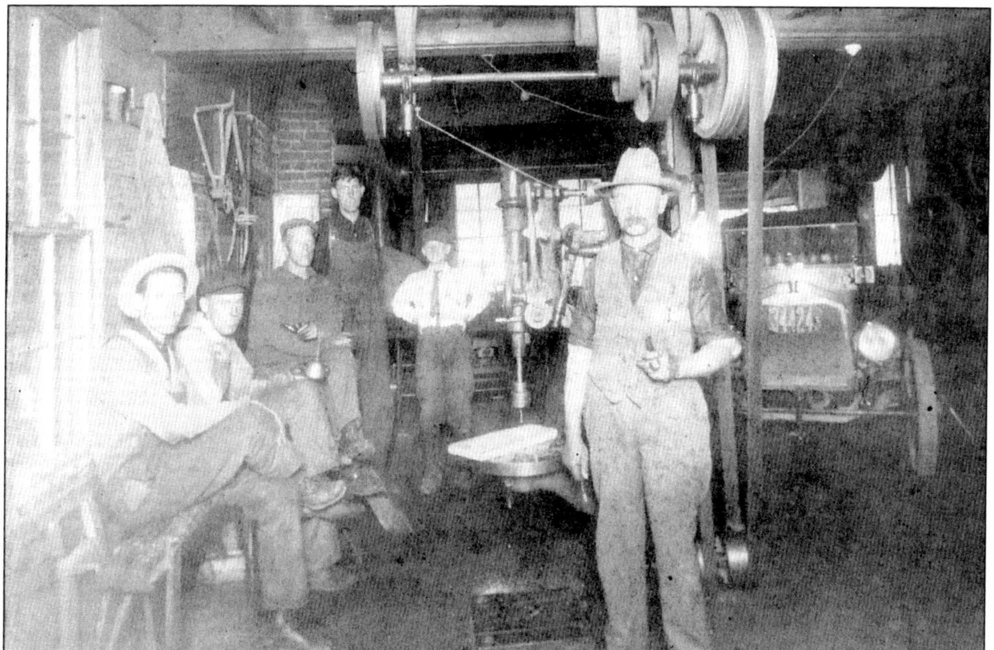

BRADLEY BROTHERS GARAGE. In the early part of the 20th century, Bob and Lan Bradley converted their father's Chesterton planing mill (in the current Art Gallery on Fourth Street) first into a bicycle repair shop, then into one of the region's first auto repair shops, and finally into a machine and welding shop. Lifelong area resident Howard Johnson later expanded his uncle's business, which merged with Wilbar Manufacturing in 1964. Pictured above, from left to right, are Bob Bradley, his brother-in-law Art Johnson, unidentified man, Lan Bradley, unidentified boy, and Frank Wannegar, the Porter town marshal.

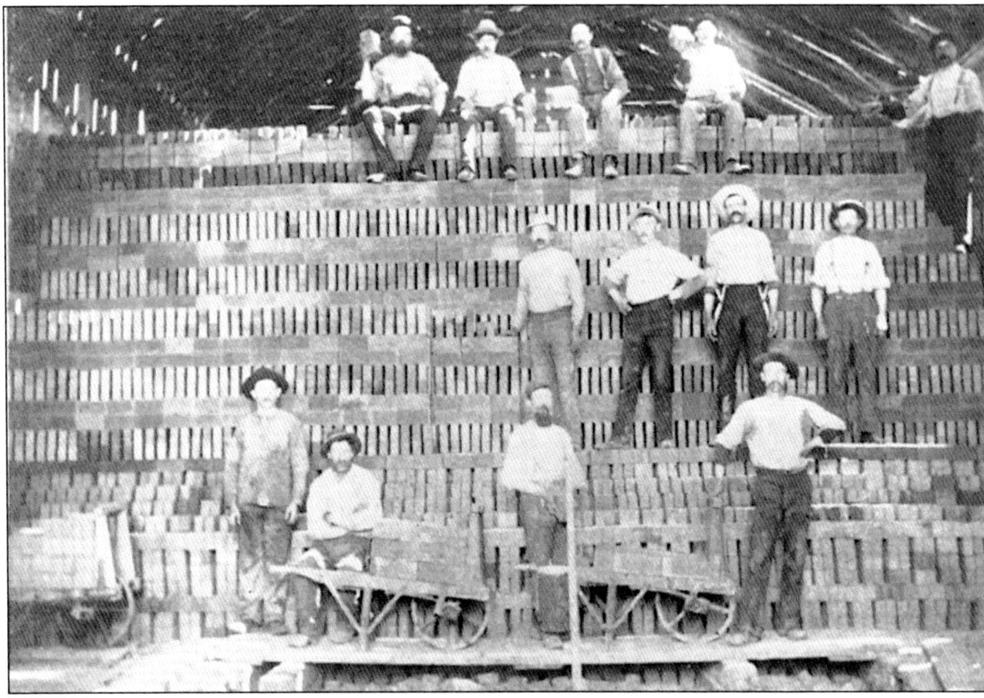

Brickyard Workers. From its beginnings in the late 1860s, the Porter brick industry grew to include at least eight different brick-making operations, many along Waverly Road. Attracted by the availability of local clay, these companies produced bricks that were used throughout the Midwest, and helped rebuild Chicago after the fire of 1871. In 1890 the Chicago Hydraulic Pressed Brick Company bought up several defunct brickyards and produced up to 50,000 bricks a day. The operation closed in the 1920s due to the exhaustion of the local clay supply, competition from cement blocks, and several damaging fires at the plant.

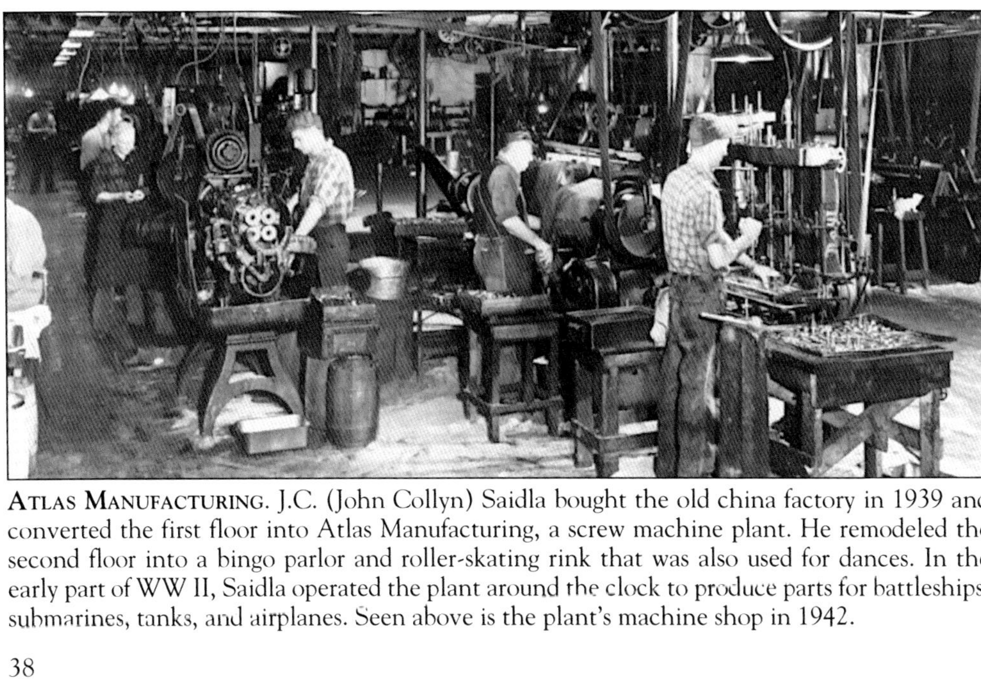

Atlas Manufacturing. J.C. (John Collyn) Saidla bought the old china factory in 1939 and converted the first floor into Atlas Manufacturing, a screw machine plant. He remodeled the second floor into a bingo parlor and roller-skating rink that was also used for dances. In the early part of WW II, Saidla operated the plant around the clock to produce parts for battleships, submarines, tanks, and airplanes. Seen above is the plant's machine shop in 1942.

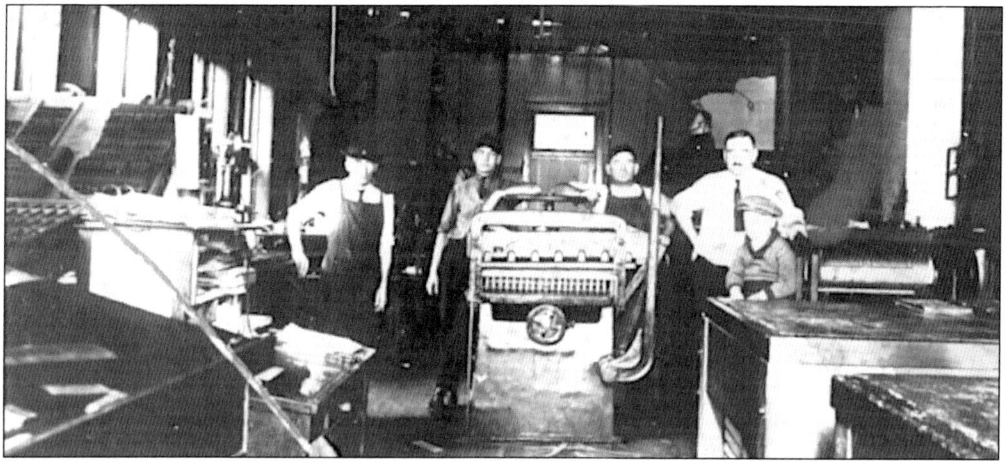

Chesterton Tribune Print Shop. John G. Graessle, owner and editor of the *Chesterton Tribune* from 1923 until his death in 1928, is seen on the right in this early photograph of the newspaper's print shop. Founded by Arthur Bowser in 1884, the *Chesterton Tribune* is the oldest continuously published independent newspaper in Northwest Indiana. Current publisher Warren H. Canright and editor David Canright are the son and grandson of long-time owner W.R. Canright.

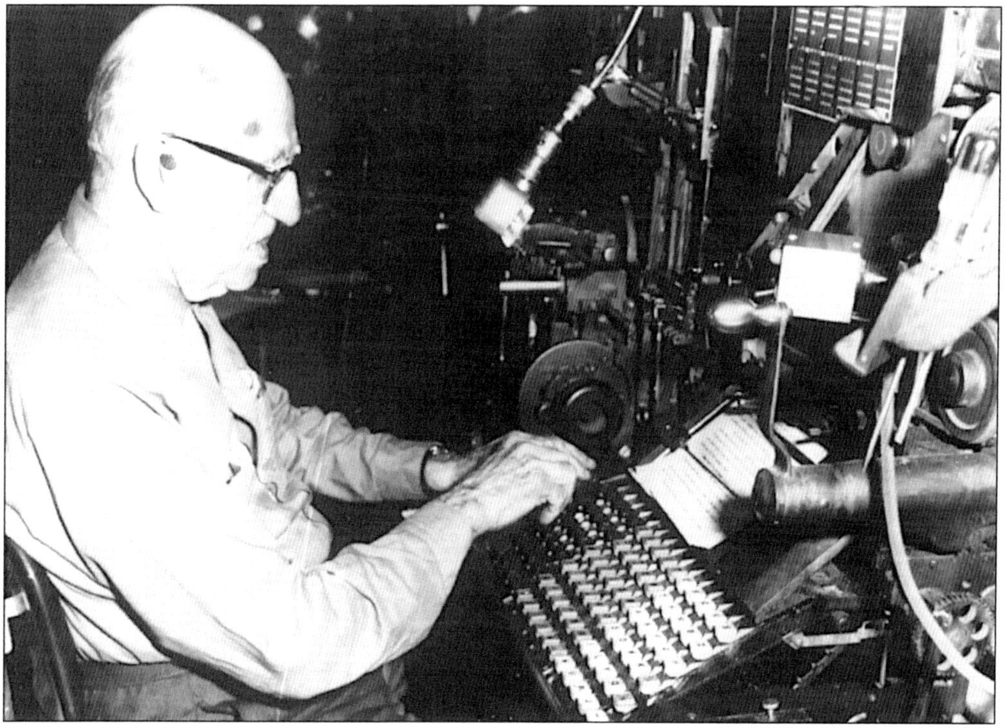

W.R. Canright, Editor. In 1907, the *Chesterton Tribune* was the first newspaper in Northwest Indiana to go from hand set to Linotype. W.R. Canright, owner and editor of the *Chesterton Tribune* from 1928 until his death in 1975, is shown above in 1970, setting type at a Linotype machine. The Linotype set type in hot lead from which the newspaper was printed. Later in 1970, the newspaper replaced its four Linotype machines with an eight-page offset press and photograph and typesetting equipment.

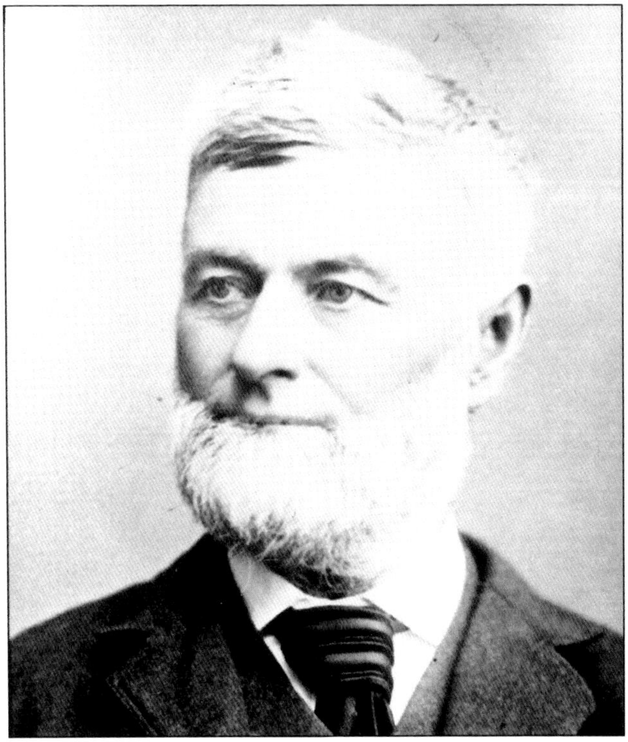

GEORGE C. MORGAN, BANKER. The son of pioneer Jesse Morgan managed the family farm until 1890, when he founded Chesterton Bank with John Gardner of Valparaiso. In 1902, seven years after George C. Morgan's death, Mr. Gardner sold his interest in the bank to Charles L. Jeffrey and E.L. Morgan, George Morgan's son. In 1910, the bank was incorporated as a state bank. Its name was changed to the Chesterton State Bank in 1930, when it received a state charter.

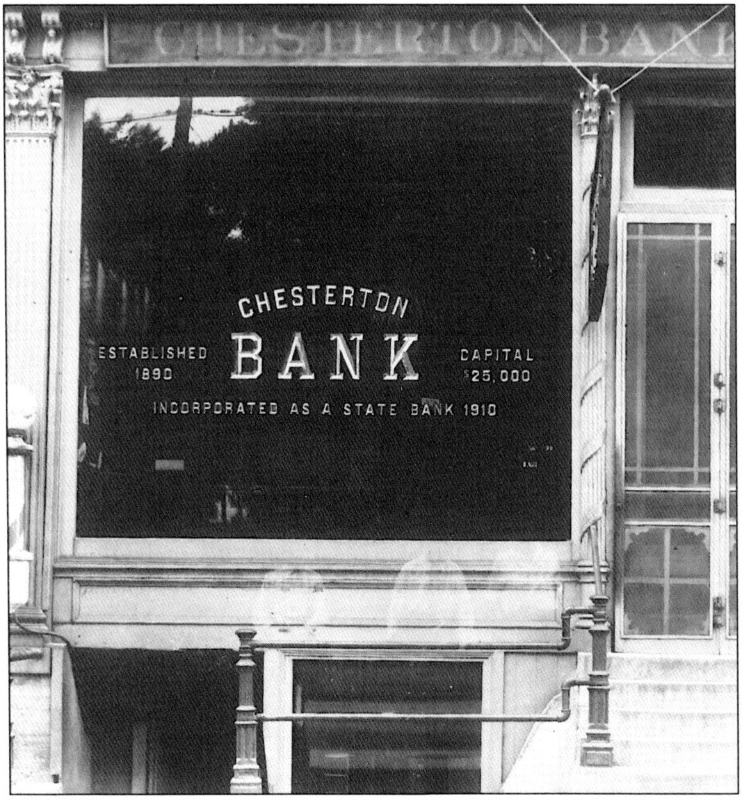

CHESTERTON STATE BANK. The bank was first established in 1890 in the Wolf & Young building on Broadway. The building, erected in 1874, was the first downtown brick building and the first to have a plate-glass window, as seen in this photograph. The bank doubled in size after a 1958 remodeling that incorporated the bakery that adjoined it on the west. The bank celebrated its 100th anniversary in 1990 and soon thereafter was sold to INB Bank.

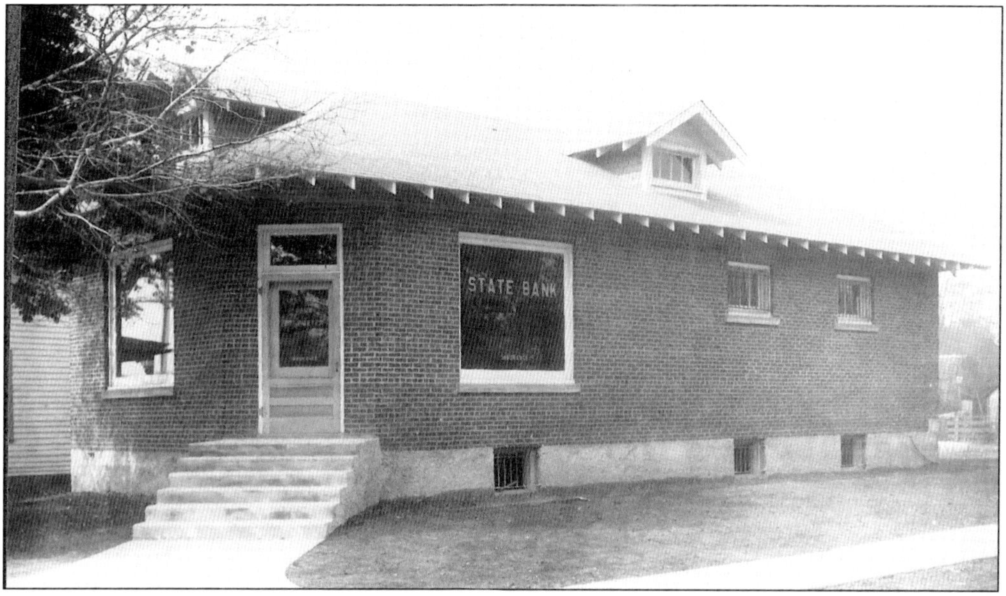

First State Bank of Porter. *Above*: The bank opened for business in October 1920. This is the main branch, located on the corner of Lincoln and Francis Streets in downtown Porter. *Below*: Photographed the same year, these workmen are constructing the vault for the bank. Local attorney Mox Ruge joined the bank in 1934 and served as president until 1967. He was succeeded by his son, James D. Ruge, in 1970. The original building has been remodeled several times, and the bank has added branches in Chesterton and Pines.

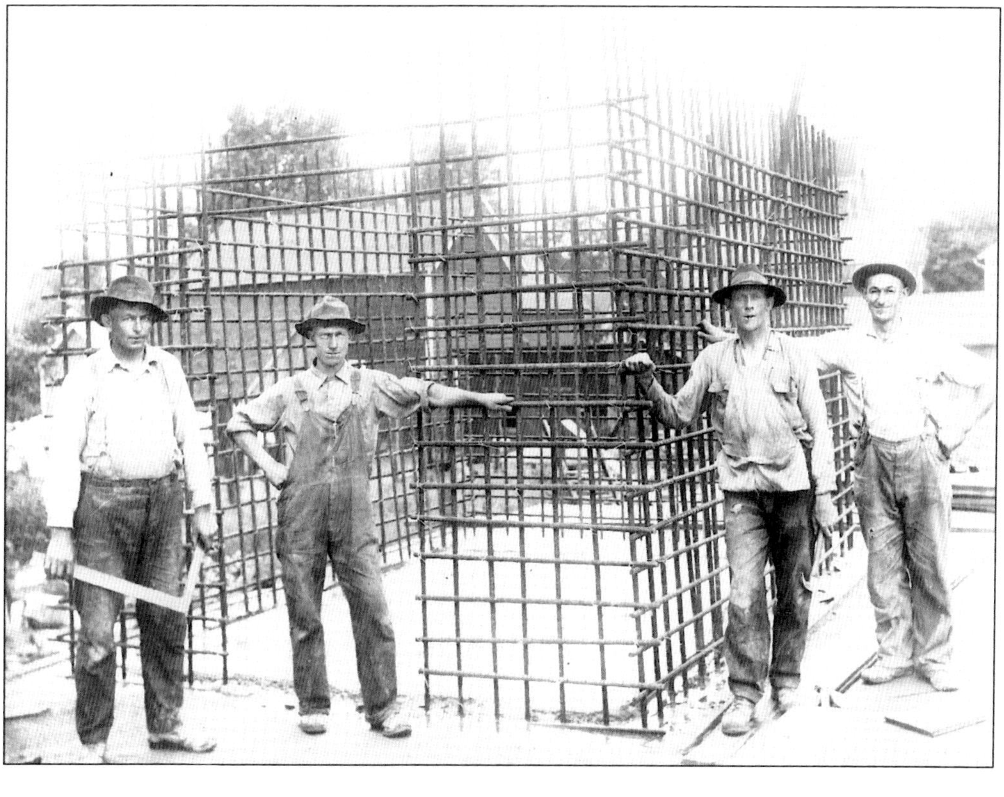

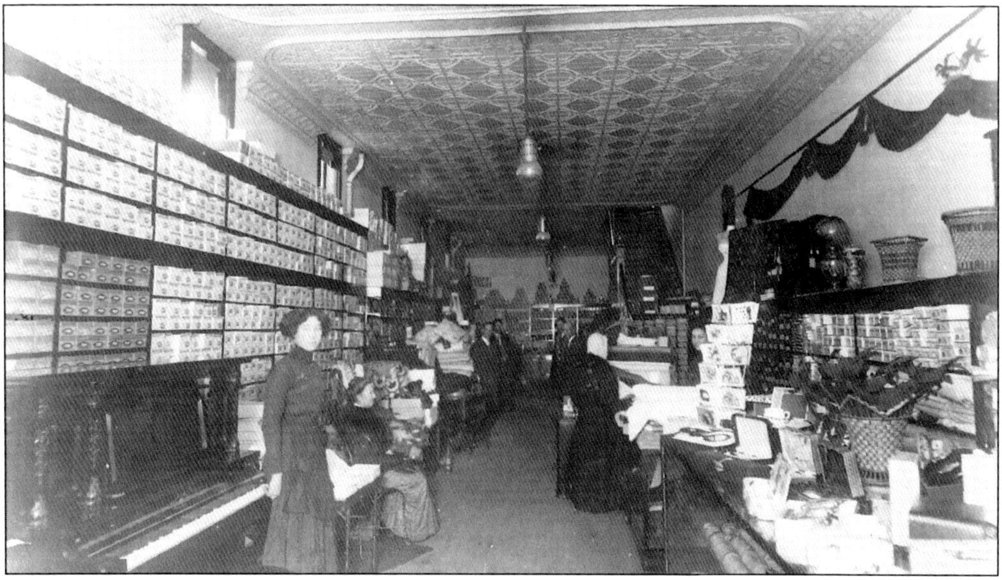

Smith Store Interior, Chesterton. Elias Thomas built the brick store at the southwest corner of Broadway and Calumet in 1888. After a fire in 1911, it was remodeled by new owners Myron and Harry Smith with huge showcase windows, a massive oak staircase, a pressed-tin ceiling, and an ornate cast-iron exterior staircase. Seen above in this c. 1912 photograph are Pearl Slont, Myron Smith, Harry Smith, and several unidentified customers.

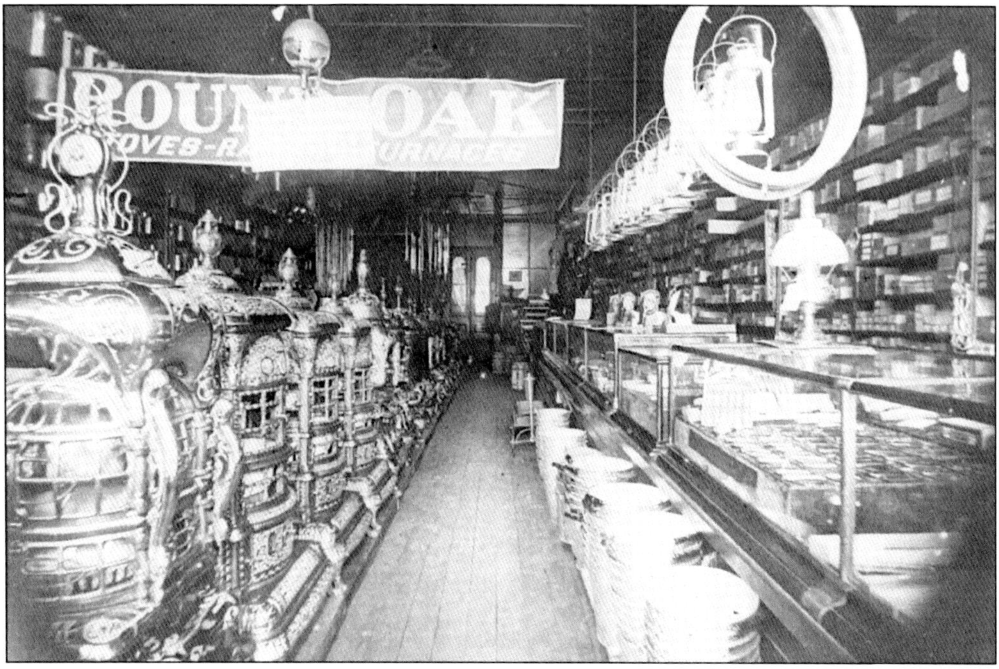

Bartel's Hardware, Interior. From 1884 until 1977, 115 Broadway housed a succession of hardware stores. The most recent, from 1892 to 1977, was Bartel's Hardware. From 1884 on, the store also held a tin shop for the manufacture of stovepipes and gutters. The tin shop was later donated by descendants of the Bartels to Billy Creek Village in Rockville, IN. The hardware store's original hand pump remains in what is still a retail space.

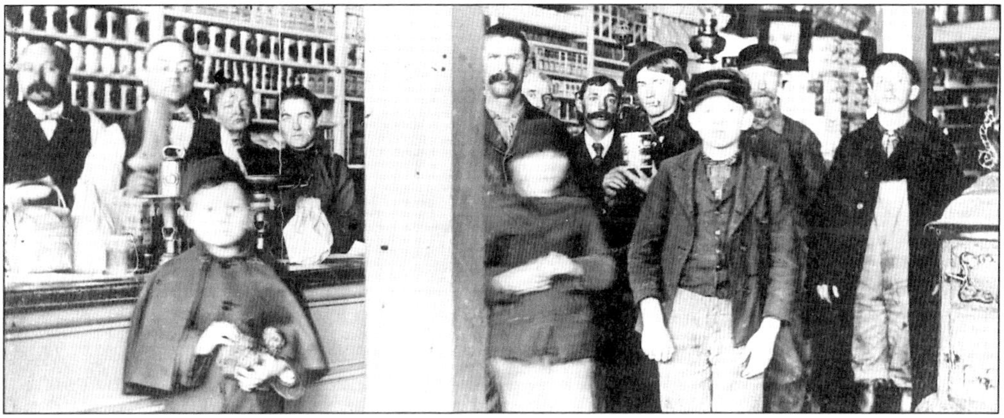

Busse's Store, Porter. This 1898 photograph shows customers and employees in the Union Block Department Store owned by John Busse. Busse married Hannah F. Hageman in 1884 and became a prominent local businessman and civic leader. He allowed many Porter families to buy groceries on credit during hard times and later became a partner in the Porter Riverside Land Co., which deeded land formerly occupied by the brickyards to the town for Hawthorne Park.

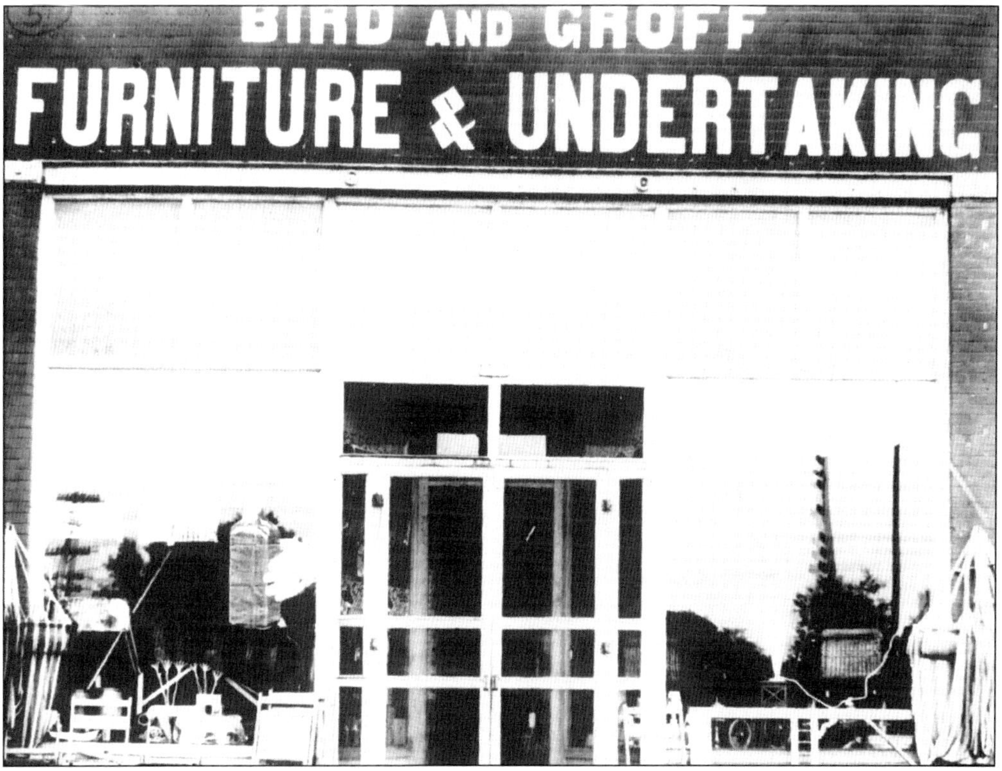

Bird and Groff, Chesterton. In the 19th and early 20th centuries, furniture stores were often operated with undertaking businesses. Edward Bird and Felix Groff opened the above business in 1915, which still stands, at 203 Broadway. In 1927, Mr. Groff bought the Jeffrey home at the northeast corner of Second and Jefferson and moved his family and his business to the new location that today is still a funeral home. Groff sold the building and his undertaking business to Fred Edmonds in 1939.

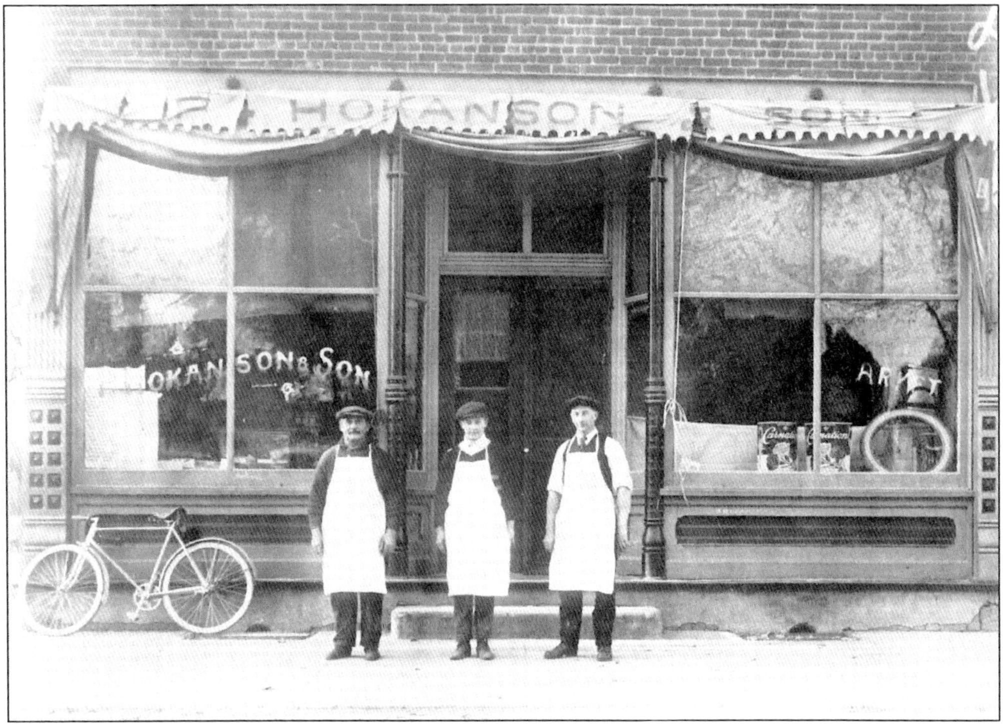

HOKANSON MEAT MARKET, PORTER. Three generations of the Hokanson family, Swedish immigrant Peter, grandson Alvin, and son Victor Hokanson, are pictured in front of their market at 200 Franklin Street, Porter, which they purchased in 1906. The Hokanson butcher shop grew to include groceries and produce. In 1943, the family-owned store became the first self-service grocery in the area. In 1954 Alvin and Arthur Hokanson relocated to 805 Broadway in Chesterton and opened Broadway Food Mart, which they operated until 1958.

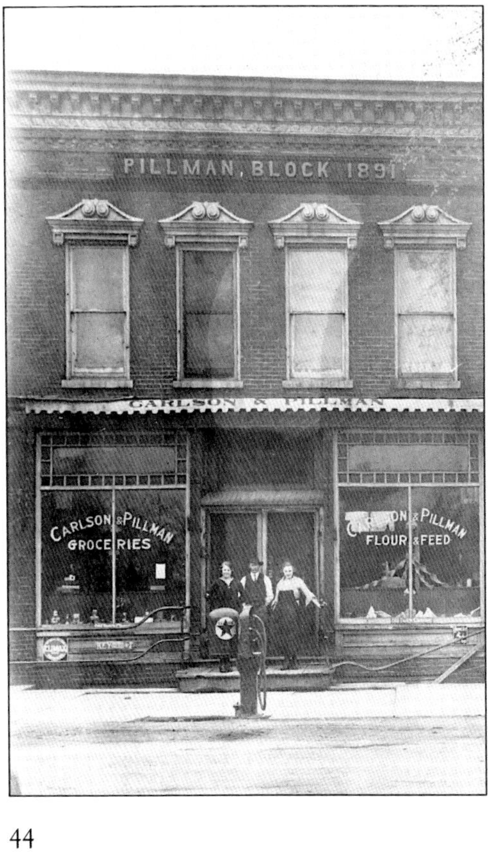

CARLSON & PILLMAN STORE, PORTER. In 1891 August Pillman founded a grocery business at 212 Lincoln Street that was later operated by C.E. Jacobson from 1898 to 1912. August's son, Arthur, formed a partnership with his brother-in-law Alec Carlson in 1915 that lasted until 1937. In this 1921 photograph, Arthur is seen between Dena Foss (left) and Adele Borg Isaacson (right). Mr. Pillman continued to operate the store into the late 1950s.

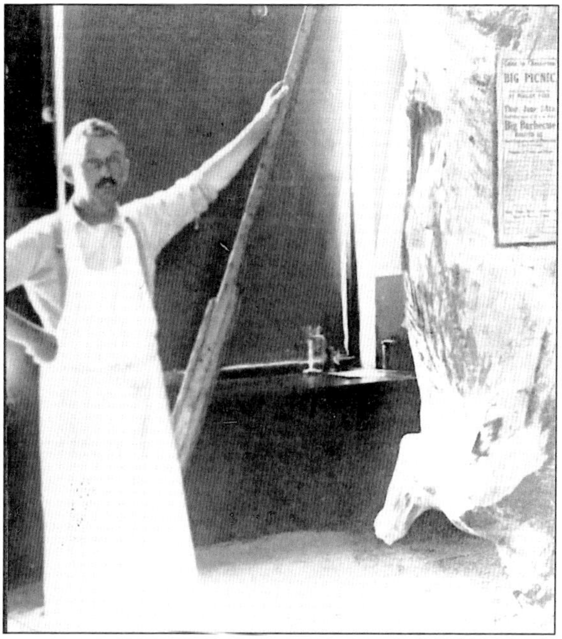

DENNIS HARRINGTON, BUTCHER. The City Meat Market was established by Dennis Harrington and his partner, Fuller, in 1901. Harrington is seen standing by an 800-pound ox carcass, which was the main attraction at the June 24, 1915, Morgan Park barbecue. According to a caption originally printed in the *Chesterton Tribune*, the meat cost 19¢ a pound wholesale, "bone, gristle, and all."

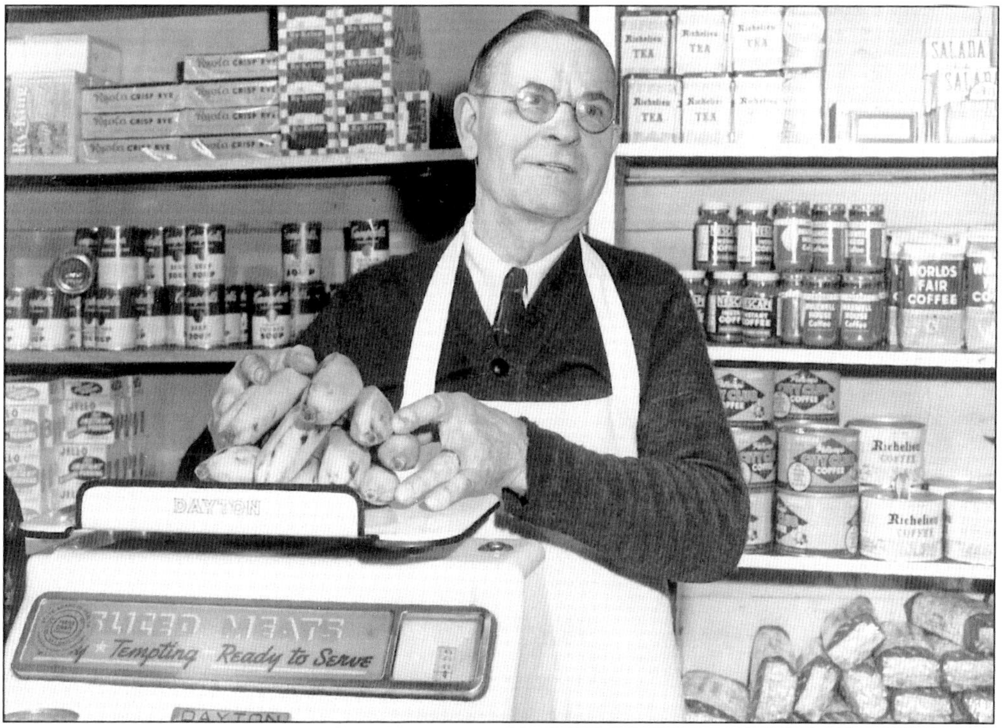

H.F. CARLSON, GROCER. H.F. Carlson was 85 when the above photograph was taken in 1959 for the *Chesterton Tribune*. Born in Sweden, he immigrated in 1891 and moved to Chesterton in 1908. He ran a general store in the Main Street Building at Broadway and Calumet; in 1935, he moved the business to the Johnson Building at 203 Broadway. He is seen in his store in 1959, before self-serve chain grocery stores such as A&P moved in, putting the smaller stores out of business.

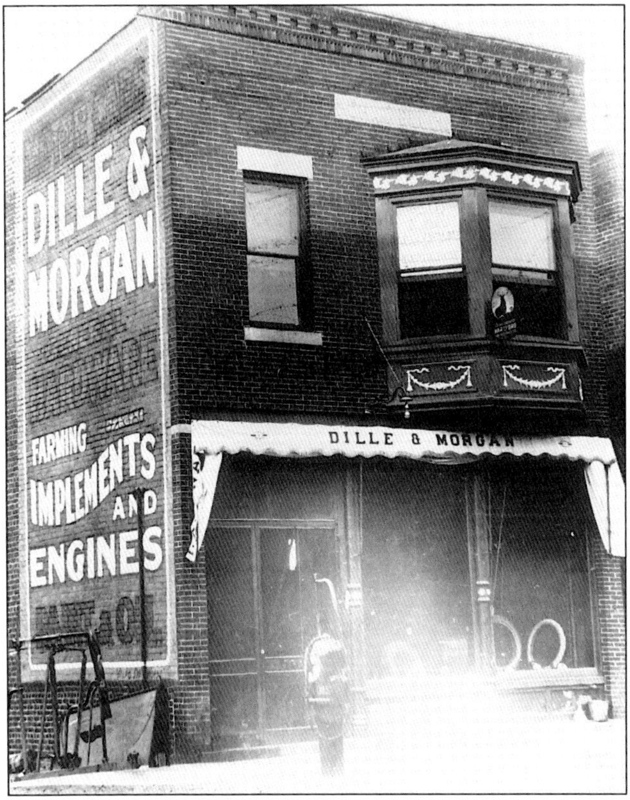

Dille and Morgan Hardware, Chesterton. John Dille and Bennett Morgan bought the Hoham building seen here c. 1913 for their growing hardware business. Mr. Morgan bought out his partner in 1922 and changed the name of the business to Morgan Hardware. Note the gasoline pump in front of the store and the "Dille & Morgan" sign on the side of the building. In the 1970s, Morgan's son, Robert, sold the business to Bill and Norma Scobey, who later sold it to Hugh and Eva Hopkins.

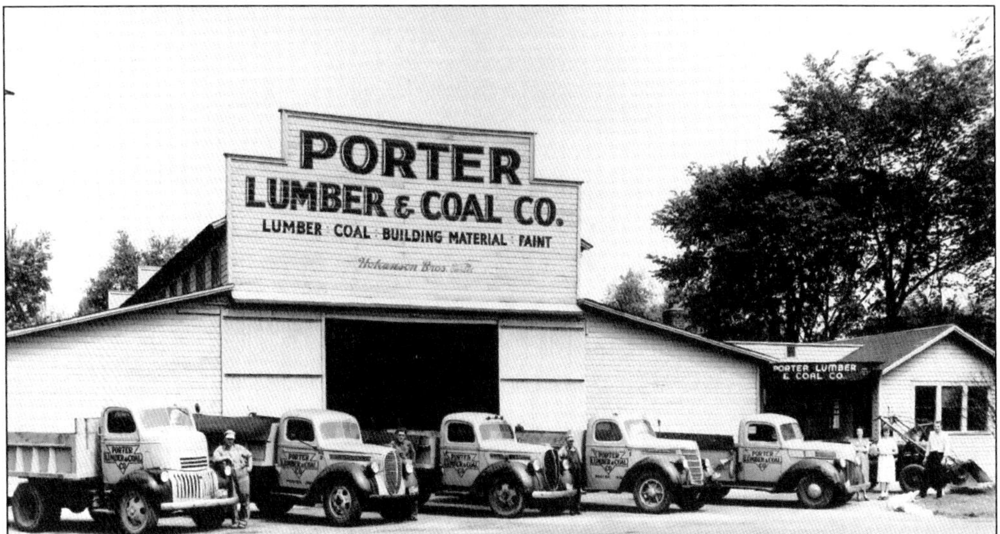

Porter Lumber. In 1946, Alvin, Arthur, Maynard, Virgil, and Clarence Hokanson, sons of successful local merchant Victor (and Anna) Hokanson, purchased Emil Anderson's coal and lumber business, located at 340 Lincoln Street, and renamed it Porter Lumber and Coal. In 1953, they acquired the lumber company founded by local builder Joseph H. Ameling and re-established it as the Chesterton Lumber and Supply Company with Clarence Hokanson as manager. The business was later sold to the Radke family.

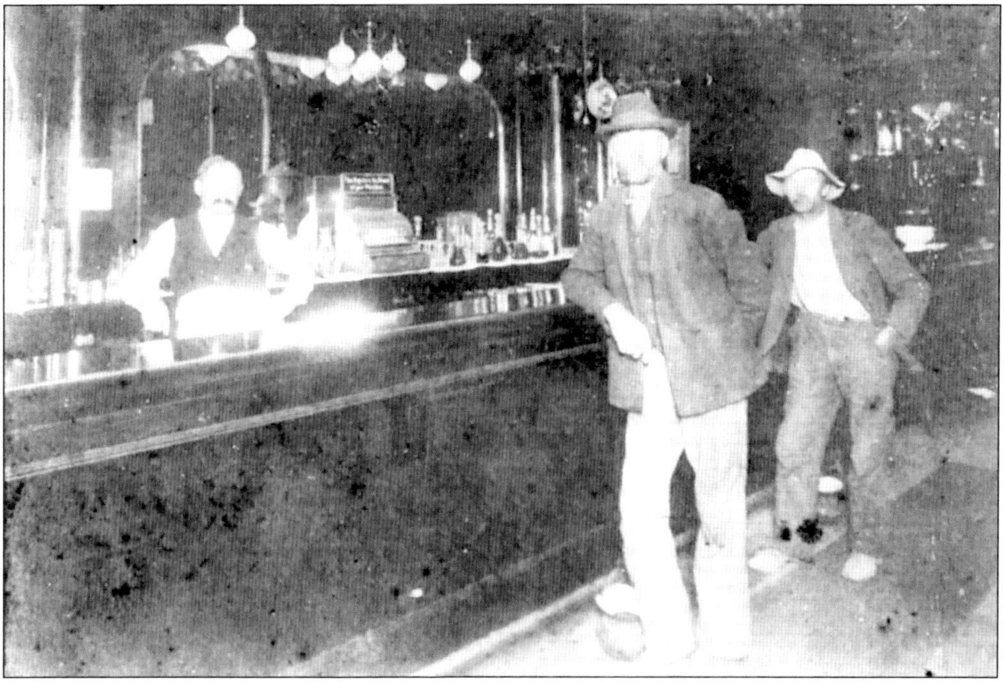

HENRY GOTENS IN SALOON, CHESTERTON. Henry Gotens and William Ameling opened a hotel on Main Street (now Broadway), in 1908, during a period when the "Drys" had won a local option election to close all local saloons. In 1909 another election reversed the results and the partners opened a saloon in their hotel, which they operated together until 1915, when Gotens (seen behind the bar in the above photograph) retired from the business. Note the individual spittoons placed at the customers feet.

PATRICK FLANNERY, SALOON OWNER, CHESTERTON. P.J. Flannery, seen in this 1940 photograph, started in the saloon business with A.O.J. Krieger in 1903. In 1910 Flannery and his brother Tom bought the business and operated it together for many years at 125 Calumet. Both brothers were avid athletes and played on the Chesterton Tribunes baseball team, beginning in 1900. The business bearing their name still operates at the same address, which from 1908 to 1909 housed the Lyric Theatre, the town's first movie theatre.

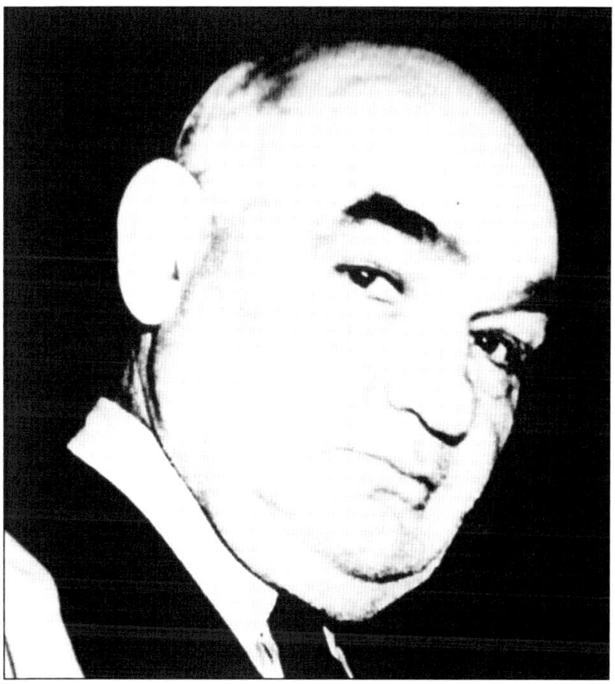

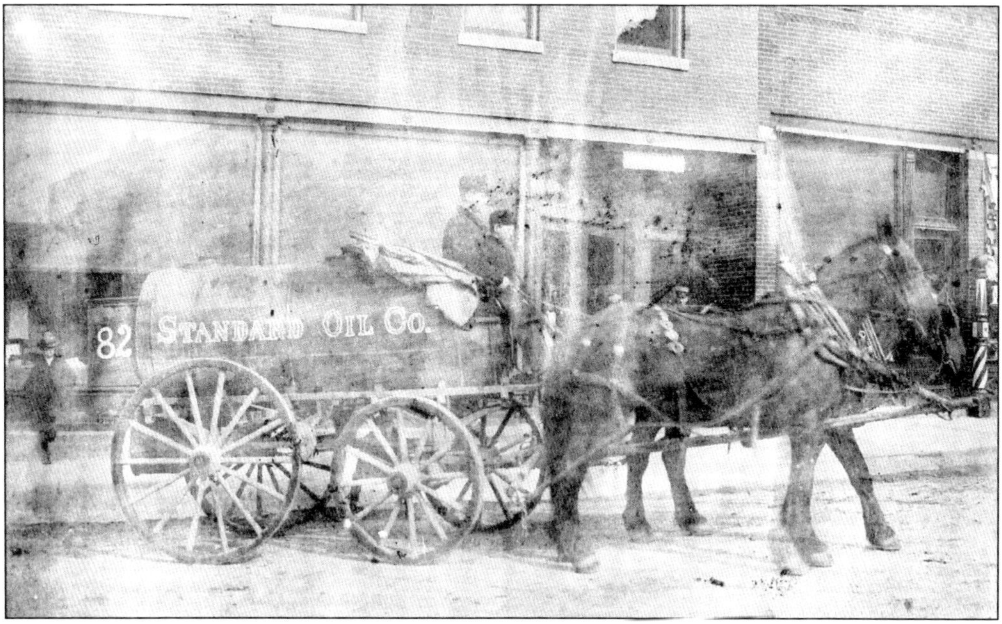

STANDARD OIL DELIVERY WAGON, CHESTERTON. Before the advent of motorized trucks, produce was transported locally by a wide variety of horse-drawn wagons. The above Standard Oil wagon is shown in 1907, in front of the post office. To the right is Sundeen's barbershop at 121 Calumet, a building that has housed a barbershop continuously since that year.

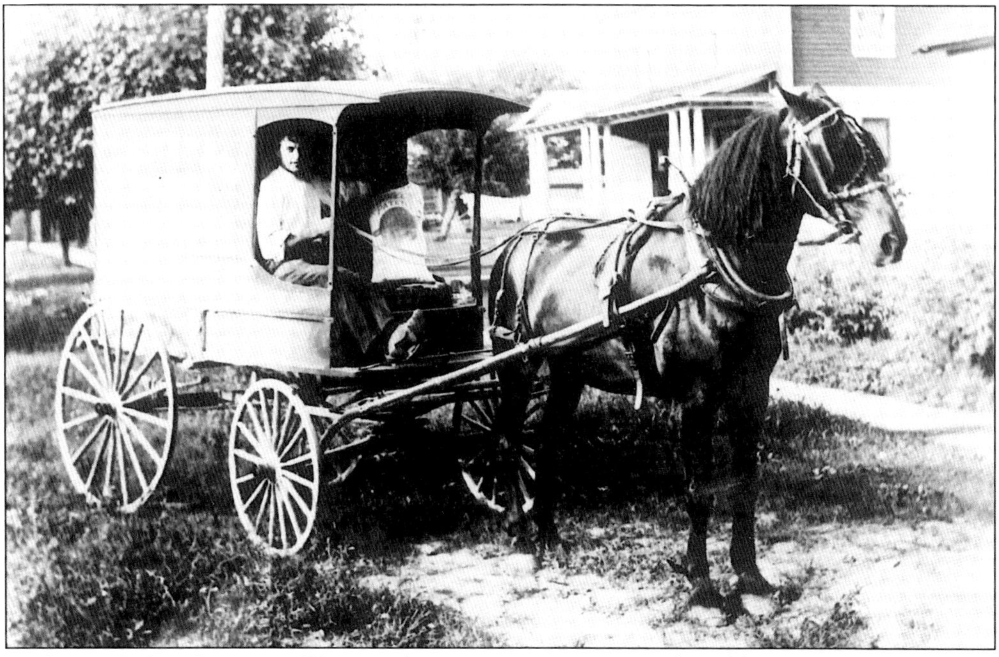

M. SMITH & SON DELIVERY WAGON, CHESTERTON. Myron Smith and his son, Harry, delivered groceries and dry goods in the horse-drawn cart seen here, in front of Roy Hubbard's home at 221 Second Street. In 1911 Harry Smith became one of the first retailers in the area to sell automobiles. The Smith family operated the general store on the southwest corner of Broadway and Calumet from 1905 until it was sold in 1975.

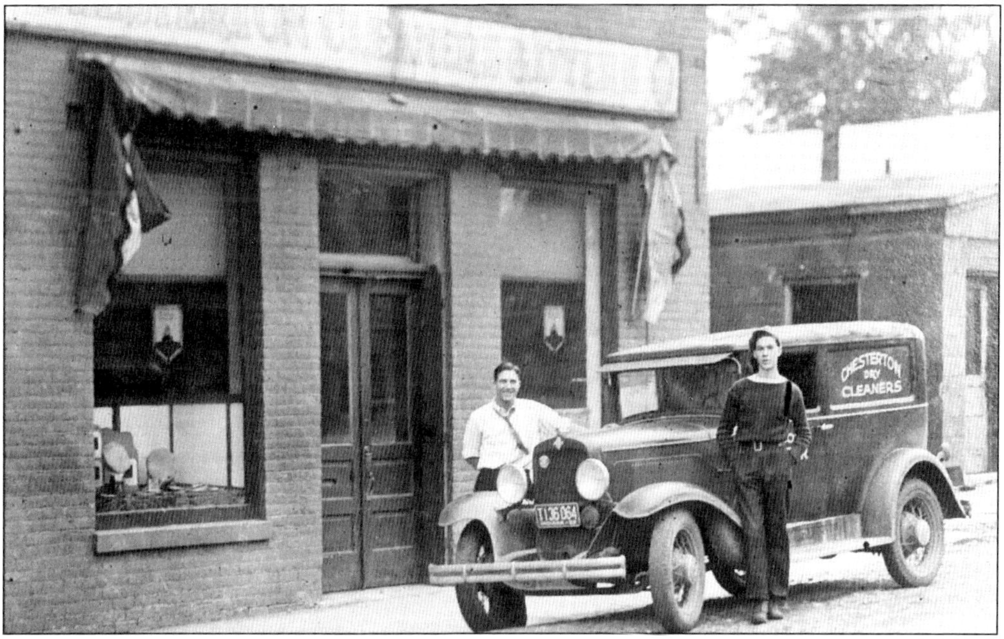

LESLIE PRATT DRY CLEANING. Leslie Pratt bought the Chesterton Cleaners and Dyers at 103 Second Street in 1930 from Felix Groff. In 1931 Pratt, pictured to the left of his delivery van, added a line of men's clothing. He built a new store at 213 Broadway in 1940, which he operated with his wife, Mary, until her death in 1991 and the sale of the store in 1992. A well-known performer himself, Pratt also taught singing lessons in the area for many years.

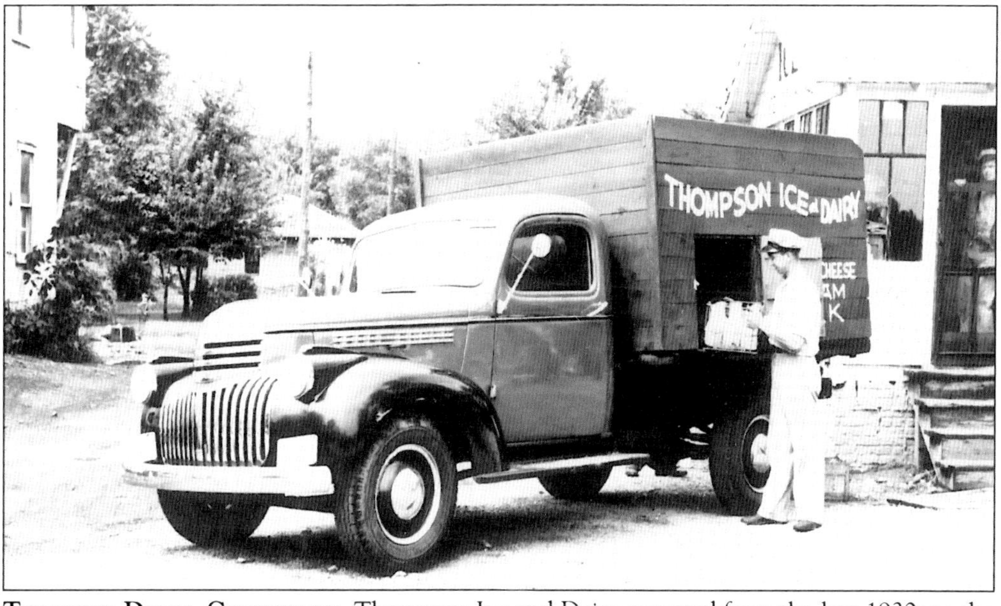

THOMPSON DAIRY, CHESTERTON. Thompson Ice and Dairy operated from the late 1930s to the late 1950s in an era when home delivery of milk was the norm. In addition to the delivery of dairy products and ice, Thompson operated a dairy fountain at 221 N. Calumet, in a building that now houses a photography shop.

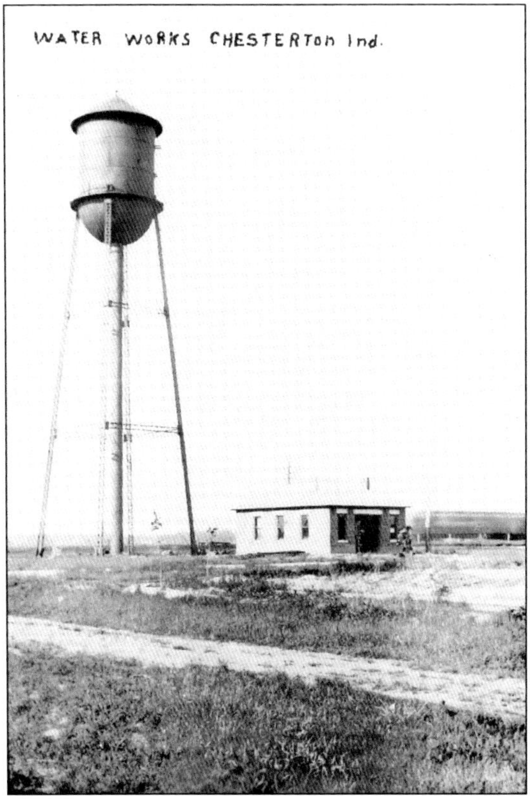

Chesterton Water Works. In 1907 Chesterton granted a franchise to the Home Water Company for the installation of a water system for the town. The pumping station, located at Seventh and Broadway, was powered by a 25-horsepower engine. The company also laid water mains throughout the town and installed 26 fire hydrants. The water tank was 100 feet high and held 50,000 gallons of water.

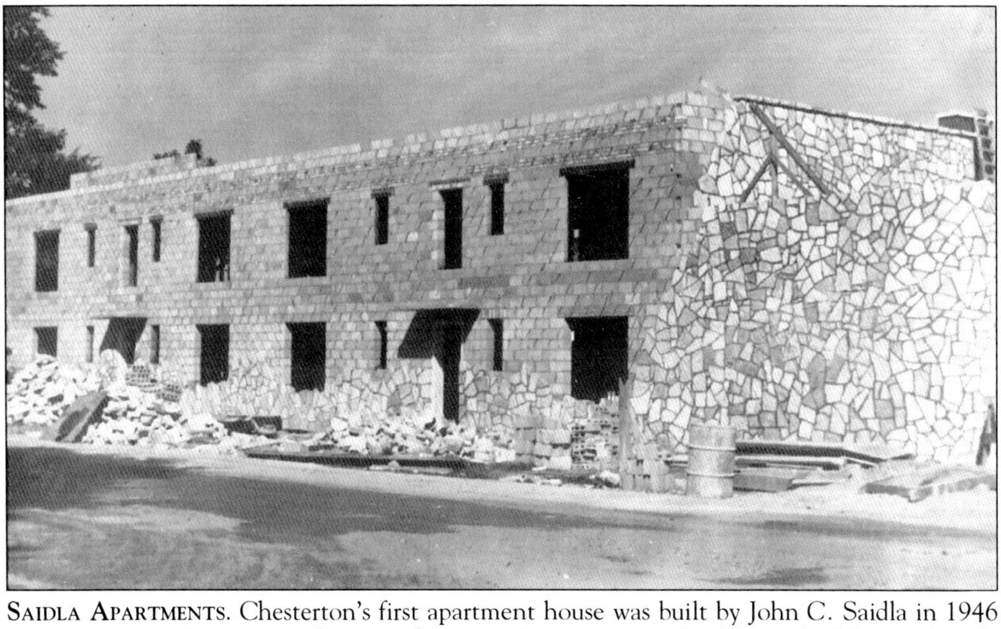

Saidla Apartments. Chesterton's first apartment house was built by John C. Saidla in 1946 as a response to the post-war housing shortage. Apartments in the 12-unit building on Ninth Street and Indiana Avenue were rented to GIs and their families for about $50 a month. Saidla also built a skating rink and pottery/photography studio next to the apartments. The second building is now the home of a gymnastics center.

Four

CHURCHES

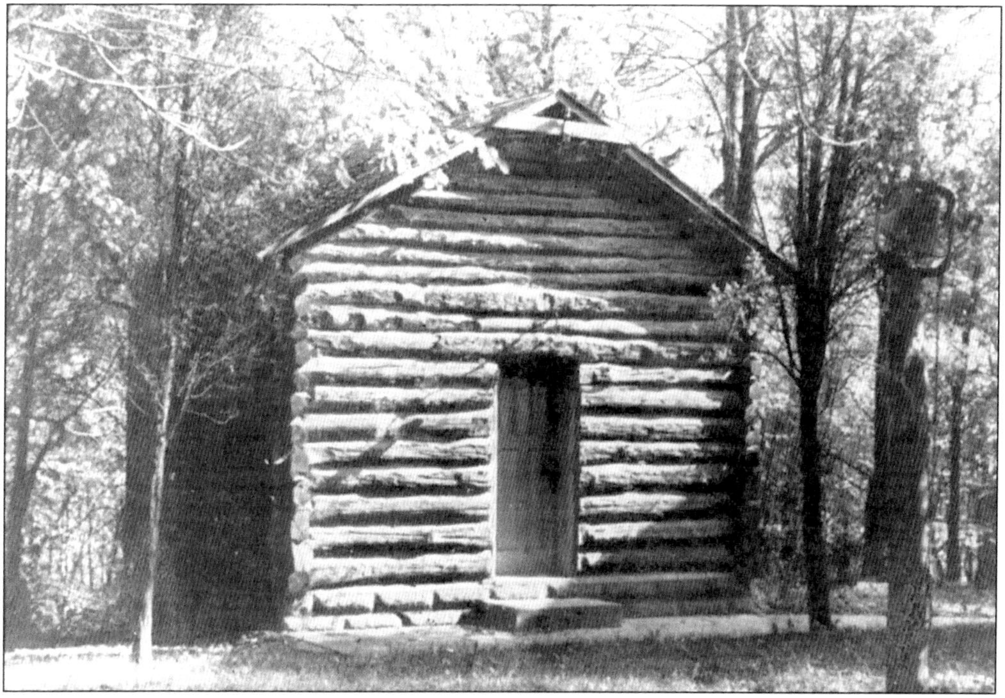

BAILLY CHAPEL, PORTER. According to Francis Howe, in 1869 her mother Rose Bailly Howe, the daughter of fur-trader Joseph Bailly, renovated what had been the Bailly Homestead's original kitchen into the small log chapel seen above. The family used the building for prayer and devotions, following the tradition of family home worship established by Joseph Bailly and his wife, Marie, in 1832. Religious observance in the home was the norm in the early years of settlement, as traveling Roman Catholic priests and, later, Protestant circuit riders passed through the area infrequently.

In the second half of the 19th century, a number of immigrant groups settled in this area, drawn by the promise of jobs and farmland. The German, Swedish, and Irish brought their own social and religious customs and traditions with them. Each group established churches in Westchester Township, with services often being conducted in their native language, a practice that continued until the 1920s.

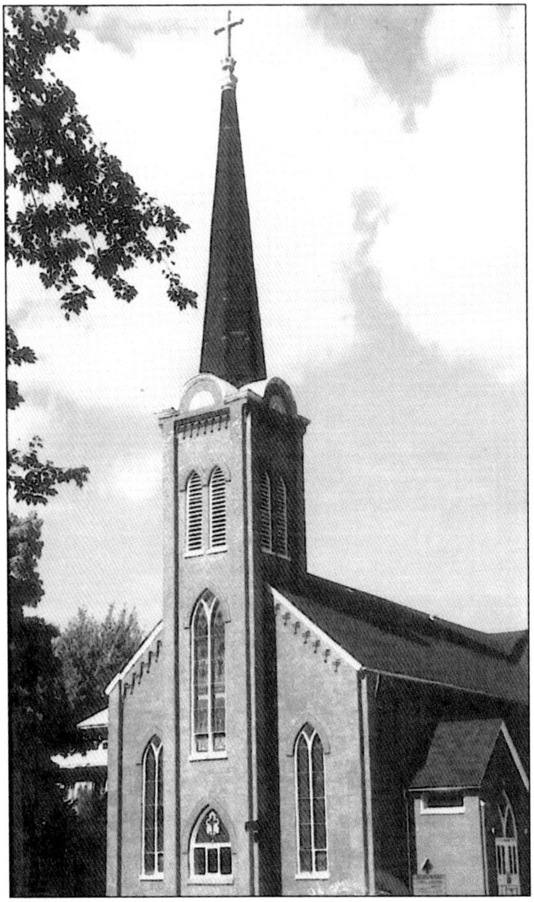

ST. PATRICK CHURCH, CHESTERTON. Father Kilroy, a missionary and pastor from LaPorte, organized the first Roman Catholic parish in Chesterton in 1858. A small frame church was built at the corner of Calumet Road and Michigan Street to serve the large number of Irish workers who had come to this area to build the railroads. In 1867, Father John Flynn was appointed as the first pastor of the new St. Patrick parish. A larger brick church at the corner of Third Street and W. Indiana Avenue was built in 1875. It served several generations of area Catholics until the 1980s, when a larger church was built on N. Calumet Road. The landmark building was destroyed by fire in 1998.

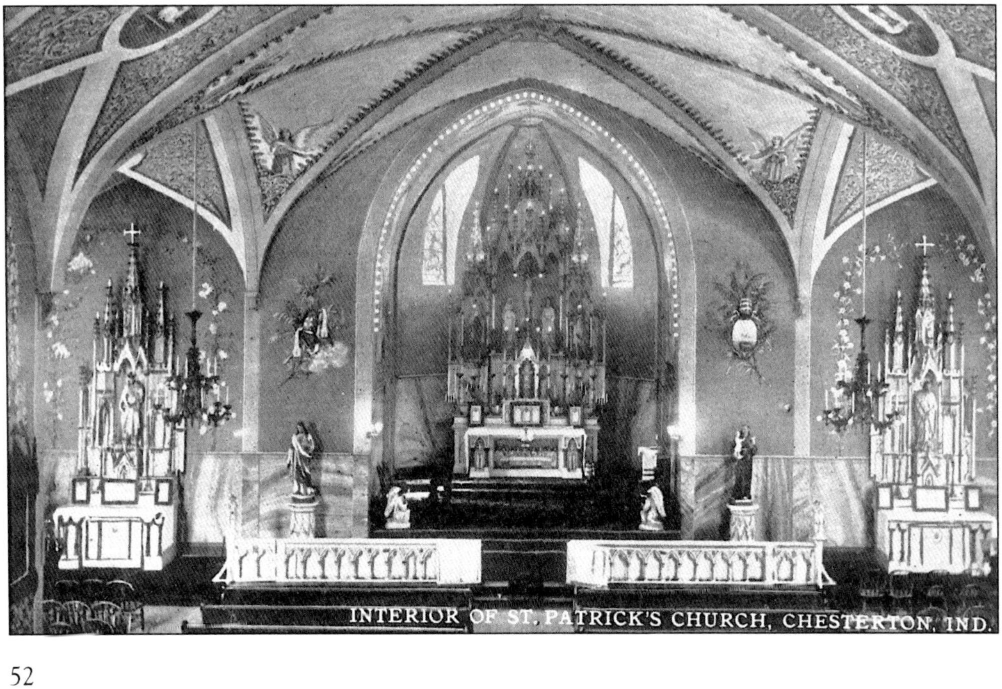

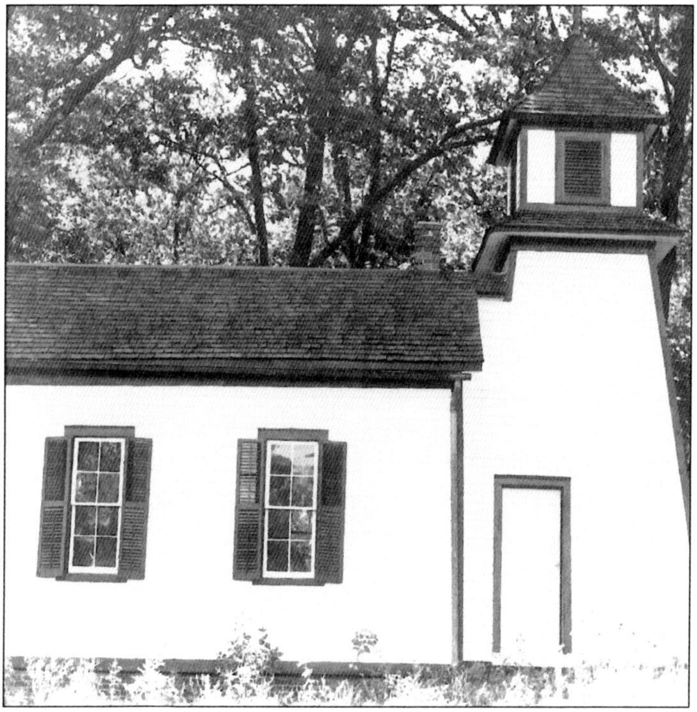

Burstrom Chapel, Porter. In 1880 Swedish immigrants in the Baillytown area renovated a tool shed, donated by Frederick Burstrom to serve as a school for local children. The school was closed in 1885, when the public school at Baillytown opened nearby. *Augsburg Svenska Skola*, a summer school taught in Swedish, was held in the building each year until 1912. Now owned by Augsburg Lutheran Church and known as Burstrom Chapel, the building was renovated in the 1930s and was often used as a chapel for midweek services until 1956.

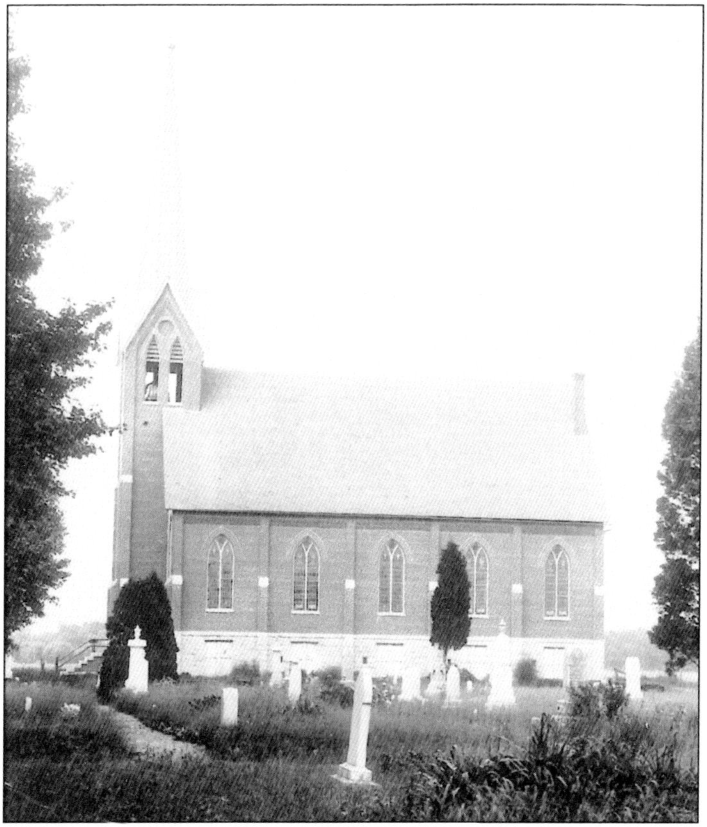

Augsburg Evangelical Lutheran, Porter. The area's first Lutheran church was organized in 1858 by Swedish settlers in the Baillytown area of Porter. The first church building was erected in 1864. Until the 1920s, services at the church were often held in Swedish. The church seen here was built in 1900 but was destroyed by fire in 1933. The church was rebuilt in 1938, and an educational wing was added in 1962. The original cemetery in the above photograph remains south of the present church.

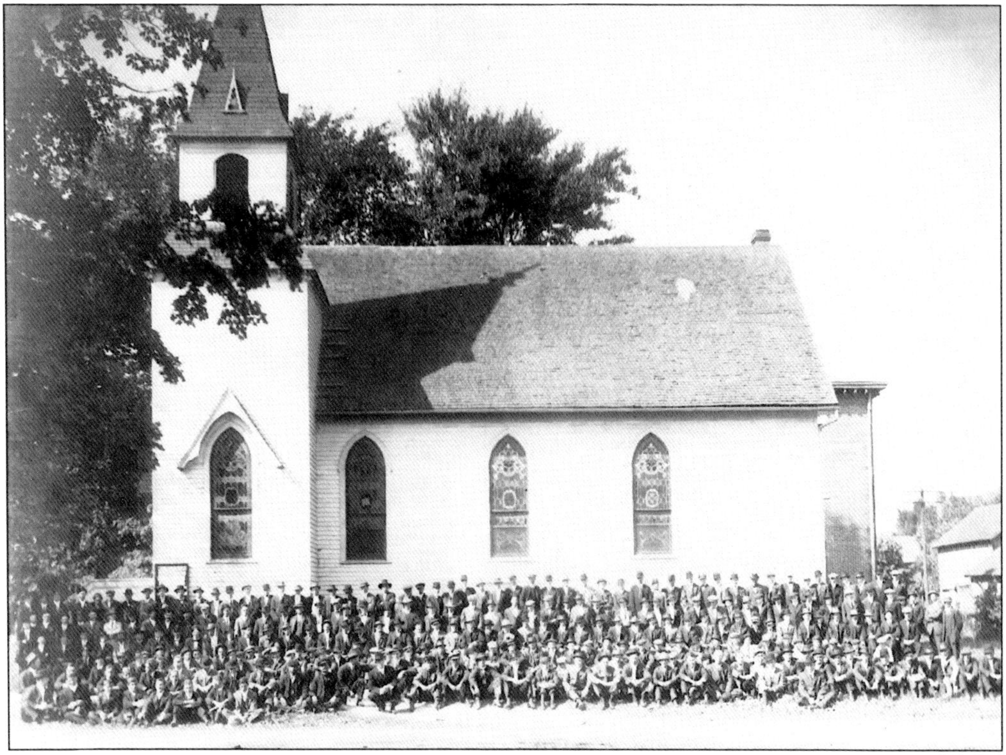

First United Methodist, Chesterton. The men's Bible class, which numbered 299 men, are shown posed outside the First Methodist Episcopal Church at the corner of Second Street and Indiana Avenue on September 27, 1914. The church was completed in 1865 and served the congregation until 1926, when the new church building at Second Street and Porter Avenue, seen below, was constructed. The name of the church was changed to First United Methodist in the 1950s, following a merger with the Swedish Methodist Church. The congregation has continued to expand with the purchase of adjacent properties in the 1950s and the addition of an educational wing in 1965.

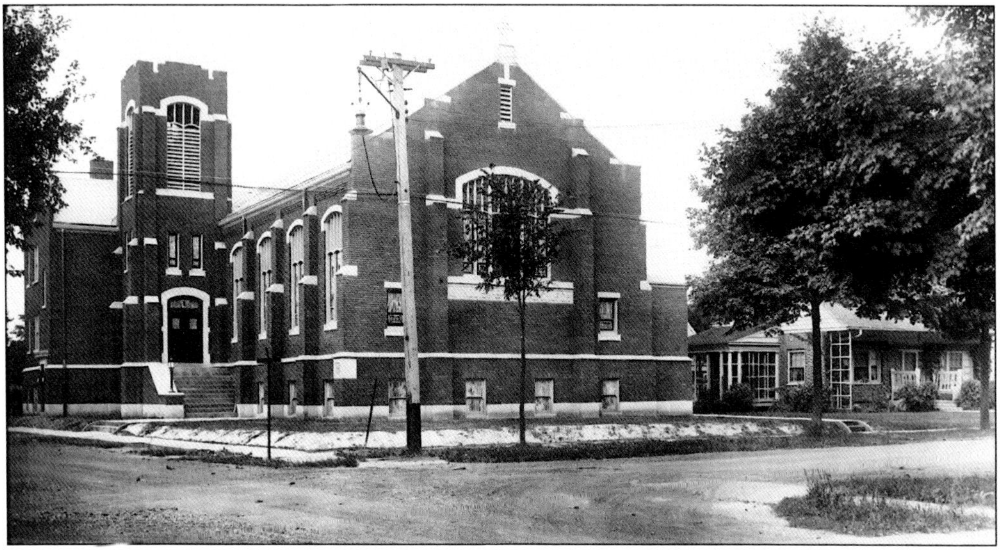

BETHLEHEM LUTHERAN, CHESTERTON. In 1879 a group of Swedish worshippers from Chesterton left Augsburg Lutheran Church to form their own congregation in town. The brick church seen here, located at 135 Lincoln Avenue, was completed in the mid-1880s. Substantial improvements and additions were made in the 1960s, including the removal of the parsonage to make way for educational and church offices and additional parking.

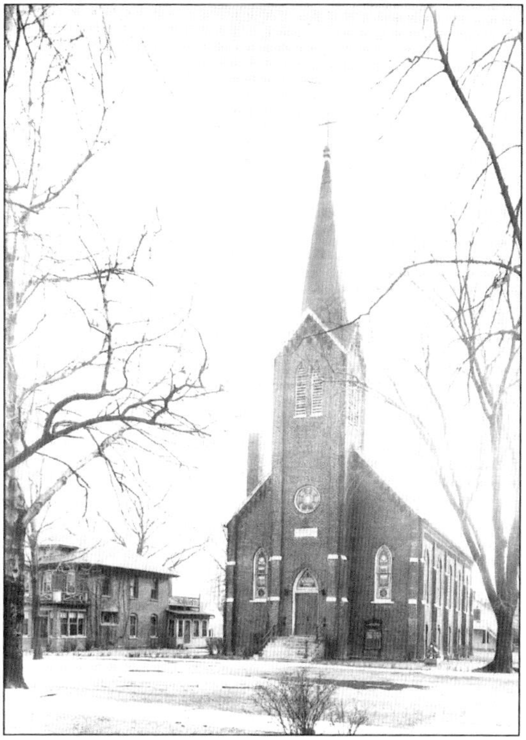

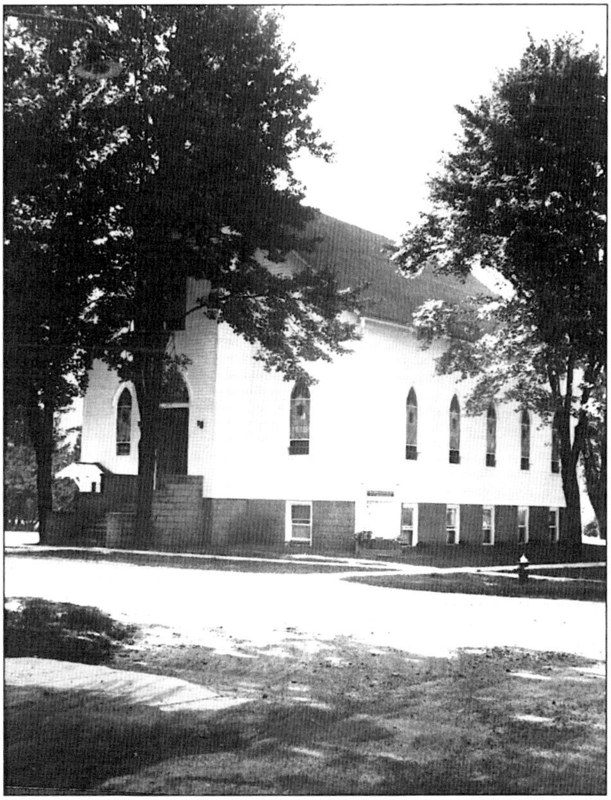

ST. JOHN'S UNITED, CHESTERTON. The church seen here, located at 215 Lincoln Avenue in Chesterton, was established by local farmers and brickyard workers. Originally known as the German Evangelical St. John's Church, services at the church were held in German until the mid-1920s. The congregation officially became St. John's United Church in 1958. In 1972 a larger congregation resulted from a merger with the Presbyterian Church of the Dunes.

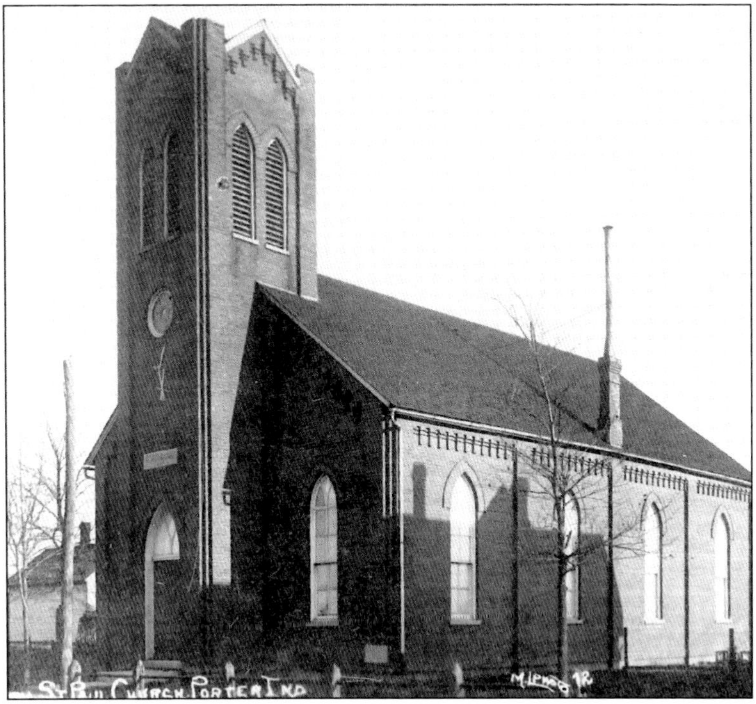

ST. PAUL LUTHERAN, PORTER. In 1887 German immigrants who worked at the nearby Porter brickyards, built the church seen here on Francis Street in Porter. The building was constructed of Porter brick donated by William Beam. In 1964 the congregation moved to a new building on County Road 1100 North, Chesterton; the Old Pathway Baptist Church now occupies the original church.

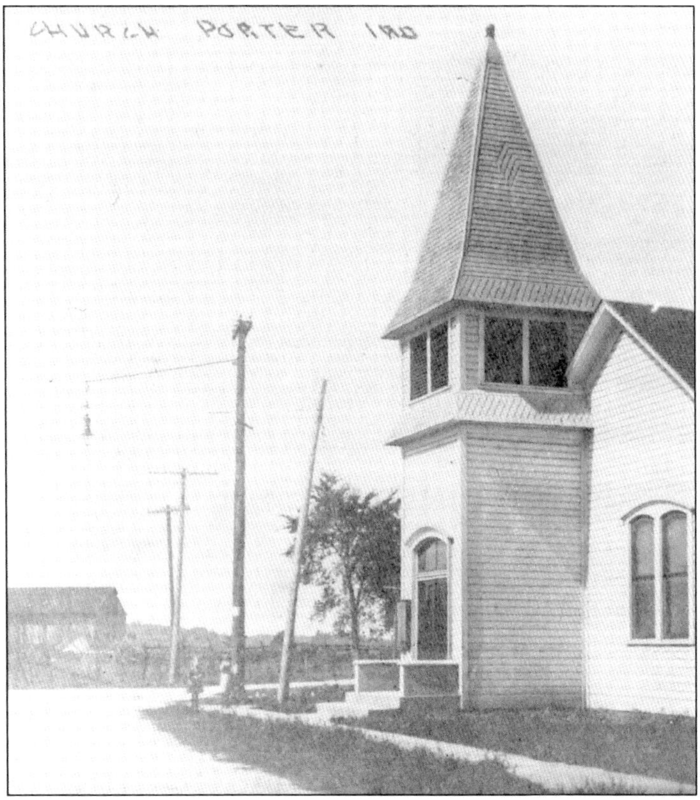

PORTER CONGREGATIONAL. The church was established at the corner of Beam Street and Wagner Road in 1891 by Rev. W.H. Brooks, who began preaching at the brickyards seen here in the background. Known as the "little white church on the corner" or the "English church," it became the First Evangelical United Brethren Church in 1922. Declared unsafe, the building was demolished in 1940 and replaced by a new church, completed in January 1943. In 1968 the congregation became part of the United Methodist denomination and is now known as Porter United Methodist Church.

SWEDISH METHODIST, CHESTERTON. Established in 1879, the congregation met in the "English" Methodist church on Indiana Avenue until its own building, a remodeled schoolhouse, was completed in 1881. The church building seen here was constructed at 117 Lincoln Avenue in 1905. In 1937 the church became known as the Lincoln Avenue Methodist Episcopal Church and later merged with the nearby First United Methodist Church. The building subsequently housed the first church, Christ Scientist, and retail businesses.

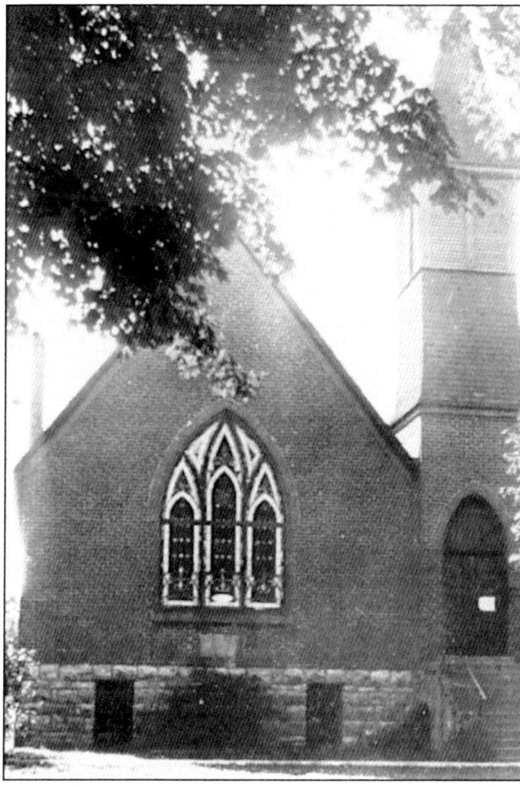

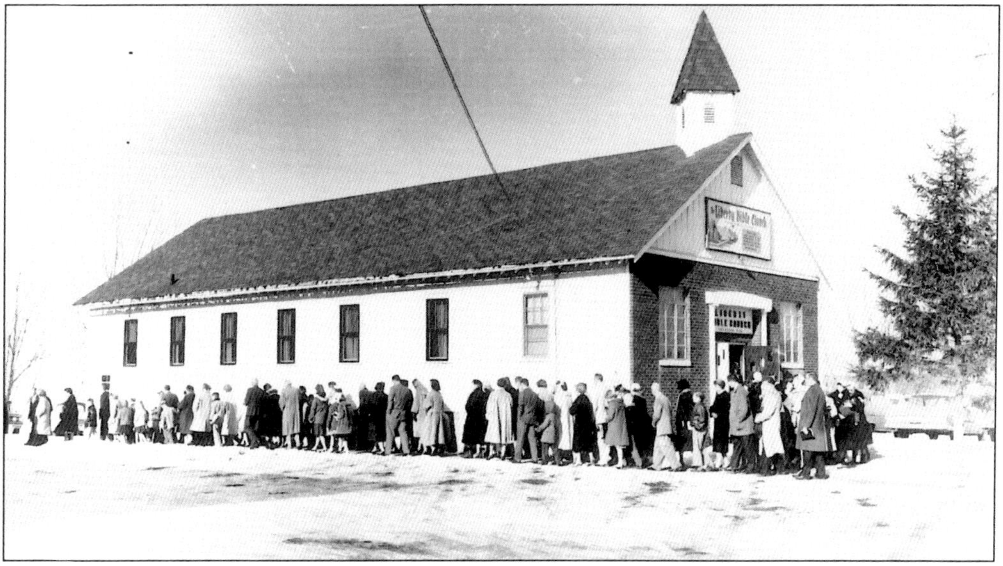

LIBERTY BIBLE, LIBERTY TOWNSHIP. From its beginnings in 1927 as the Liberty Township Sunday School Association, the church, affiliated with the Evangelical Free Church of America since 1959, has continued to expand. Construction of a large church building was begun in 1954. Church members are shown above, leaving the old church once the new sanctuary was completed in 1960. An educational unit was also added in the late 1960s to meet the needs of a growing congregation.

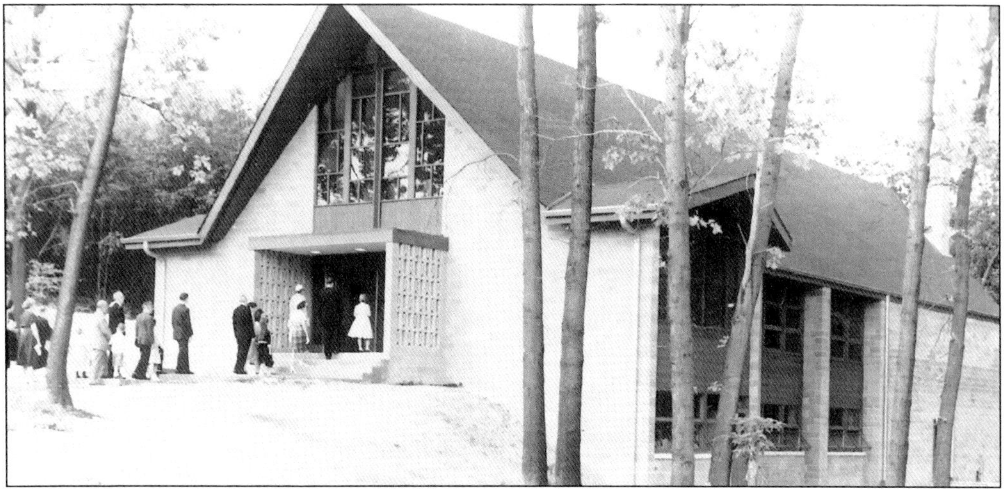

PRESBYTERIAN CHURCH OF THE DUNES. Located on Highway 12 at Kemil Road, the structure seen above was built in 1960 to replace the Old North Church of the Dunes (Presbyterian) in Beverly Shores, home of the congregation since 1940. Indiana Dunes National Lakeshore purchased the building in 1970 for use as their headquarters. The congregation formed a shared ministry with St. John's United in Chesterton, which resulted in a merger of the two groups in 1972.

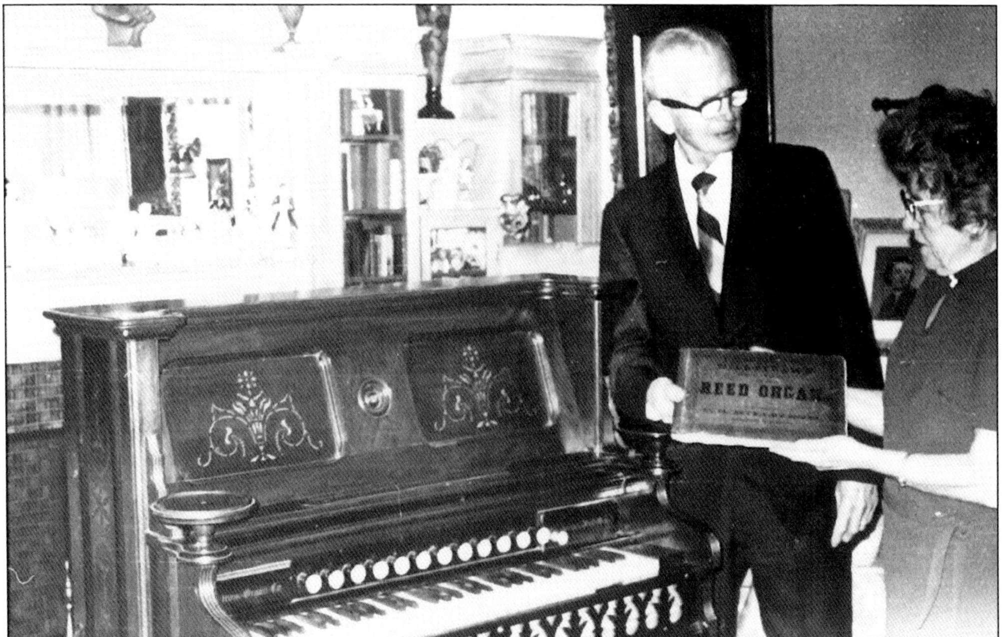

BETHLEHEM LUTHERAN ARCHIVES, CHESTERTON. Mrs. Warren Carpenter is shown donating a Hillstrom Organ to the church archives in 1972. Church member Elmer Vedell (also pictured above), along with Russel Lee and Terry Dietz, organized and maintained the archives, a collection of more than 600 historical artifacts, books, and photographs relating to the history of the church and Westchester Township. Local history items from the archives were later donated to Westchester Public Library. The church donated the organ to the Westchester Township Historical Museum in 1997.

Five

Community Organizations

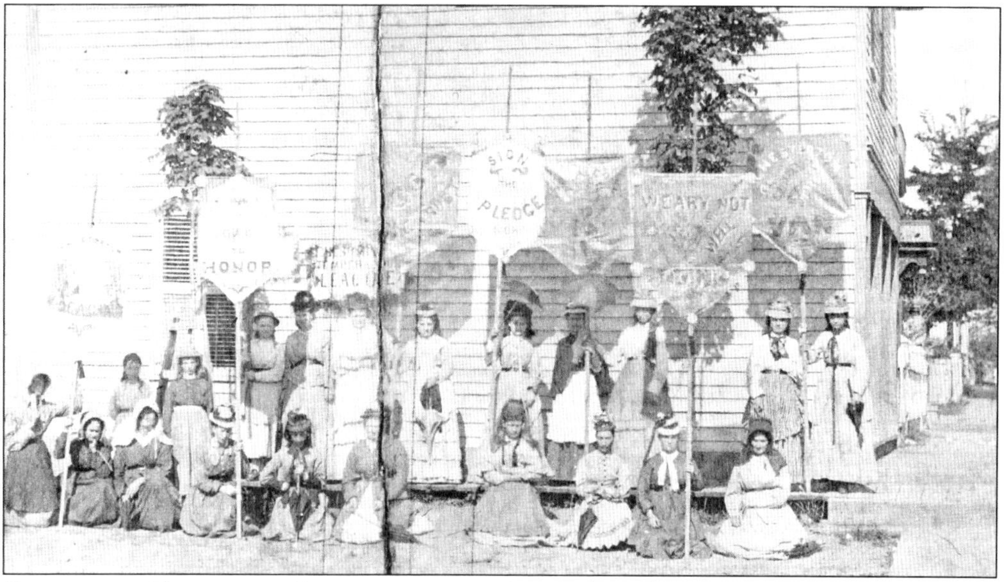

Chesterton Temperance League, c. 1873. Pictured on the corner of Second Street and Broadway are members of the Chesterton Temperance League. Women throughout the country held marches in their communities during the latter part of the 19th century, pleading with liquor sellers to close their businesses, but met with only limited and short-term success.

The earliest settlers in Westchester Township had little time to pursue social and recreational activities, concerned as they were with facing the challenges of life on the frontier. Between 1850 and 1910 the population of Westchester Township grew from a mere 360 to 2,953 residents. As communities were established and prospered, citizens formed a wide variety of civic and social groups to improve the quality of life in their communities. In addition to the organizations pictured here, those formed in the latter part of the 19th century included the Knight of Pythias, the Independent Order of Foresters, the Sons of Temperance, the Grange, the Good Templars, the Modern Woodsmen, and the Masonic Lodge.

Residents continue this civic tradition today, with a great variety of organizations committed to helping others in the community and beyond.

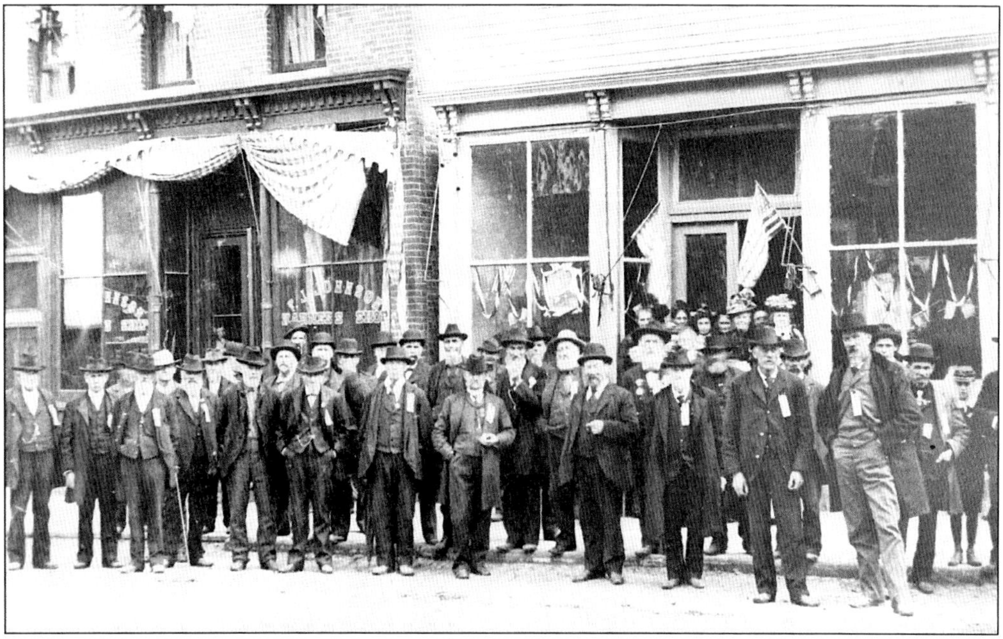

Grand Army of the Republic. Pictured on Calumet Road at the turn of the century are members of the GAR, A.B. Wade Post No. 208. The organization of veteran soldiers and sailors who served in the Union Army during the Civil War was organized in Chesterton in 1883 and boasted a large membership. By 1912, only 12 members remained.

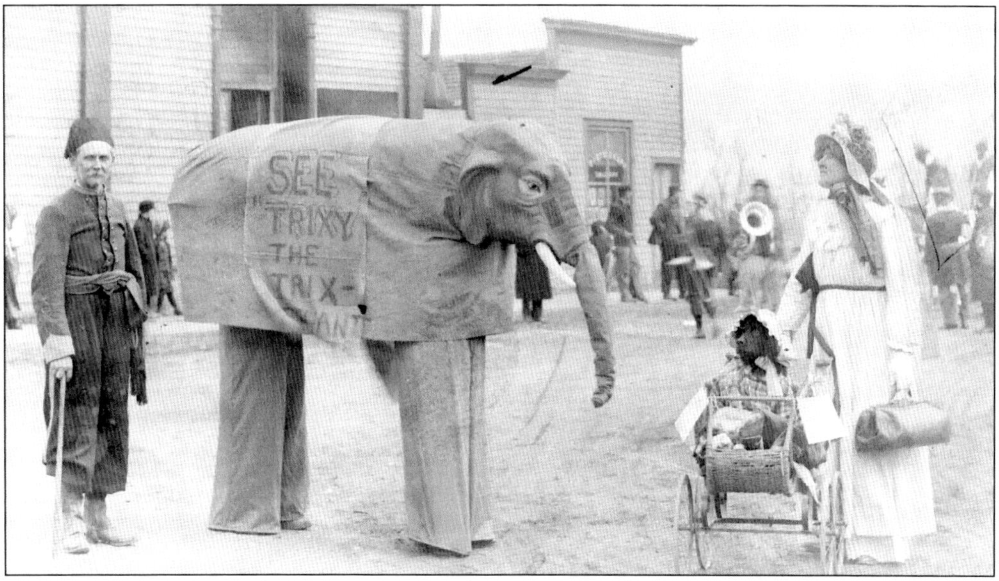

Men's Aid Parade. This picture was taken at N. Calumet Road and Grant Street in Chesterton, *c.* 1909. The Men's Aid Society was best known for its annual parade featuring oddly dressed men, and its minstrel shows. The group began as an April Fool's joke in 1907, with the men hosting a dinner as a benefit for the Ladies Aid Society of the Methodist Episcopal Church. The event proved so popular that the parade and shows were a yearly tradition until the early 1930s.

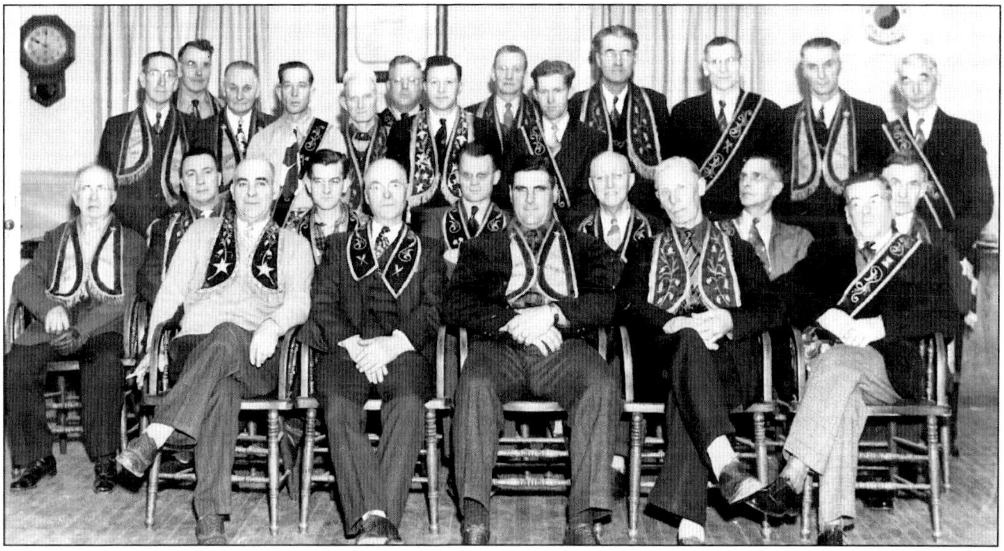

INTERNATIONAL ORDER OF ODD FELLOWS. Members of Chegemink Lodge, I.O.O.F. posed for this photograph during a meeting in early 1949. The organization was chartered in 1855 and met for many years at 132 1/2 S. Calumet. The Rebekahs, the women's auxiliary of the I.O.O.F., organized a chapter in Chesterton in 1907.

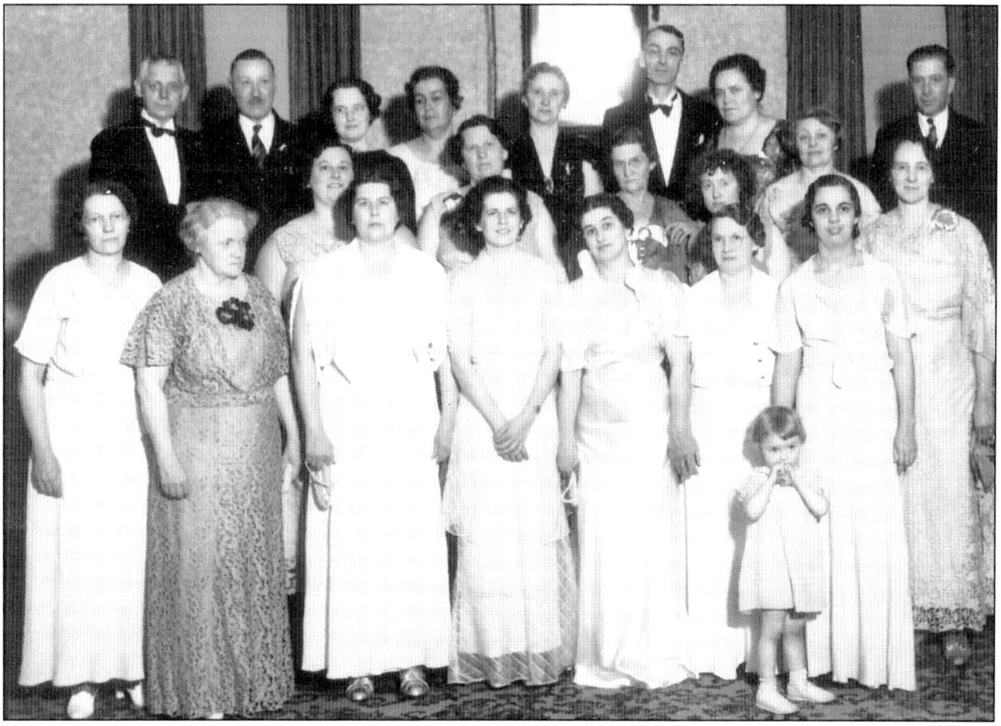

ORDER OF THE EASTERN STAR. The Chesterton chapter of the women's auxiliary of the Masons was photographed in November 1937 during a social event. The local Eastern Star chapter was organized in 1902, with Etta Osborn as worthy matron. The chapter had grown to 108 members by 1912. The Calumet Lodge of the Masons, chartered in Chesterton in 1868, was the second Masonic lodge established in Porter County.

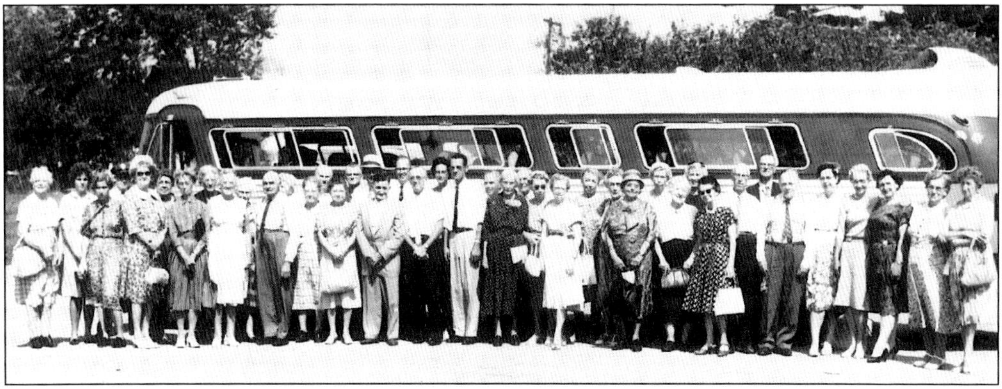

Duneland Historical Society. Members are pictured during an overnight trip to Spring Mill State Park in June 1961. Organized in 1948 by a group of local citizens interested in learning more about the history of this area, the Society has contributed to the collection and preservation of local history through public programs, the publication of a newsletter, tours, and placement of several local historic markers. The Society continues to be actively involved in historical research and programs.

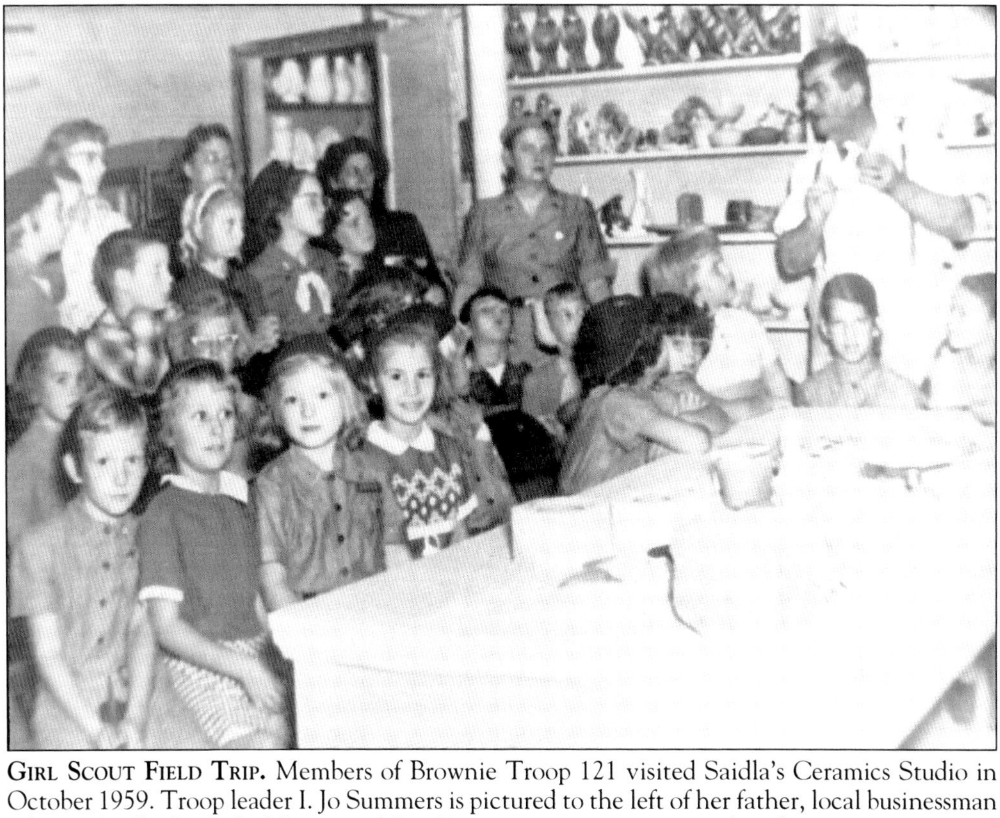

Girl Scout Field Trip. Members of Brownie Troop 121 visited Saidla's Ceramics Studio in October 1959. Troop leader I. Jo Summers is pictured to the left of her father, local businessman John C. Saidla. Both Girl Scout and Boy Scout groups were organized in this area in 1921, and scouting has continued to be a popular activity for many local girls and boys.

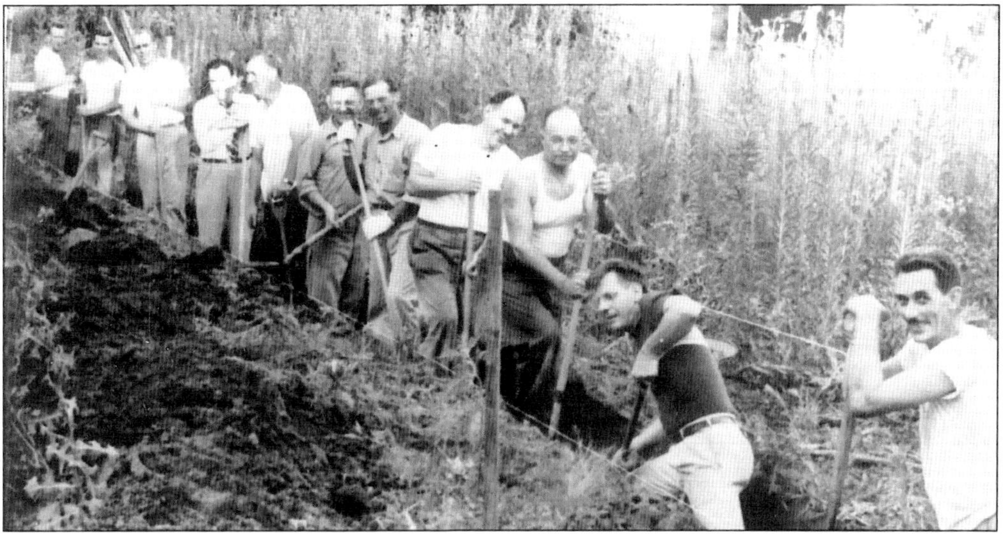

Lions Club Building. On July 26, 1950, members of the local Lions Club pitched in to dig trenches for the foundation of their new building. Pictured, from left to right, are Henry Radiger, John Radiger, Larry DeKoker Jr., Dr. Cassidy, Larry DeKoker Sr., Phil Anderson, Milt Stephens, Howard Johnson, Sam Newton, Ralph Anderson, and Jim Marshall. The Lions Club building was constructed at 411 S. Fifth Street and now houses the Instructional Materials Center for the Duneland School Corporation.

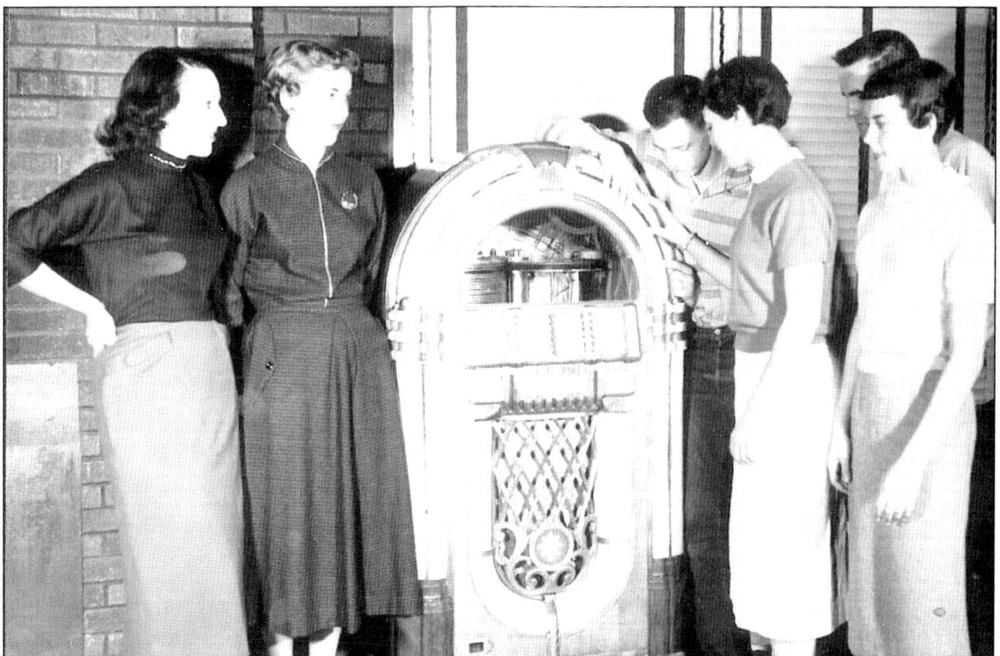

Youth Center, 1957. Members of the Junior Women's Club are shown donating a jukebox to the Youth Center in the Lions Club building in 1957. The Chesterton Women's Club, founded in 1934, and the Junior Woman's Club, which had its beginning in 1950, have been active supporters of many community projects, including the public library, the Food Pantry, the Art Gallery, and the local park system.

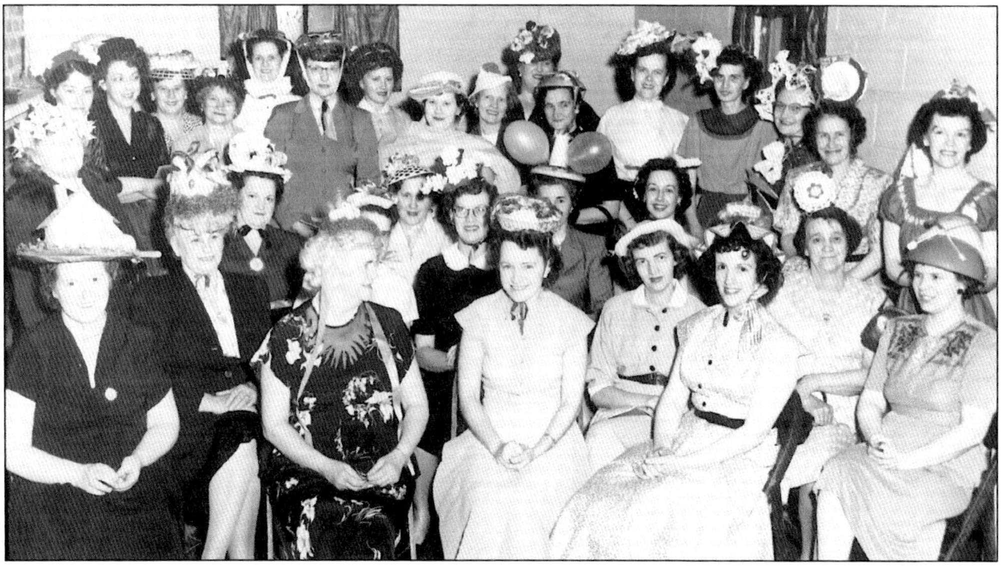

Westport Home Economics Club. In the spring of 1954, members of the club modeled their original Easter bonnet creations, which were auctioned off to raise funds for the group's project, the construction of a community building. The Westport Community Club opened later that year on S.R. 149. The idea of organizing a town in the Westport area is said to have originated with this group. (Arthur E. Anderson photograph.)

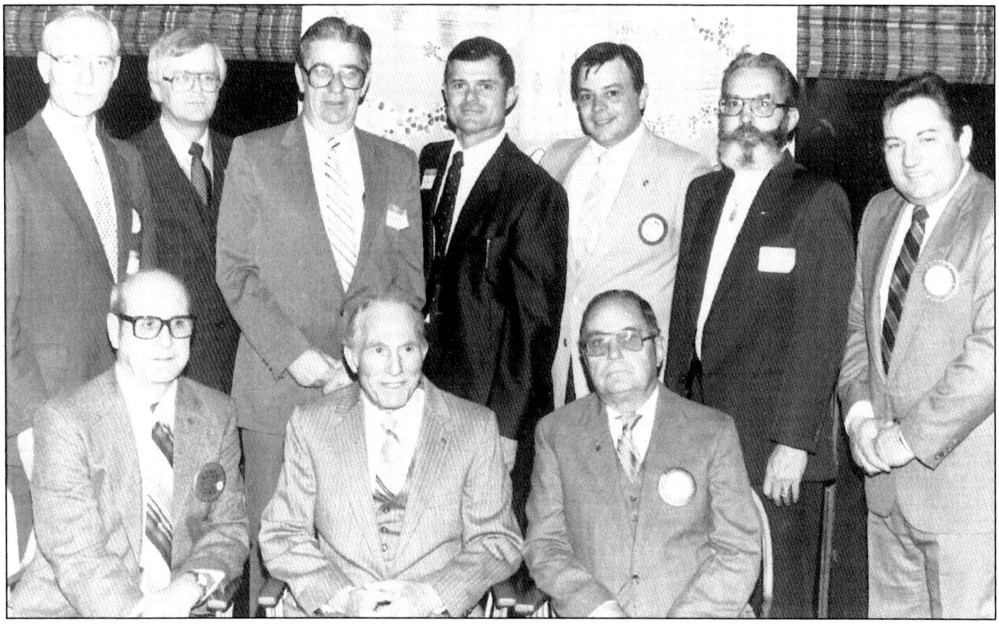

Chesterton-Porter Rotary Club. Past presidents of the local Rotary Club gathered in 1985 to celebrate the group's 25th anniversary. Pictured, from left to right, are as follows: (seated) George Kriviskey, Leslie Pratt and Dee Hand; (standing) Bob Dunbar, Richard Parker, Bill King, Jim Read, Mike Anton, Joe Callahan, and Terry Hiestand. The local chapter of Rotary International was formed in 1960 with James M. Read as charter president. The club continues its active involvement in community affairs, contributing to local causes and the Rotary Foundation, and sponsoring student exchange programs.

Six

Dunes and Parks

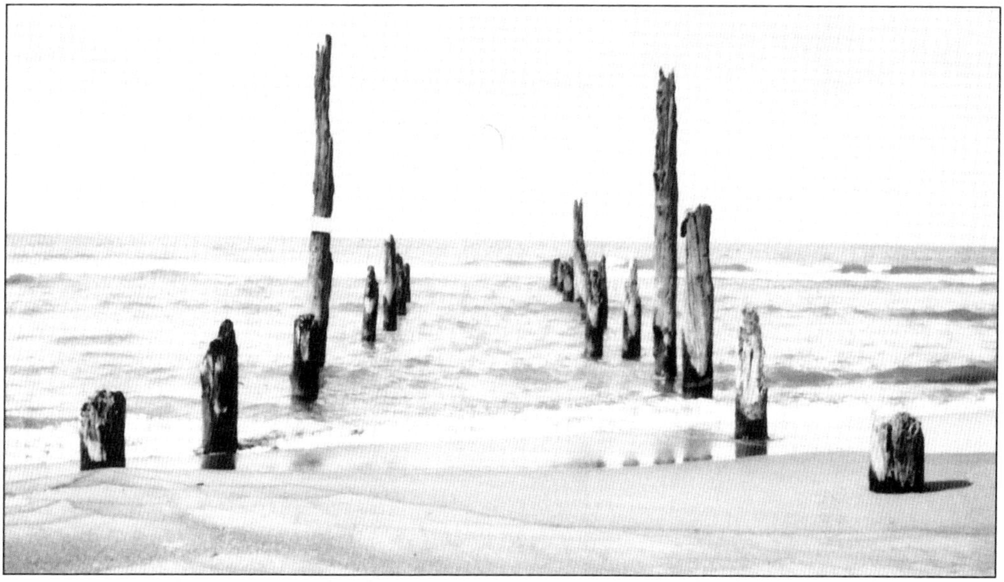

Lumber Dock, Tremont. In the above 1925 photograph, rotting stumps were all that was left of a Lake Michigan dock located about one half mile east of the present State Park Pavilion. The dock was once part of a thriving lumber business centered in Tremont and Furnessville in the mid-1800s. Heavily timbered with white and red oak, cherry, elm, and white pine, northern Westchester and Pine Townships produced wood for railroad fuel and ties and finished boards for the building trade. Lansing Morgan, a major early landowner, ran one of several Furnessville sawmills. A track ran between the mill and his dock with special cars to accommodate lumber. Morgan owned two ships on Lake Michigan that he used to transport his lumber. He lost one of his ships at a dock in the Chicago fire of 1871.

Pioneer dreams of a major harbor and city on Lake Michigan in Westchester Township faded in 1837 with the failure of City West, which was to be located about where the Indiana Dunes State Park campground now stands. Despite continuing talk of industrializing the Dunes through the turn of the century, the area gradually became a recreational center, attracting both local residents and Chicago visitors. Eventually the beautiful landscape was recognized as a unique and valuable resource, and efforts developed to save the dunes. Thanks to the dedicated work of many conservationists, residents and visitors alike now enjoy the Indiana Dunes State Park and the Indiana Dunes National Lakeshore.

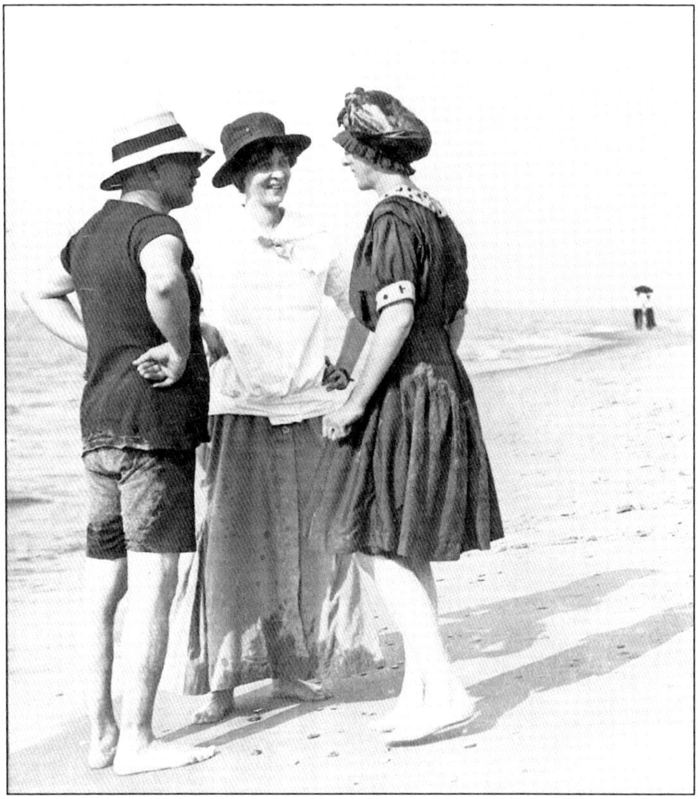

"Confab on the Beach." Members of the Prairie Club, founded in Chicago in 1908, enjoy the beach near their Indiana Dunes beach house in this 1914 photograph. Members of the Prairie Club worked to establish forest preserves in Chicago and also organized nature hikes throughout the Chicago metropolitan area, including a walk in the Indiana Dunes in 1908 that attracted 338 hikers. (Prairie Club Archives at Westchester Public Library.)

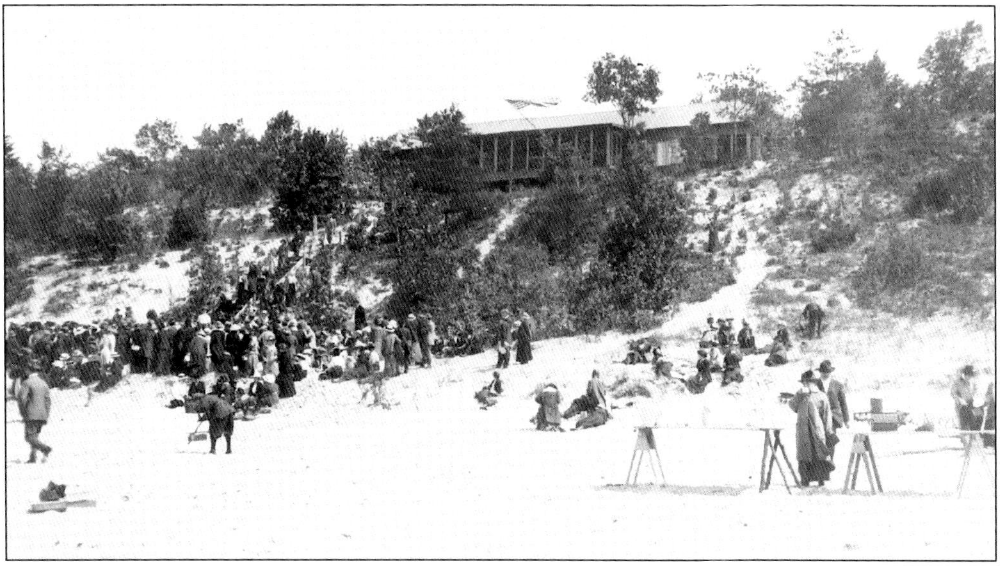

Prairie Club Beach House. The above photograph shows some of the Prairie Club members who gathered on October 21, 1913, to dedicate their new beach house. It was set on a shore dune almost due north of the Tremont Station of the South Shore Railroad, in what is now the Indiana Dunes State Park. The structure was used by Prairie Club members until 1967. (Prairie Club Archives at Westchester Public Library.)

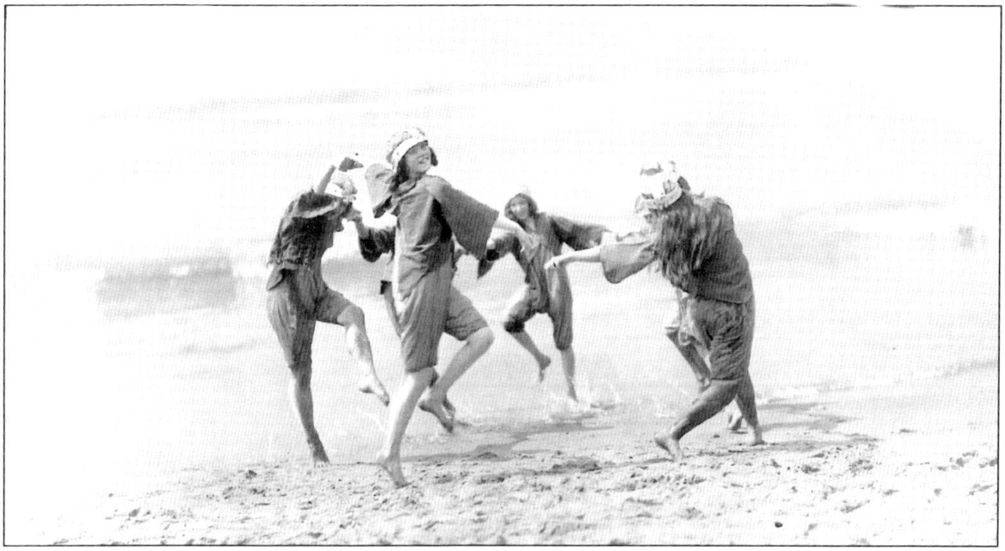

DANCE OF THE SHORE BIRDS. The above interpretive dance formed part of the Historical Pageant of the Dunes, produced in 1917 by the Prairie Club and other organizations in support of the creation of an Indiana Dunes national park. Although the early national park movement failed, public attention was drawn to the area, and in 1923 the Indiana State Legislature passed a bill creating the Indiana Dunes State Park, which opened in 1925. (Prairie Club Archives at Westchester Public Library.)

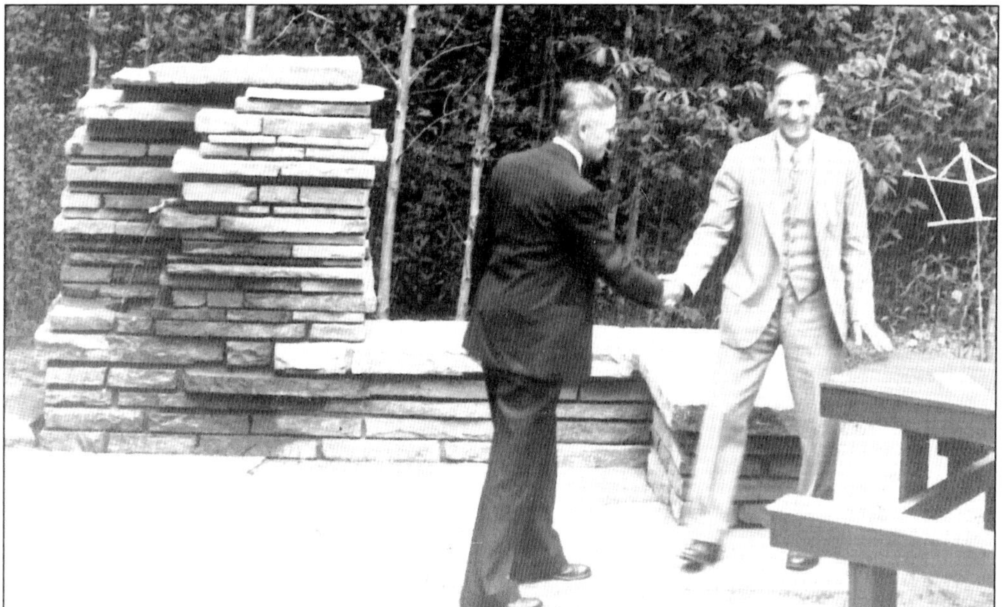

DEDICATION OF THE PRAIRIE CLUB FOUNTAIN, INDIANA DUNES STATE PARK. In the above photograph, taken on May 30, 1932, Prairie Club President O.C. Bruhlman, on the right, is shown presenting the Prairie Club memorial drinking fountain to a representative of the Indiana Department of Conservation. Designed by member and well-known landscape architect Jens Jensen, the fountain commemorated the Prairie Club's discounted sale of its dune land to the State in 1926. (Prairie Club Archives at Westchester Public Library.)

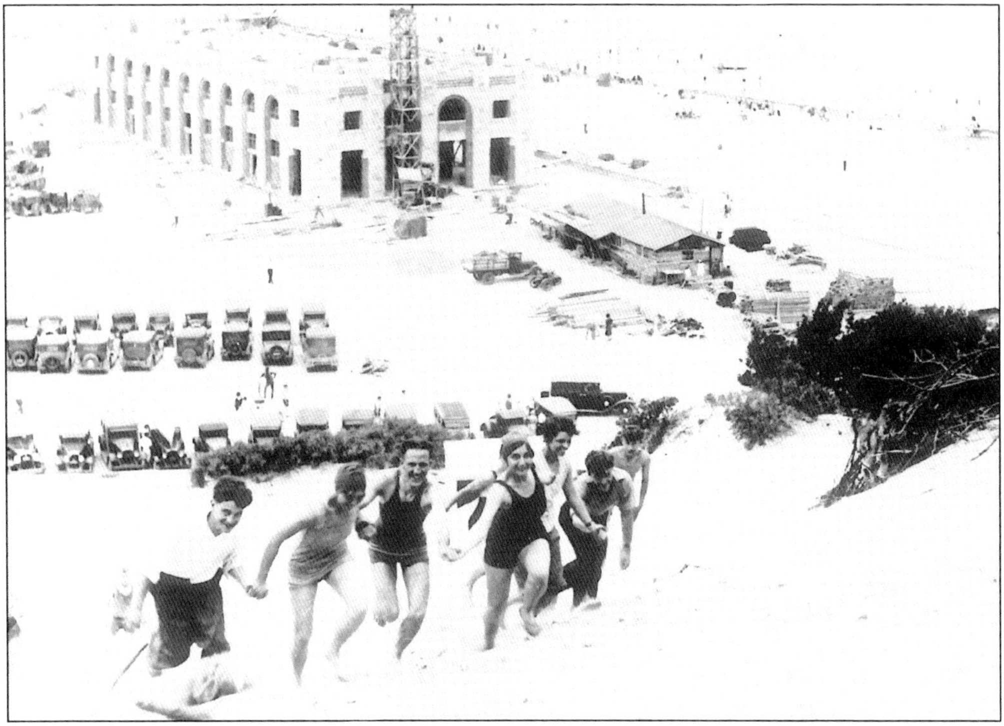

Construction of the State Park Pavilion, Indiana Dunes State Park. The above photograph shows the construction of the State Park Pavilion at Waverly Beach c. 1930. The State also constructed a "State Cottage," intended as a summer home for state governors. The cottage was located on a dune east of the pavilion. Seen above are swimmers climbing Devil's Slide, which was also a popular sledding hill in the winter. (Courtesy Indiana State Library.)

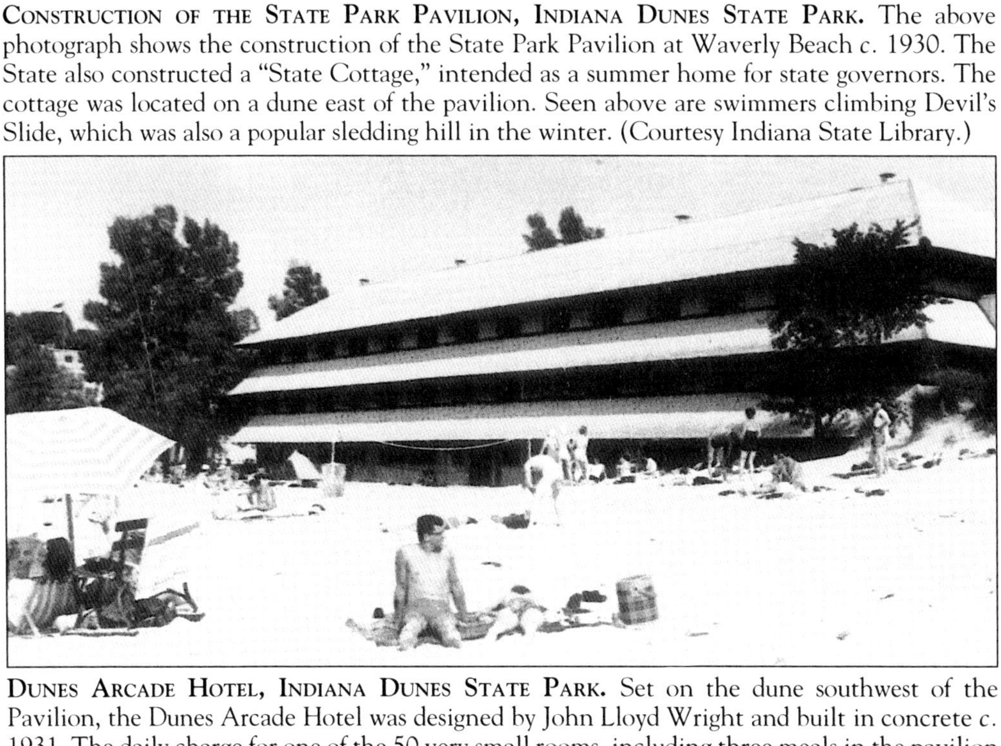

Dunes Arcade Hotel, Indiana Dunes State Park. Set on the dune southwest of the Pavilion, the Dunes Arcade Hotel was designed by John Lloyd Wright and built in concrete c. 1931. The daily charge for one of the 50 very small rooms, including three meals in the pavilion dining room, was $5.85. Ione Harrington served as manager of the hotel in the late 1940s and early 1950s. Having fallen into disrepair, the hotel was demolished in 1972.

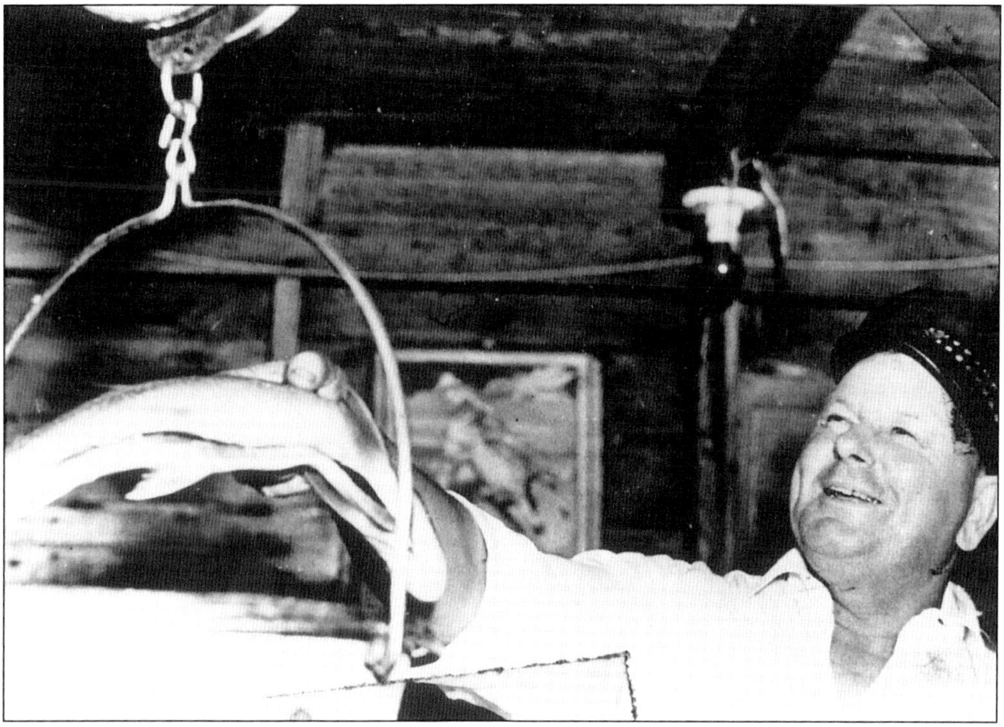

ELMER JOHNSON. Elmer Johnson, seen above, and his brother William continued the fishing business started by their father, J.P. Johnson, at Waverly Beach in 1907. The brothers were responsible for improving the road to Waverly Beach, paving the parking lot, and building a bathhouse. They fished in Lake Michigan from April until October using a flat-bottomed boat to set both pond and floating nets, with which they caught lake trout, whitefish, perch, and in the spring, herring.

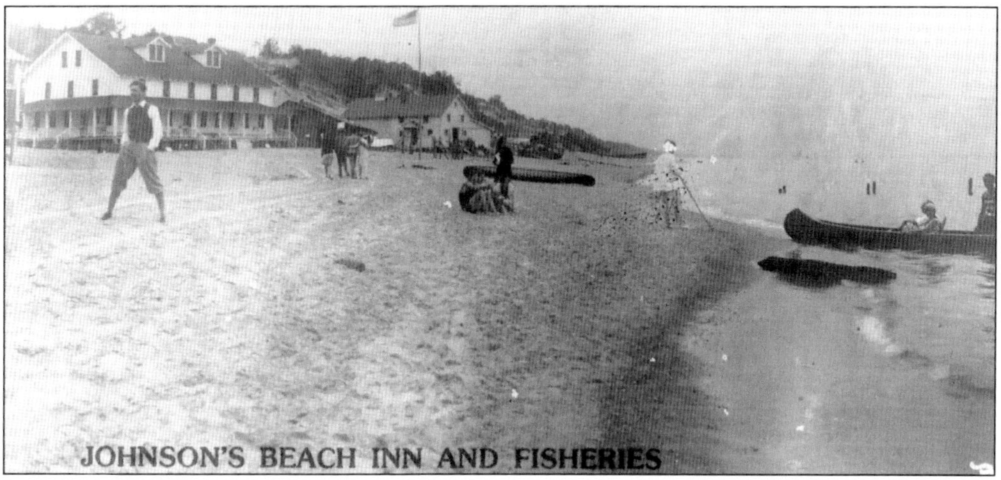

JOHNSON'S BEACH INN AND FISHERIES. After the State Park was created by the Indiana Legislature in 1923, the Johnson brothers moved their Porter Beach fishing business west from Waverly Beach to Porter Beach. At the new location they built Johnson's Beach Inn, a restaurant and hotel popular with local residents and visitors from Chicago for its excellent fish dinners. The fish market is the small house to the right of the Inn in the above photograph.

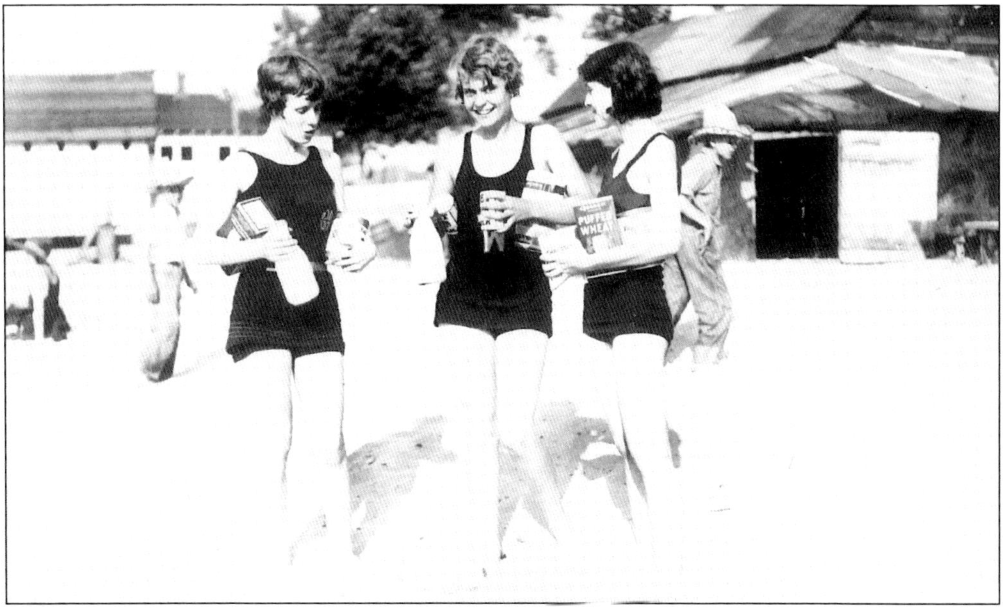

THREE GIRLS AT WAVERLY BEACH. Wearing the warm but itchy woolen bathing suits of the time, these three teenagers are shown with their arms full of snacks, preparing for a day at Waverly Beach. Johnson's fish market can be seen in the background to the right, the bathhouse to the left.

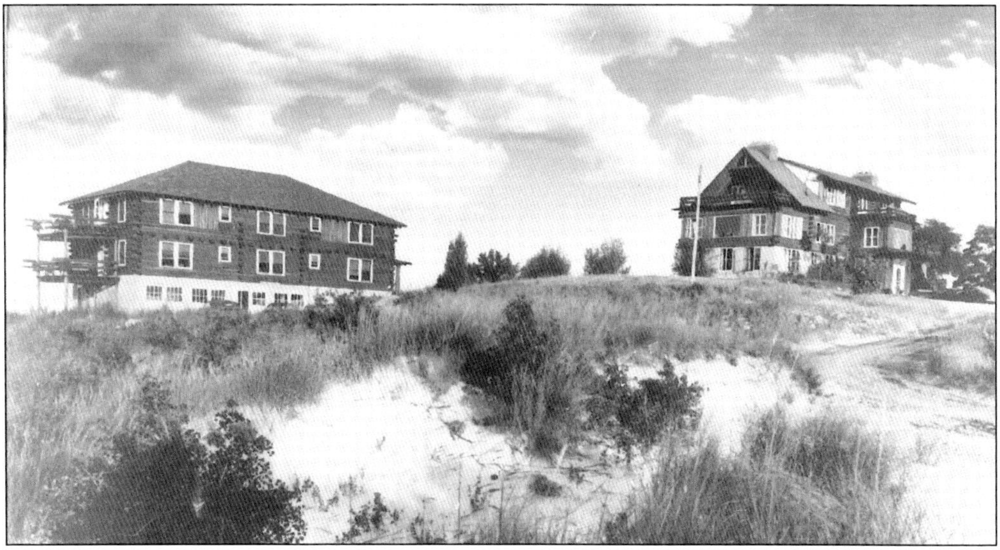

DUNE ACRES GUESTHOUSE AND CLUBHOUSE. Constructed on a high dune overlooking Lake Michigan, of logs hauled up from the South Shore Railroad, the Dune Acres Guesthouse and Clubhouse opened in 1926, three years after the town was founded on September 15, 1923. Alden Studebaker, husband of Naomi Chellberg Studebaker, built the Guesthouse, as well as almost all the houses in Dune Acres through 1941. Although the Guesthouse was later demolished, the Clubhouse was remodeled in 1990 and is still used by Dune Acres residents.

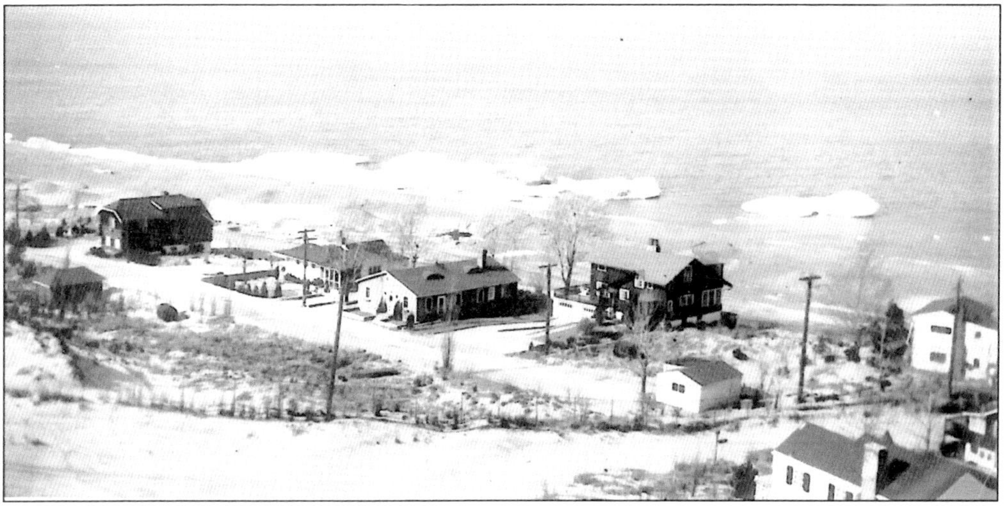

Shelf Ice in Dune Acres. This spring scene from the 1950s shows shelf ice floating near East Road in Dune Acres, as viewed from a dune in Porter Beach. A beautiful but dangerous natural occurrence, shelf ice usually forms along the southern shore of Lake Michigan from late December to late February.

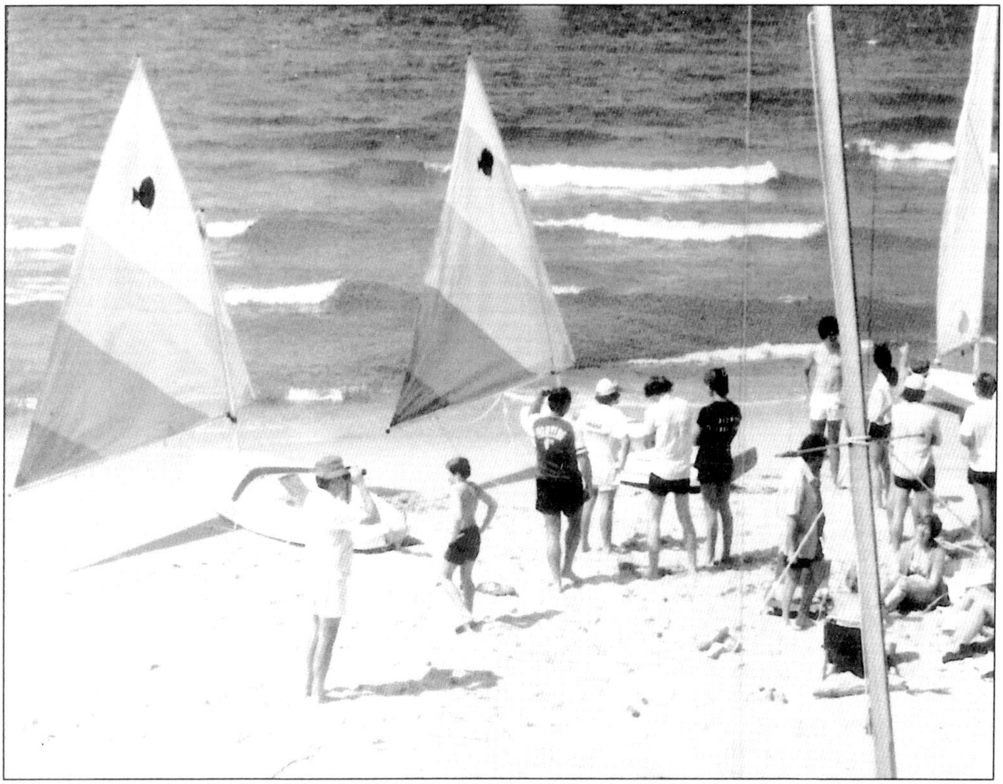

Sunday Sailboat Races. Sailing has long been a popular activity for the residents of Dune Acres. The above photograph, with two Sunfish sailboats on the left and a Laser on the right, shows residents during one of the Dune Acres sailboat races held on Sundays throughout the 1960s.

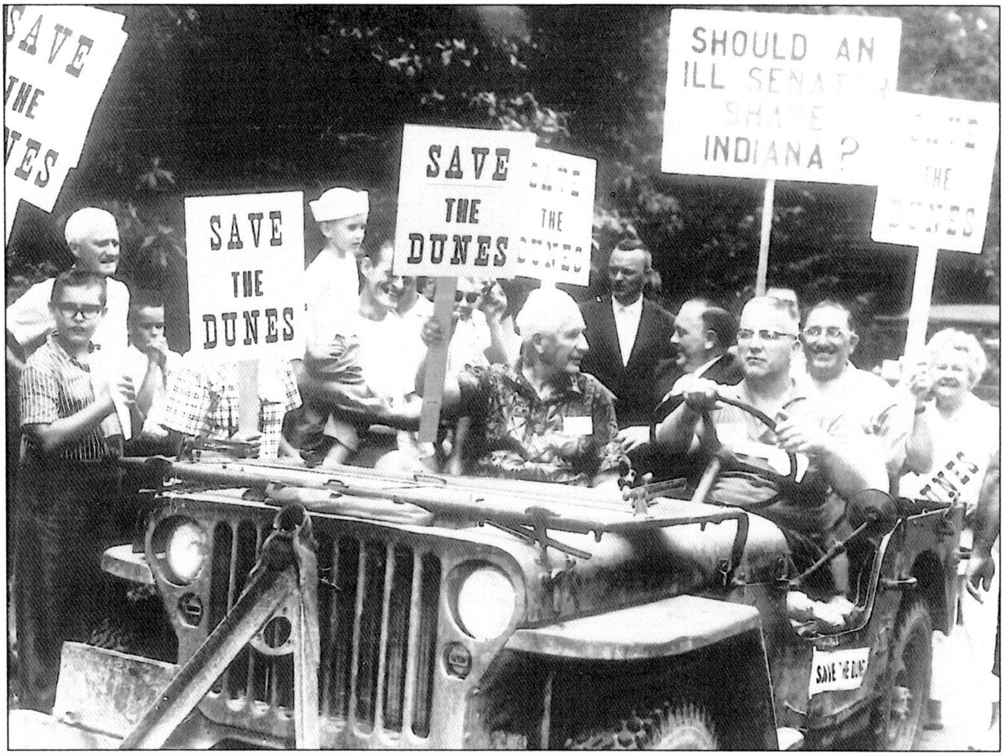

Save the Dunes Movement. Illinois Senator Paul Douglas played a major role in saving the Indiana Dunes and in the creation of the Indiana Dunes National Lakeshore. He is seen here in 1961 with Gary Mayor George Chacharis in the midst of the Dunes battle. Largely through the efforts of Senator Douglas and the Save the Dunes Council, founded by Dorothy Buell in 1952, Congress finally established the Indiana Dunes National Lakeshore in 1966.

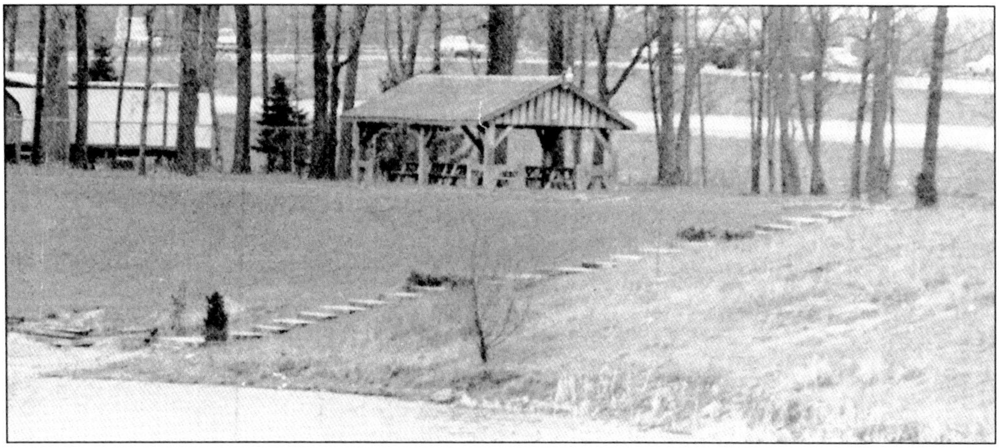

Lakeland Park, Burns Harbor. Groundbreaking for Burns Harbor's first park took place March 9, 1974. Town resident Paul Wasz is credited with naming the park; Dorothy Gillette is credited with naming Harbor Lake, formerly an unnamed borrow pit located within the park. With the help of the local Marine Corps Reserves, the park opened to the public in the summer of 1974. A supervised summer play and crafts program also began that year in the park. (Courtesy Burns Harbor Park Dept.)

Seven

Events and Disasters

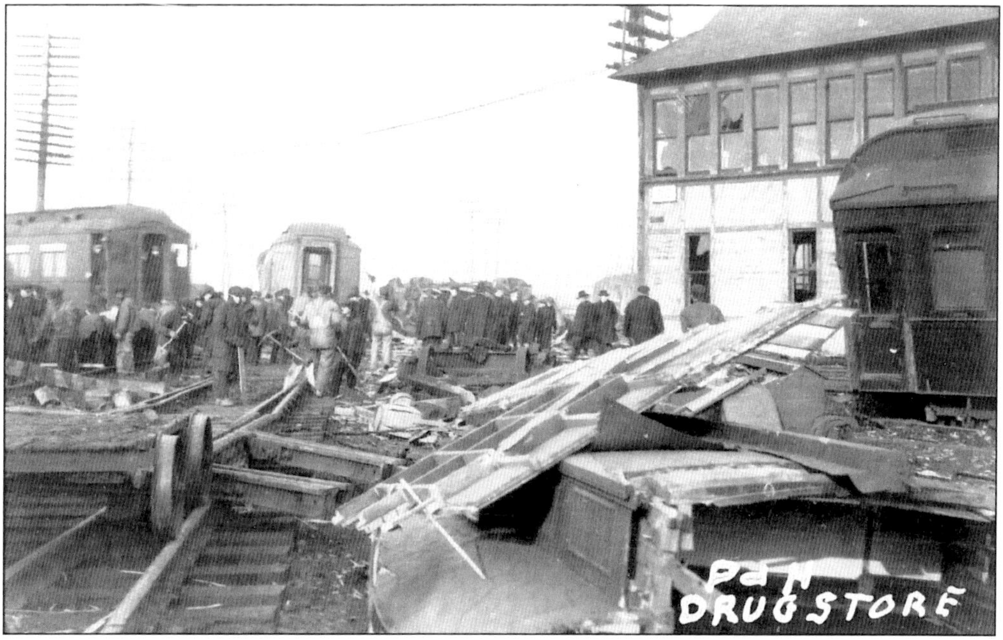

Porter Train Wreck, 1921. Railroads criss-crossing Westchester Township have brought growth to the community, but have also been the cause of many train accidents through the years. The most serious accident, pictured above, occurred on February 27, 1921, when the N.Y. Central Interstate Express from Boston to Chicago collided with Michigan Central's Canadian at the diamond intersection in Porter. Thirty-seven people were killed instantaneously by the impact, but other injuries were minimal. Inquiries followed the tragic accident, but few changes were made at the crossing until the advent of electronic signals and fail-safe switching devices.

This chapter commemorates some of the events that have created lasting memories for the citizens of Westchester Township. Although the community has seen its share of fires, train accidents, violent weather, and other disasters, its history is also marked by a great variety of celebrations, parades, and special events, many of which are included here.

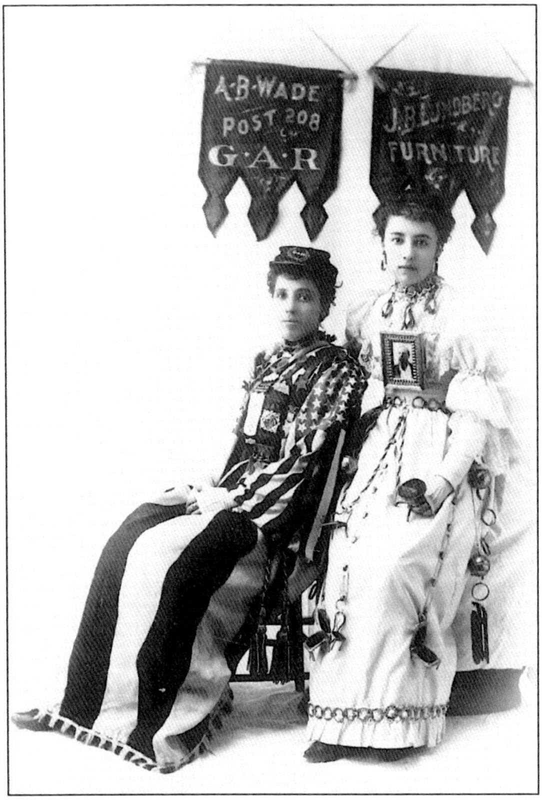

Merchants' Carnival, 1893. Francis Bookout (left), wearing an outfit inspired by the Stars and Stripes, represented the A.B. Wade Post of the Grand Army of the Republic. Eva Lundberg (right), in a costume adorned with miniature replicas of furniture, represented J.B. Lundberg Furniture Store at a carnival organized by local businesses on December 29, 1893. The highlight of the event at Moroney's Hall was a performance by 28 young women costumed in banners and decorations representing local merchants.

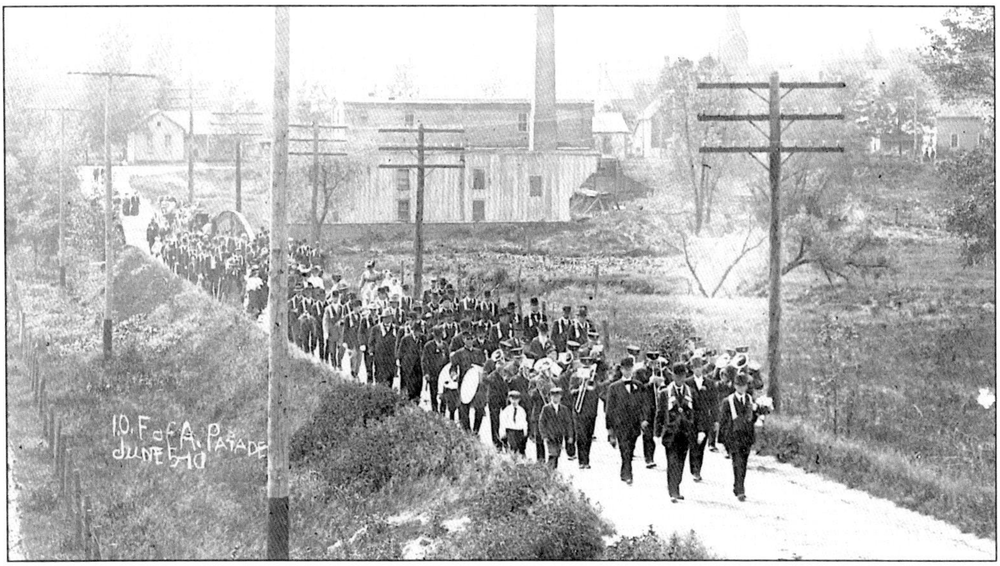

I.O.F. of A. Parade, 1910. Led by the Suman Cornet Band, members of the Chesterton Court of the Independent Order of Foresters of America and Lady Foresters are seen marching east on Porter Avenue toward the cemetery where memorial services were conducted on June 5, 1910. Visible in the photograph are the steeple of Bethlehem Lutheran Church, Blackwell Mill on the southeast corner of Porter Avenue and Calumet, and the Smith house, now a restaurant, which still stands at the northwest corner of Porter Avenue and Calumet Road.

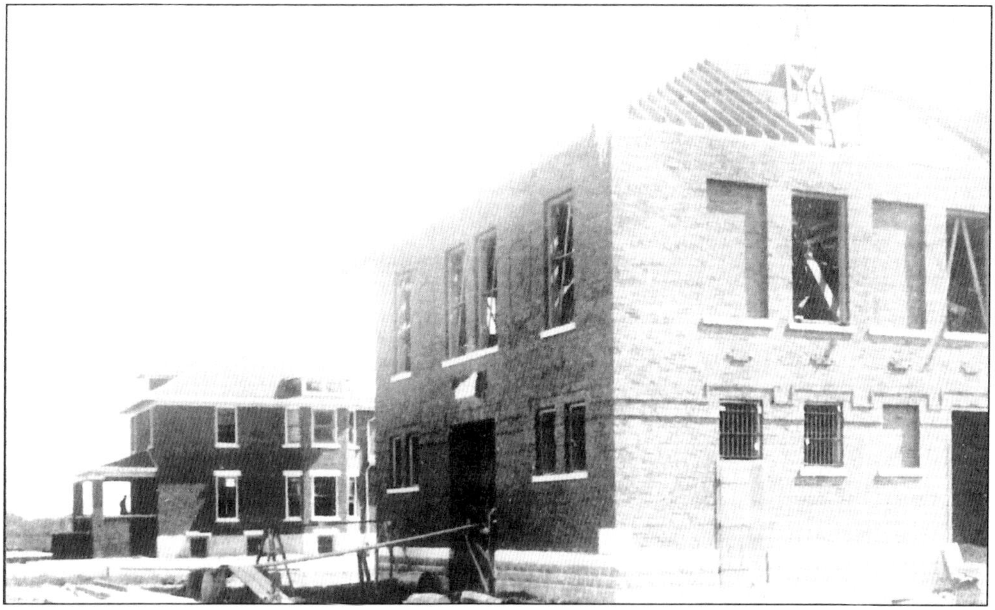

PORTER BUILDS A TOWN HALL, 1913. The town's first municipal building, located at the corner of Franklin and Francis Streets, is shown during its construction in 1913. Constructed of local brick by contractor Joseph Ameling for approximately $12,000, the structure featured a large assembly hall for public meetings, a jail, and a fire station. The town hall also housed the Porter Public Library from its founding in 1914 until 1975 when the Hageman Library, a branch of Westchester Public Library, opened at 100 Francis Street.

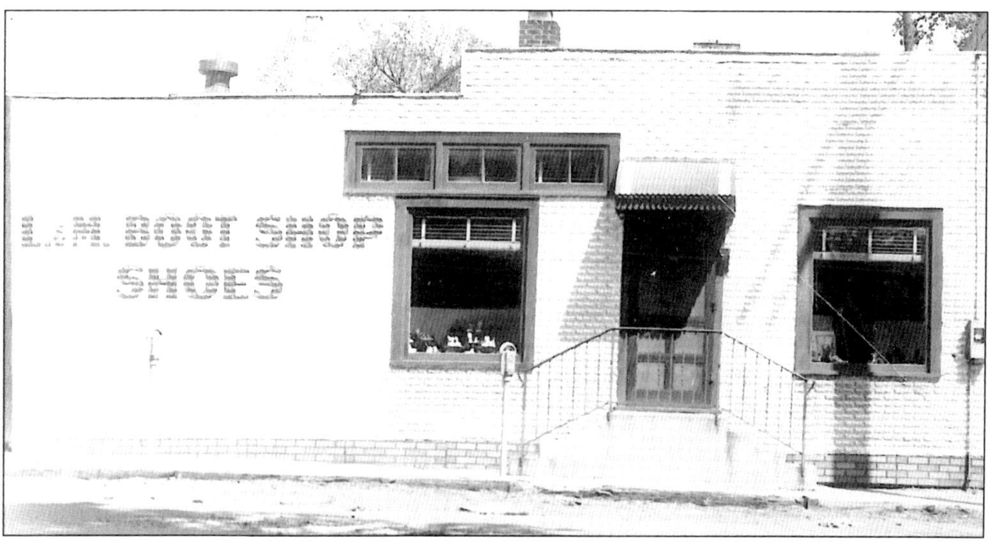

FIRST CHESTERTON LIBRARY, 1921. On July 28, 1921, Chesterton's first library opened in the Harvil Building on Broadway, seen above at a later date after it was moved to Third Street and had become the L & M Boot Shop. The library remained a contracted branch of the Gary Public Library until 1972 when the Porter Library Board voted to form a single town-township library district to be known as the Westchester Public Library.

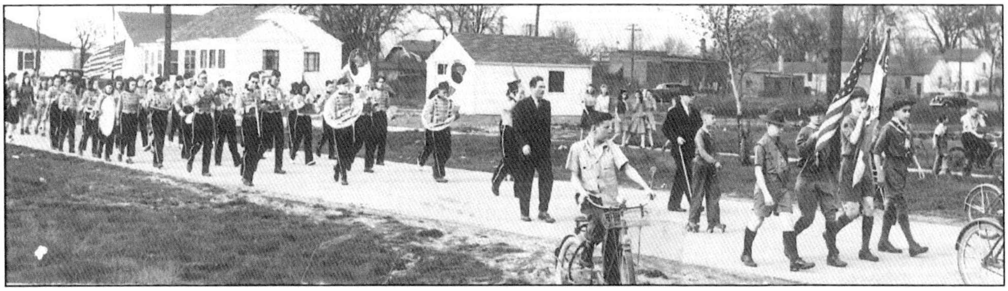

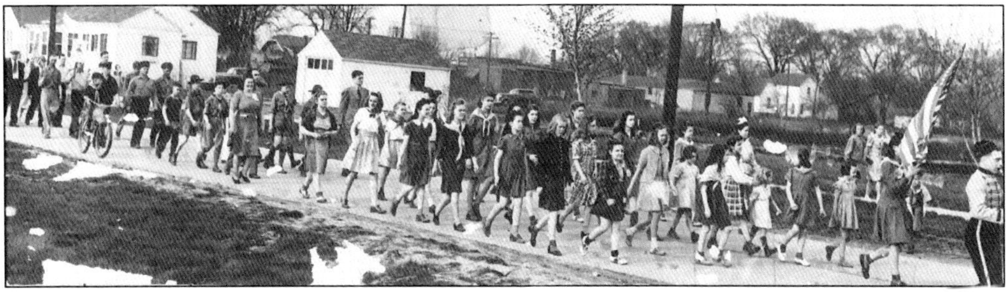

MacArthur Week Parade, 1942. Throughout World War II, local citizens and merchants participated in a variety of activities to support the war effort. In April 1942 a parade through downtown Chesterton culminated in a rally at Chesterton High School where Principal Lee E. Eve addressed "Our Duty on the Homefront." Local businesses also sponsored a bond rally and pledge drive for war savings stamps and bonds.

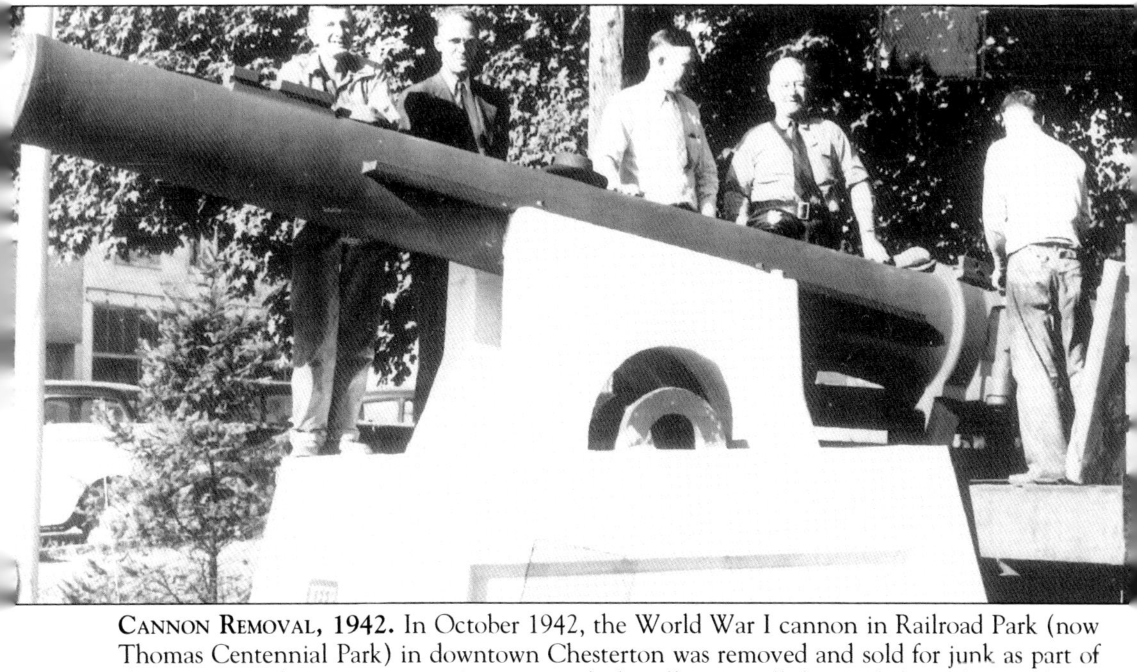

Cannon Removal, 1942. In October 1942, the World War I cannon in Railroad Park (now Thomas Centennial Park) in downtown Chesterton was removed and sold for junk as part of the war-time salvage campaign. Assisting with the effort were (left to right): Hjalmer Lafving, Frank Othrow, Royal Atkinson, and Marshal LaRoche.

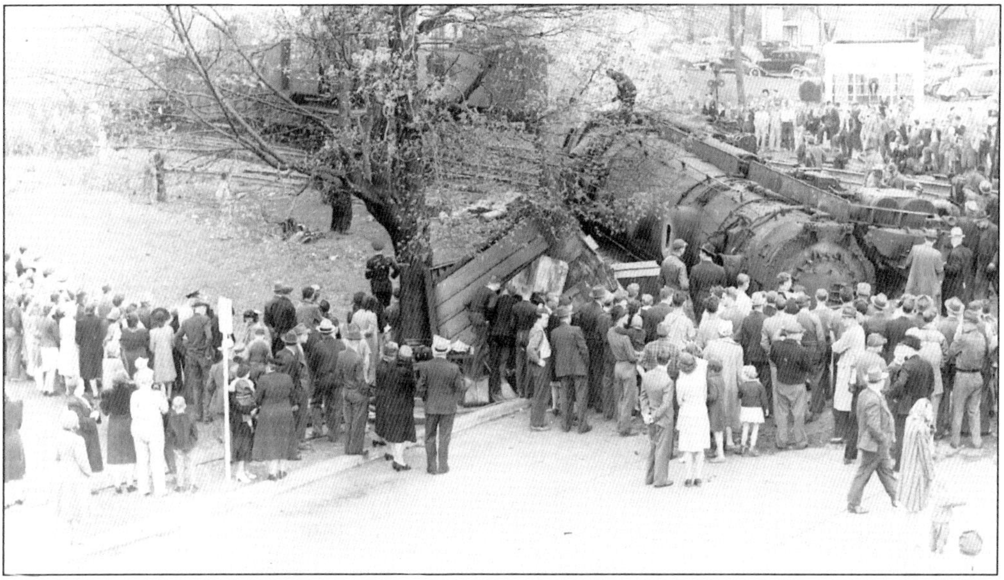

N.Y. Central Train Wreck, 1941. A freight engine derailment on April 26, 1941, at the Calumet Road crossing caused quite a stir in Chesterton. Curious onlookers came from miles around to survey the damage caused when a carload of hogs overturned and several freight cars were demolished. Local resident Don Young narrowly escaped injury when the engine struck and overturned his watchman's hut.

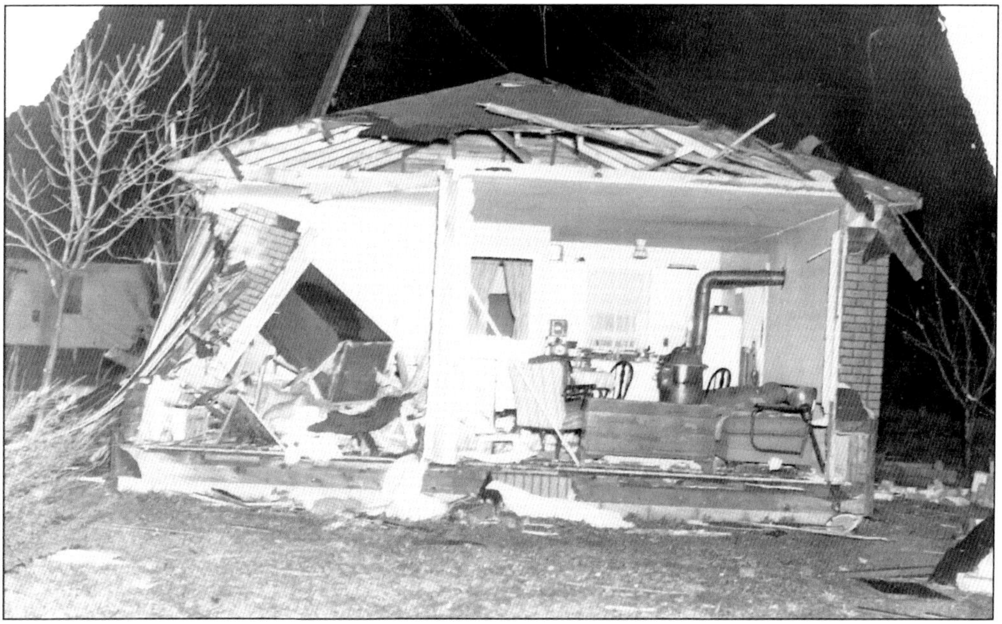

Tornado Strikes Porter, 1948. The Brainerd family home, pictured here, was completely destroyed by the tornado that swept through Porter on April 7, 1948. Trees were downed, and many buildings, including the town hall, school, and several homes, were damaged or destroyed. Fortunately, injuries were minimal and no lives were lost. The community rallied to aid those affected by the tornado, and most homes were rebuilt.

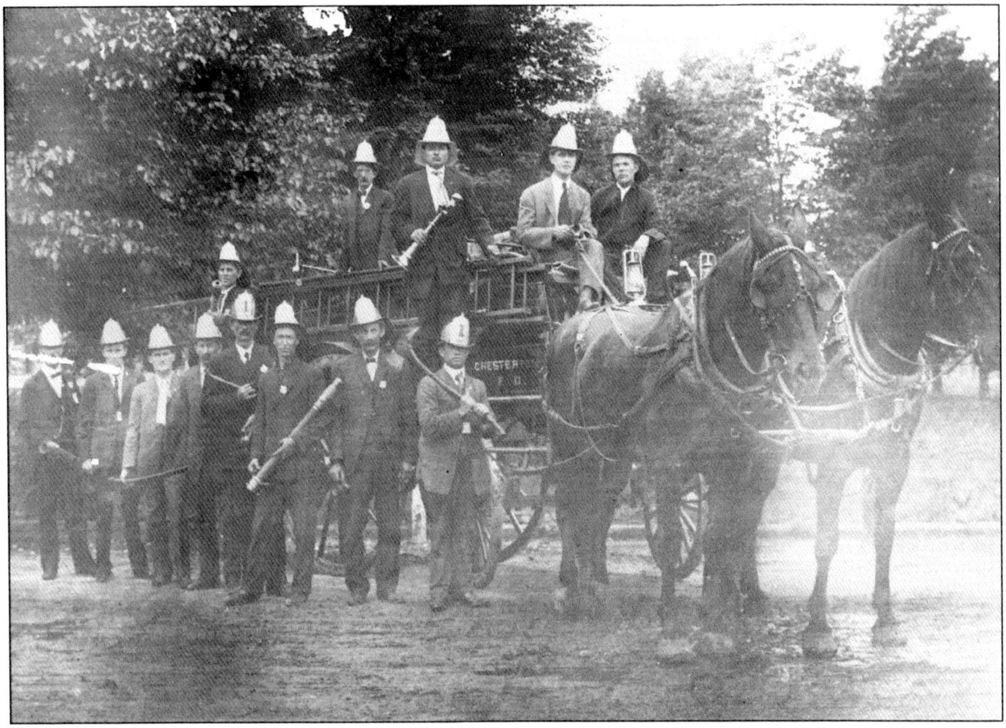

CHESTERTON FIRE DEPT. Members of an early Chesterton volunteer fire department are pictured here. The town's first fire department was organized in 1902 in the wake of a devastating fire on April 6 that destroyed 11 downtown businesses. The town board ruled that thereafter only brick buildings could be built in the business area. They also constructed a fire station on Calumet Road, purchased a 45-gallon chemical tank, and drilled a system of wells for fire protection.

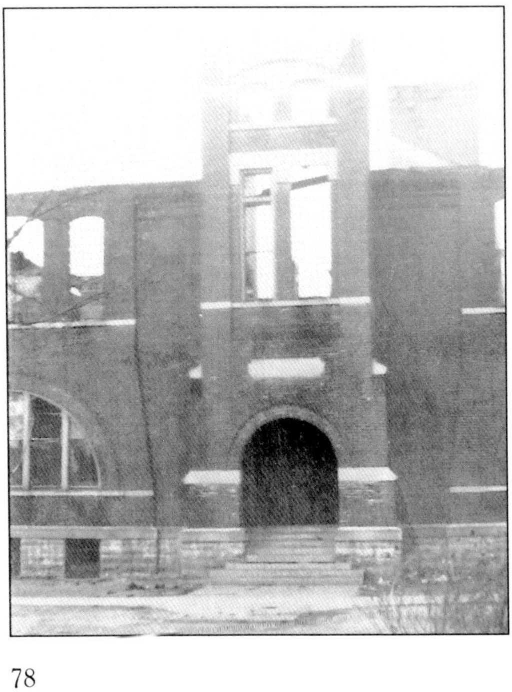

SCHOOL FIRE, 1924. Major damage to the Chesterton Grade School and nearby buildings occurred when a fire broke out on November 11, 1924. The school, which incurred more than $100,000 in damages, lost its tower and was rebuilt with substantial interior changes and a flat roof. Students were taught in the basements of local churches and at Chesterton High School while the reconstruction was completed.

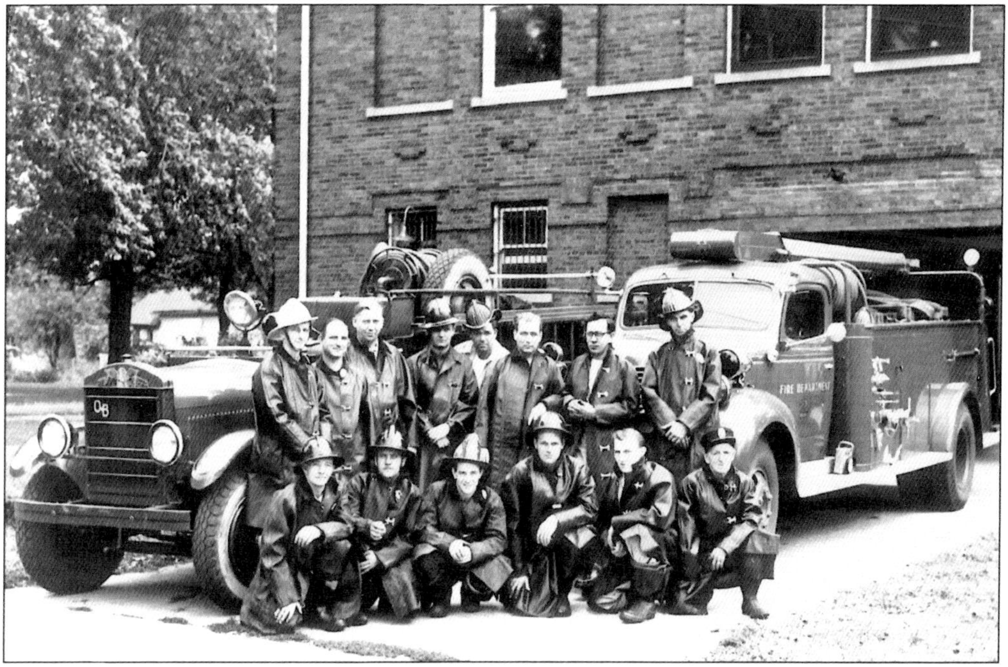

Porter Volunteer Fire Department, 1950. Firefighters pictured in this 1950 photograph are, from left to right, K. Slater, C. Hamilton, W. Slater, B. Groff, E. Hokanson, and A. "Shorty" Slater; (second row) A. Hokanson, W. Wesley, H. Hokanson, R. Lindquist, R. Swanson, L. Esmoer, C. Randler, and C. Pratt. First organized in 1908, the Porter Fire Department was housed in the town hall on Franklin Street until 1991 when a new fire station was built on Beam Street.

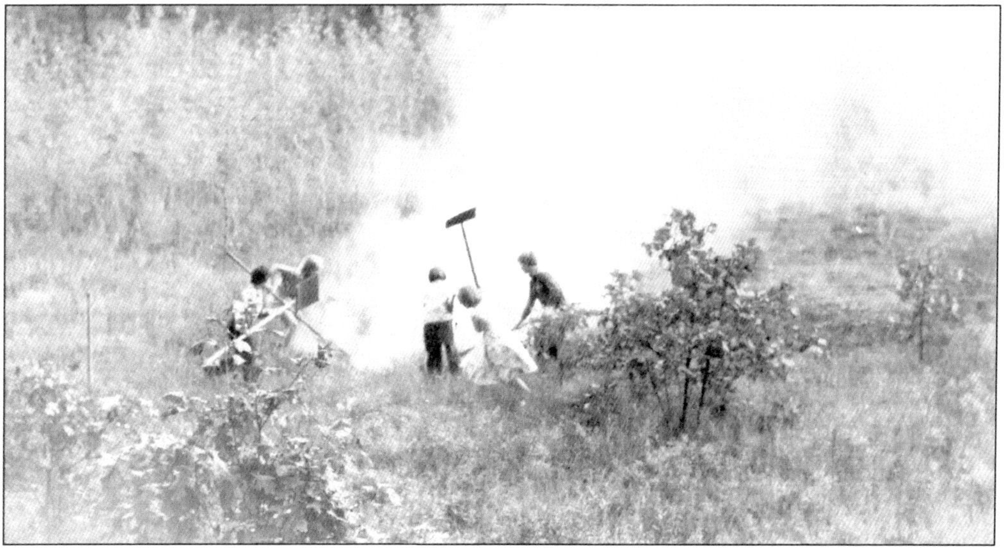

Dune Acres Firefighters. Brush fires were a common and dangerous threat in Dune Acres up to the early 1960s. Showing great courage and self-sufficiency, town residents used water tanks with hoses strapped to their backs and beaters (long poles with rubber flaps) to fight the brush fires, as seen in the photograph above. Contracts with neighboring fire departments eventually replaced the Dunes Acres volunteer fire department by the mid-1980s.

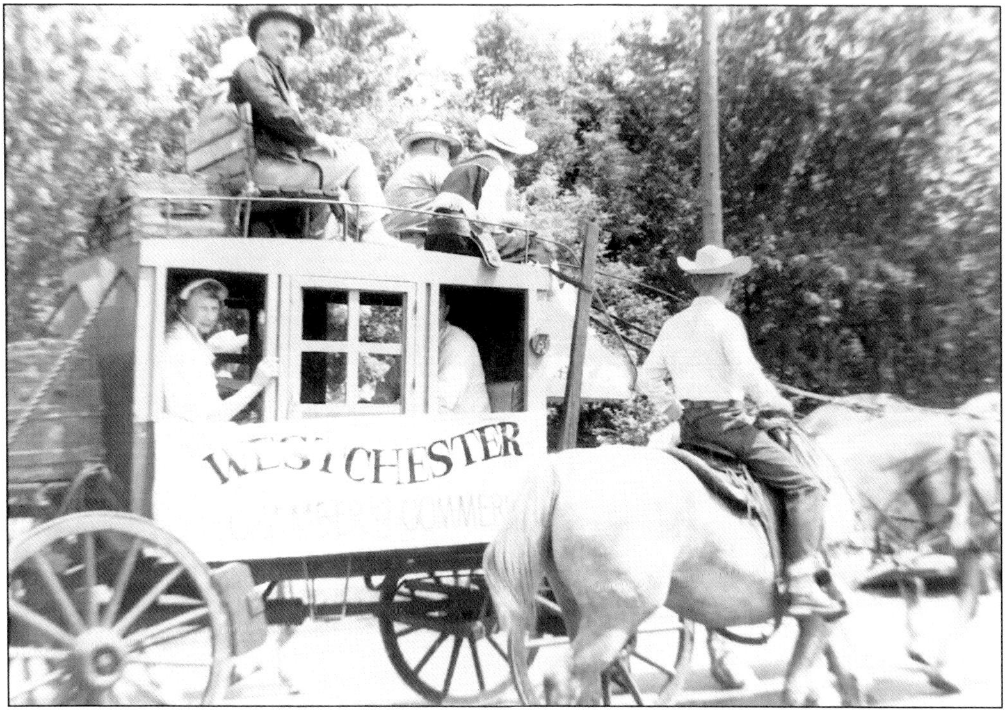

CENTENNIAL PARADE, 1952. The Westchester Chamber of Commerce entry in the August 19, 1952 Centennial parade is pictured above. The bearded man on top of the wagon is *Chesterton Tribune* writer and history buff Louis Menke, the organizing force behind the Centennial Celebration. Now known as the Duneland Chamber of Commerce, the local chapter was organized in 1921 as the Chesterton Chamber. (Arthur E. Anderson Photograph.)

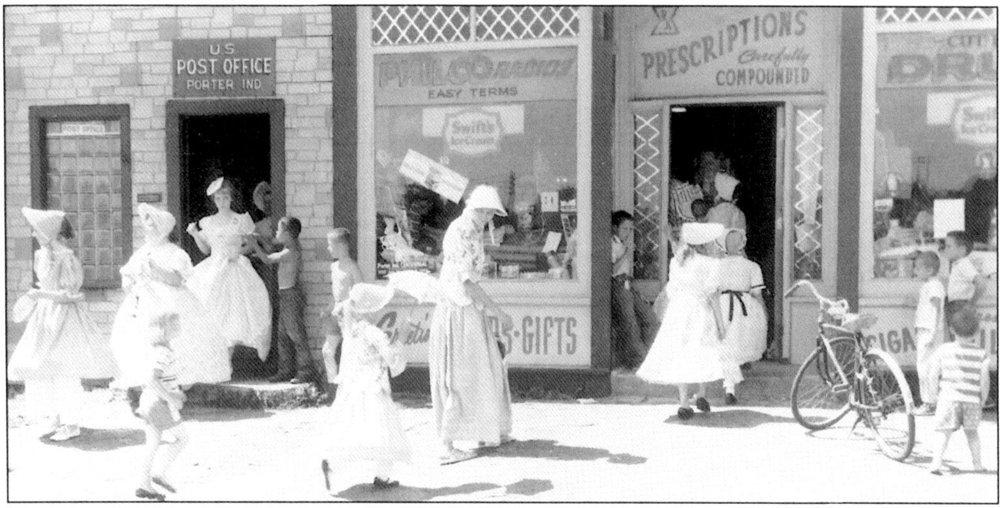

PORTER CENTENNIAL, 1958. In this photograph taken on Lincoln Street, local women and children are dressed in 1850s-style clothing to participate in the Sisters of the Swish style show. The show was one of the many events, including a parade, Centennial ball, crowning of the Centennial Queen, a visit from the governor, and a historical pageant, during Porter's Centennial Celebration in July 1958. The Centennial marked the settling of Old Porter in 1858.

CENTENNIAL FAMILIES, 1952. The two groups pictured here were among the numerous local families who dressed in 1850s-style clothing as part of Chesterton's Centennial celebration in August 1952. Pictured are Eloise Jeffrey Johnson, her husband J. Oliver, and their son John (also seen on page 90). The photograph below shows Dallas, Collyn, I. Jo., and Juli Summers. Festivities during the week-long celebration included a pageant, fireworks, a Centennial Ball, beard-growing contest, and style show. The Centennial marked the 100th anniversary of the platting of the original village of Calumet by the William Thomas family in 1852.

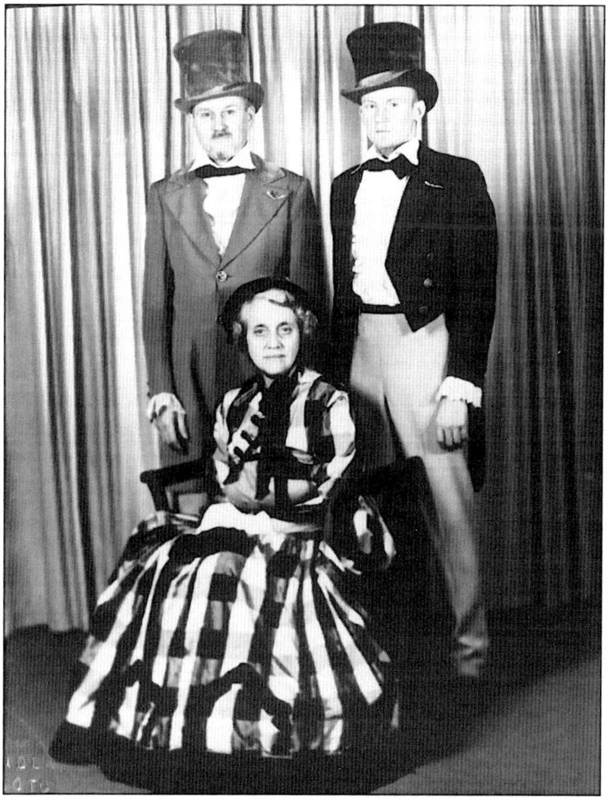

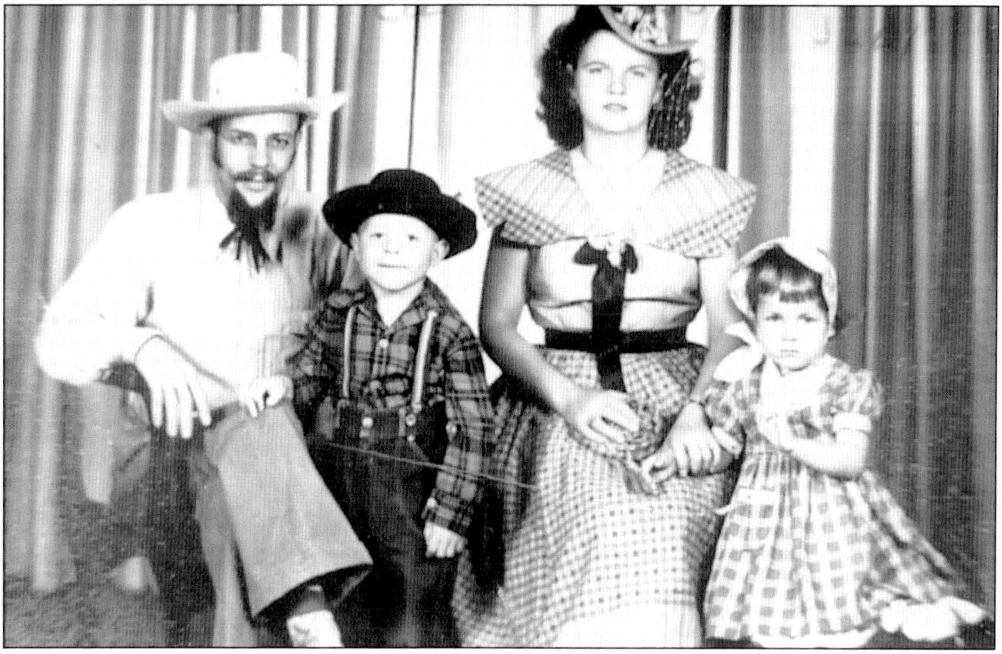

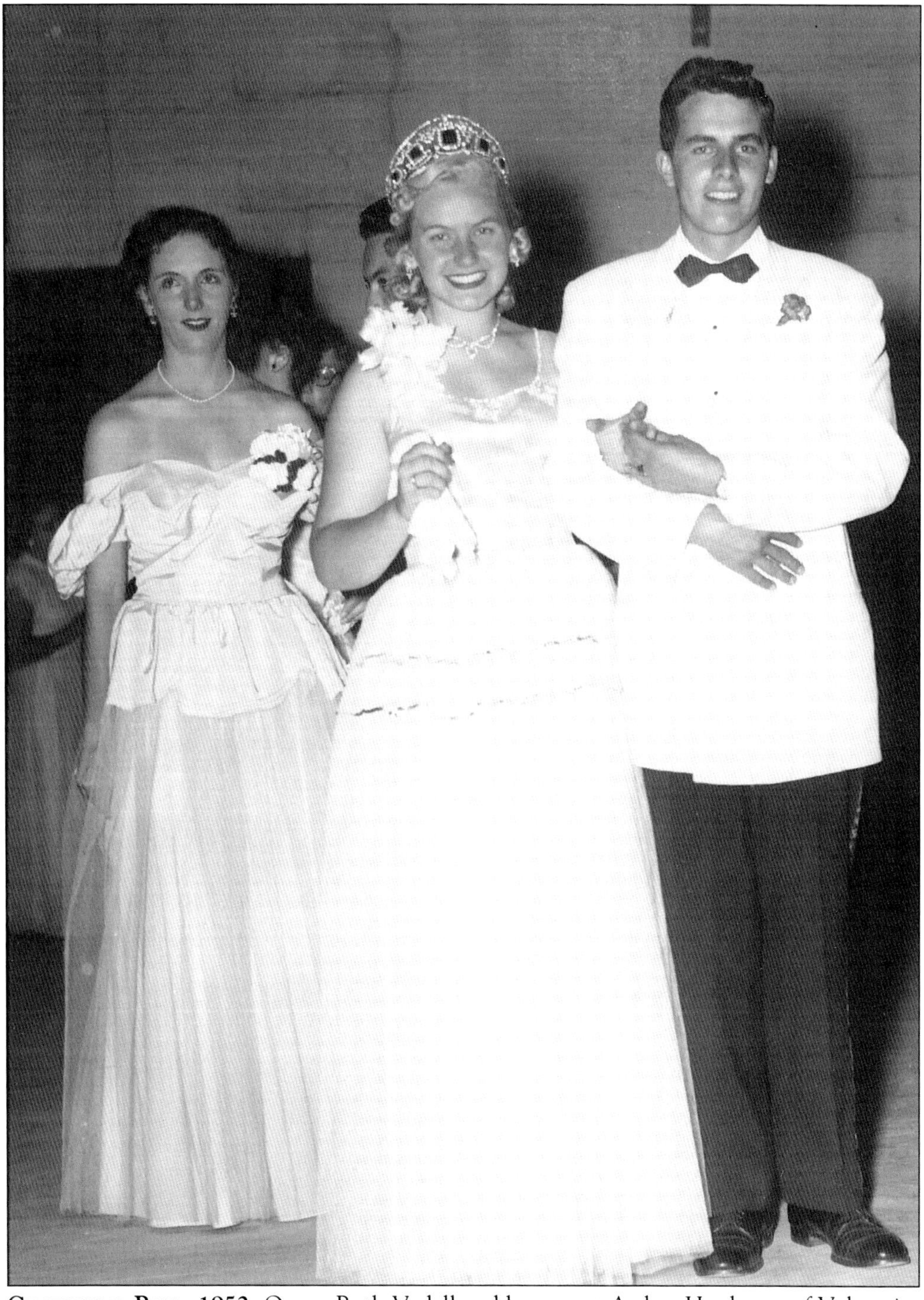

CENTENNIAL BALL, 1952. Queen Ruth Vedell and her escort Arthur Hershman of Valparaiso are joined by maiden-in-waiting Dolores Glawe for the grand march. The crowning of Miss Chesterton Centennial took place at a ball held at the Atlas Roller Rink on Friday, August 21, 1952. Local couples, attired in centennial costumes as well as summer formals, enjoyed entertainment by Bill Morthland's Band and Lenny Collier and the Three Bars.

Eight

Home Life

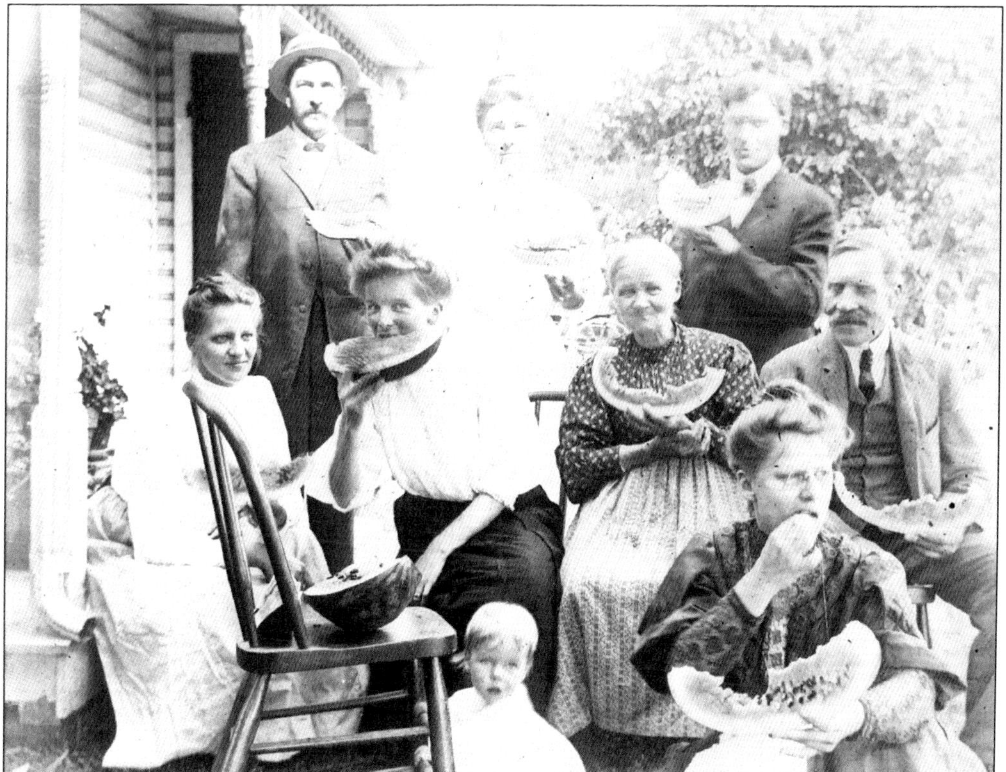

Watermelon Party. The Gustafson-Peterson families enjoy watermelon in this charming slice-of-life scene taken at their homestead in Old Porter around the turn of the century. Emily Peterson, longtime Chesterton High School teacher and Porter librarian from 1914 to 1954, is pictured in the lower right-hand corner of the photograph.

Since the earliest settlers arrived in Westchester Township, home and family have been the focus of life in this hard-working community. The photographs included in this chapter provide a portrait of the families and homes that make up the fabric of our township.

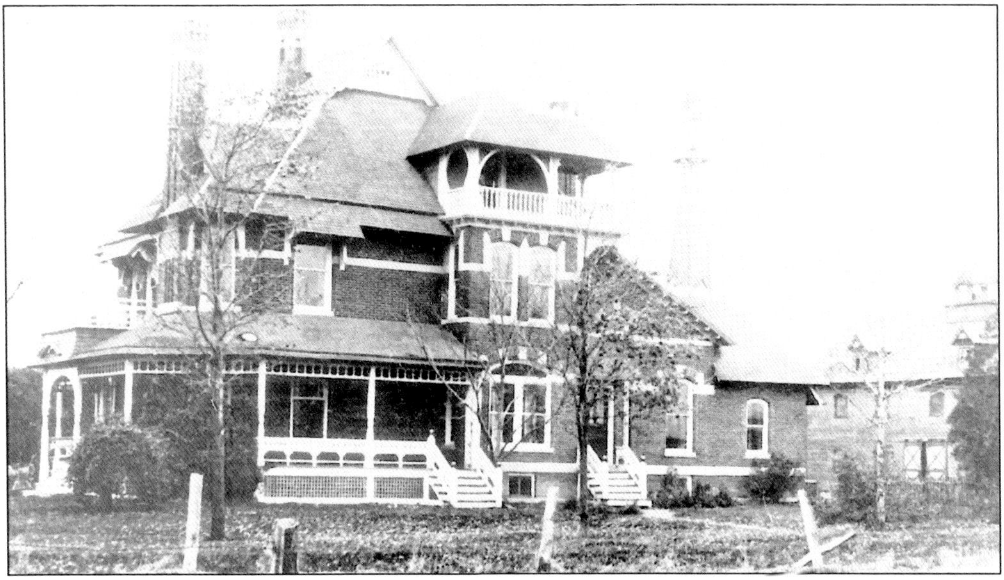

Brown Mansion, Chesterton. The red brick house at 700 W. Porter Avenue was built in 1885 for George Brown. Constructed in the Queen Anne style popular at that time, the home featured hand-carved fireplaces and oak stair railings, frescoed ceilings, gingerbread trim, and scrollwork porches on the exterior. The carriage house and windmill seen above to the right are no longer in existence. Westchester School Corporation purchased the building in 1963 and renovated it for use as the Administration Center.

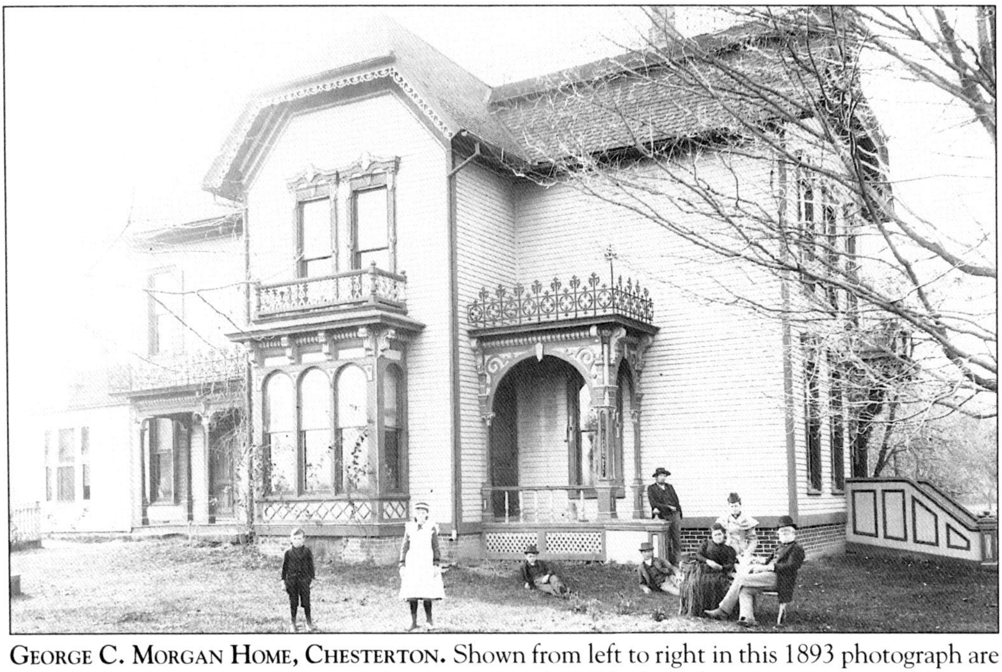

George C. Morgan Home, Chesterton. Shown from left to right in this 1893 photograph are Morgan family members Bennett, Georgie, Edward, Wilfred, Arthur, Mrs. Margaret Morgan, daughter Sarah, and father George C., son of early settler Jesse Morgan. The home, located on the Morgan farm near E. Porter Avenue (1200 N.) and Sand Creek Drive, burned to the ground in the early 1900s.

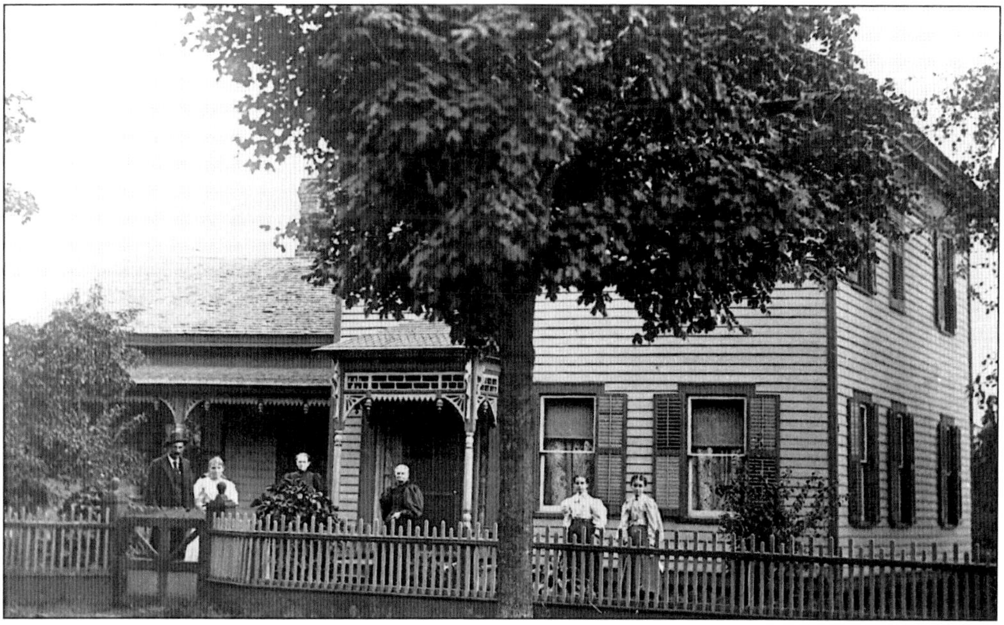

WILLIAM THOMAS HOME, CHESTERTON. Pictured here from left to right are Charles Haslett and his wife Elena Thomas Haslett, who lived in the home for many years, Jane Thomas, Grandmother Haslett, Ivy Haslett Riffer, and Nora Haslett Hubbard. The house, situated on the southeast corner of Indiana Avenue and Second Street, was built in 1858 for the family of William Thomas II. The land was sold to Chesterton State Bank in 1975, and the home was demolished.

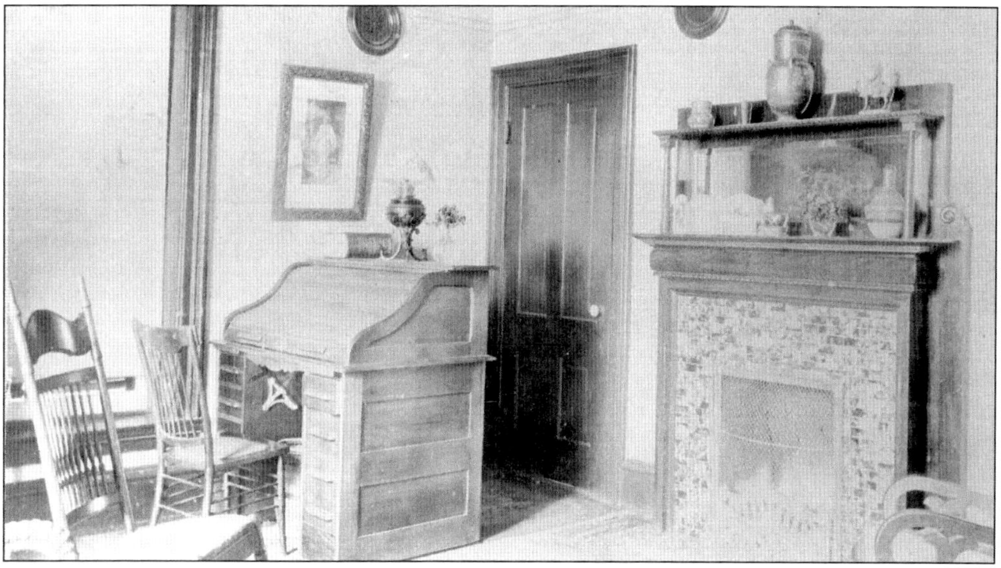

FURNESS HOME, FURNESSVILLE. The library of the E.L. Furness residence, which still stands near U.S. Highway 20 in Furnessville, is seen above. Constructed in 1881 of local brick, the Federal-style 12-room home featured a well-stocked library. The round, wooden openings visible on the walls were part of a system designed to circulate cool air from the basement of the home. The sewing chair in the foreground was donated to the Westchester Township Historical Museum.

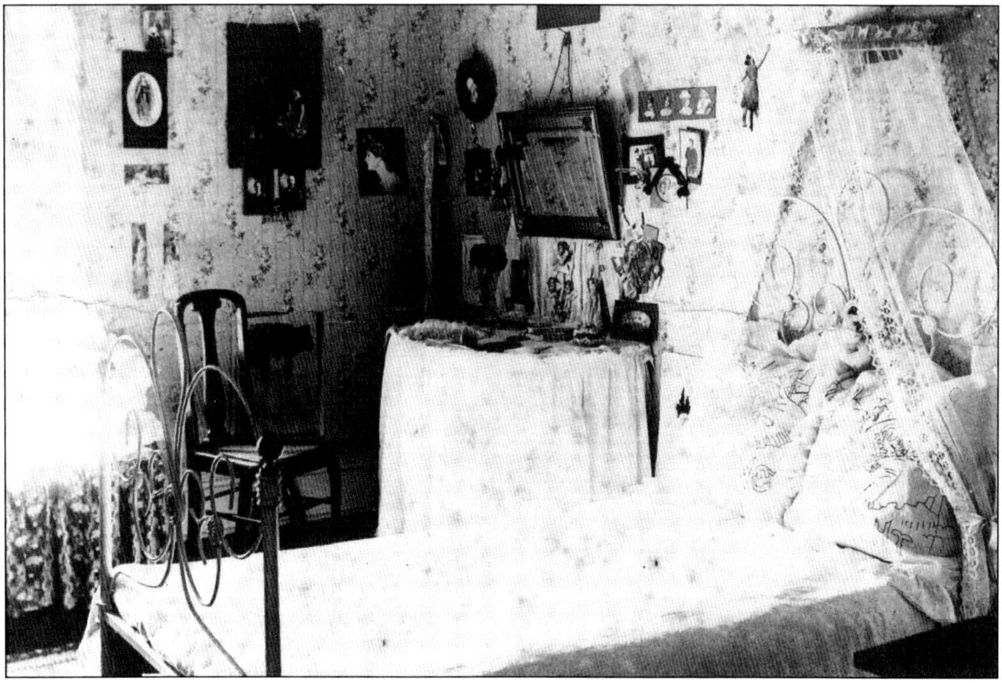

Beam House Exterior and Bedroom. The photograph below shows the home, located on Wagner Road in Porter, as it looked in the early part of the century. The original portion of the residence was constructed in the 1850s. William Beam, a superintendent at one of the Porter brickyards, built a large addition of Porter brick on the front of the house in 1883. The above undated photograph shows a bedroom in the home. The Beams lived in the house for a short time before it was sold to the Peterson family and later the Busses, who undertook extensive remodeling.

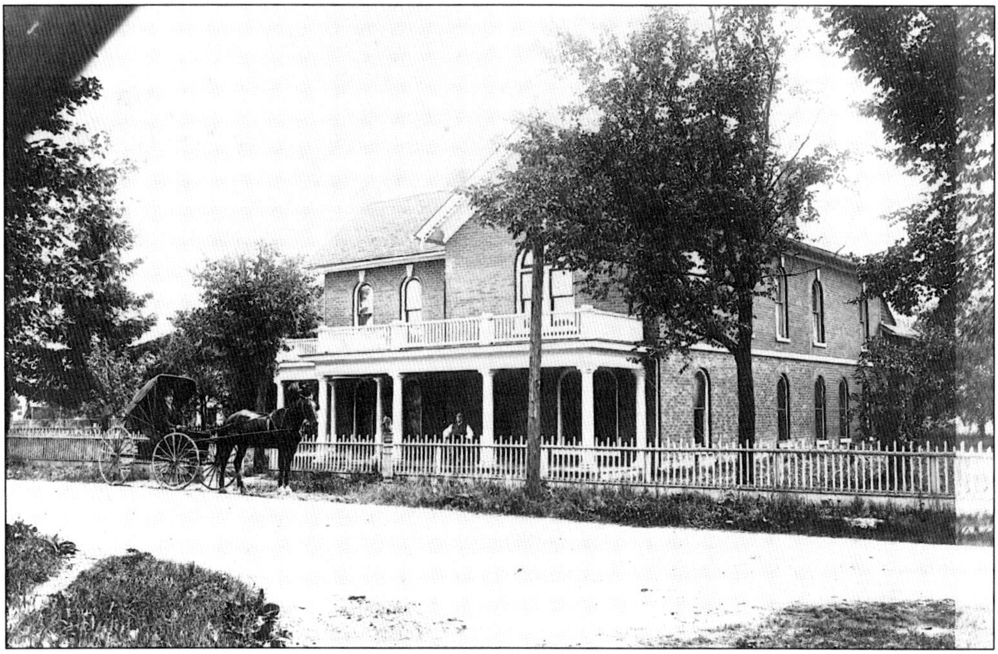

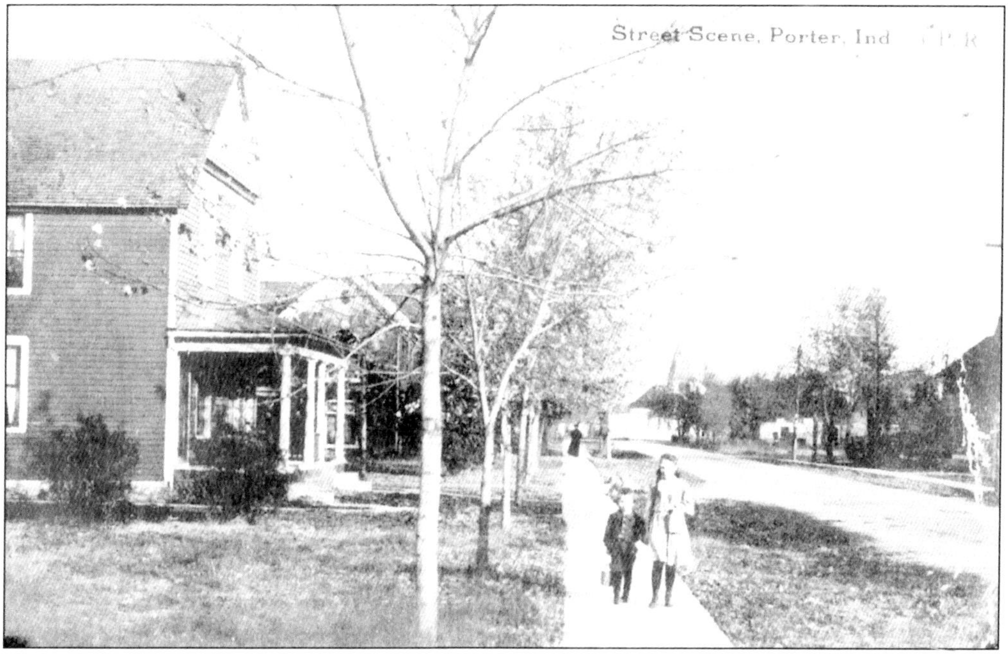

PORTER STREET SCENE. Taken looking north on Wagner Road in the early part of the century, this postcard depicts a residential section of Porter. The Porter Congregational Church can be seen on the right at the end of the road.

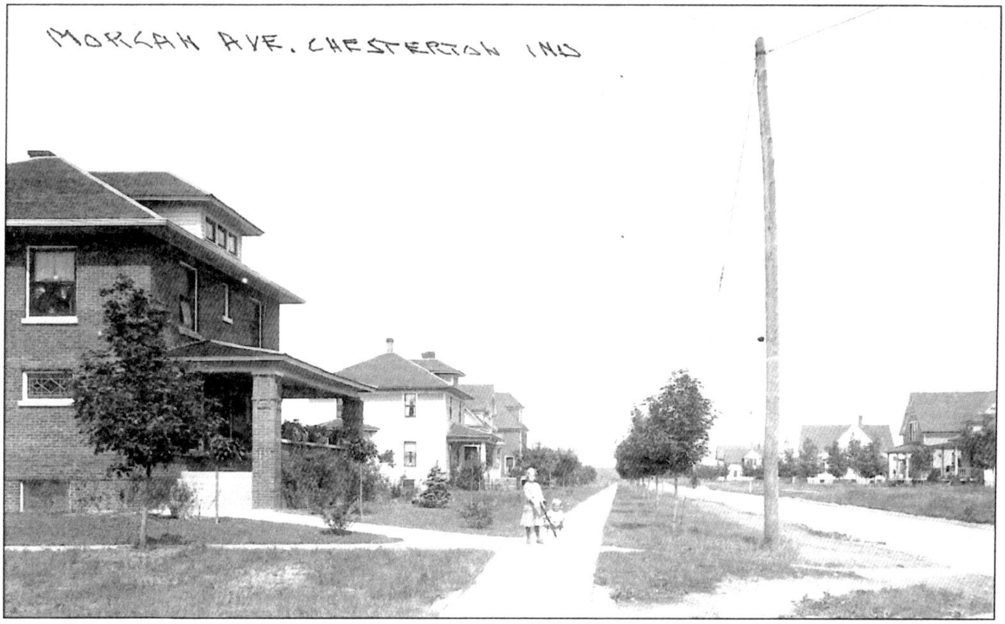

MORGAN PARK, CHESTERTON. This view, looking east on Morgan Avenue in 1914, shows the town's earliest subdivision, shortly after its development. Charles L. Jeffrey, Arthur L. Bowser, and Edward L. Morgan established the Chesterton Realty Co. and began selling lots in the subdivision in 1907. The Schwedler maple trees that were planted throughout Morgan Park are visible in this early postcard. As can be seen, the area boasted paved sidewalks, but Morgan Avenue was as yet unpaved.

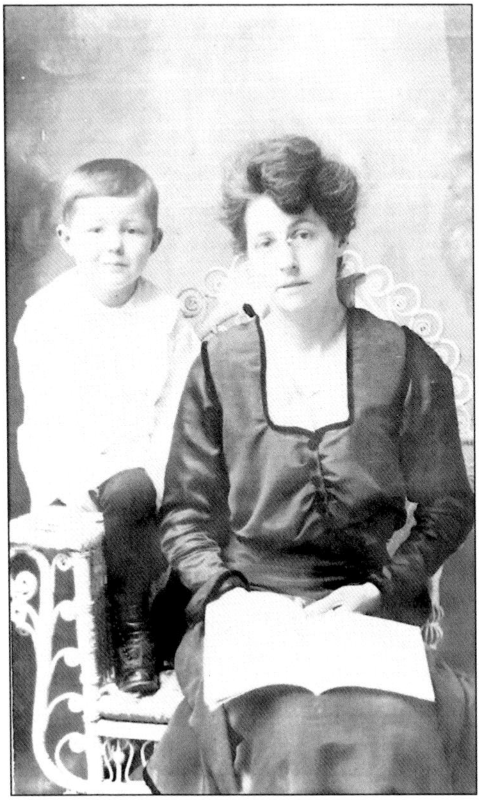

Richard and Anna Smith, Chesterton. Richard Smith posed for this formal portrait with his mother Anna Morgan Smith, *c.* 1912. Mrs. Smith was the daughter of John G. Morgan and Mary Ann Holland Morgan.

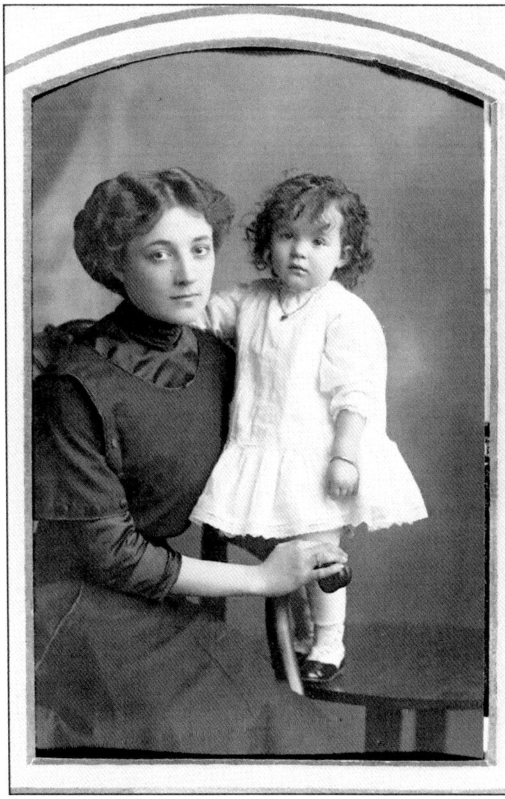

Oral Haslett and Niece Marjorie, Chesterton. In this *c.* 1909 photograph Oral Haslett is pictured with her young niece Marjorie Hubbard, the daughter of Oral's sister Nora and Roy Hubbard. Marjorie later married local merchant Arthur Hokanson. Oral Haslett, a descendant of both the Morgan and Thomas families, was a schoolteacher prior to marrying businessman Charles Smith in 1912. Following her husband's death, Mrs. Smith continued to operate their store. Mrs. Smith, who lived to age 99, had a life-long interest in local history and wrote *My Hometown*, her recollections of Chesterton's past.

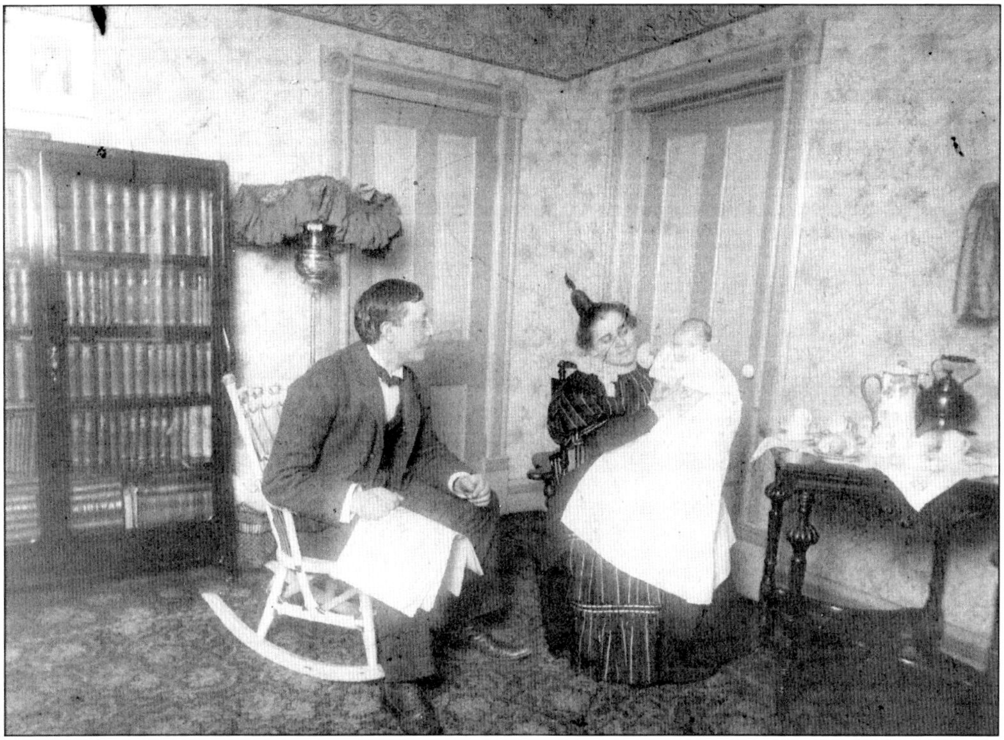

JEFFREY FAMILY, CHESTERTON. Local financier Charles L. Jeffrey is pictured with his wife Elizabeth and their young daughter Eloise in their Chesterton home in 1896. The Jeffrey home at 525 S. Second Street was later sold and used as a funeral home, which it remains today.

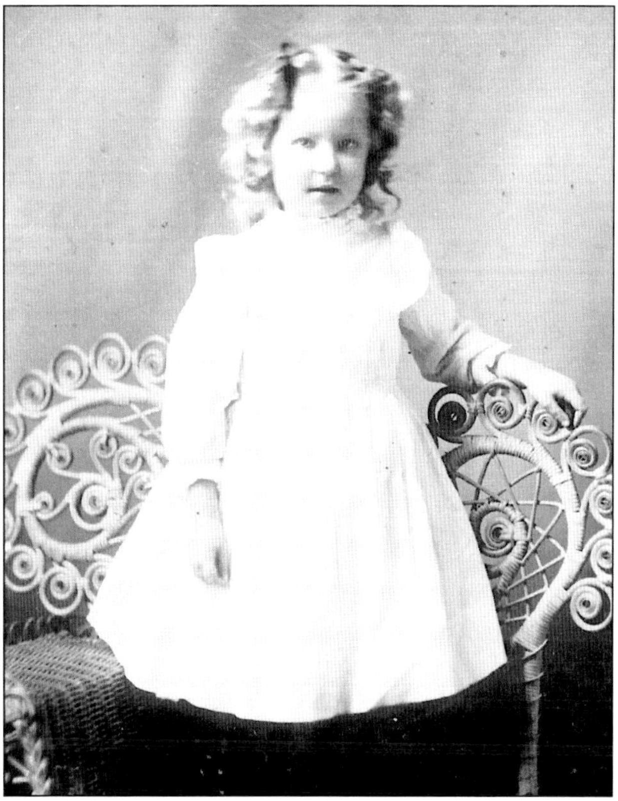

MARGARET LARSON, PORTER. This 1903 photograph of four-year-old Margaret was taken in Michigan City to send to relatives in Sweden. Miss Larson, whose family at one time worked for the Baillys, was unable to attend school at an early age due to health problems. She received instruction at the Bailly Homestead for several years from Frances Howe, Joseph Bailly's granddaughter. This experience inspired her to become a teacher, a career she pursued for 48 years until her retirement in 1968.

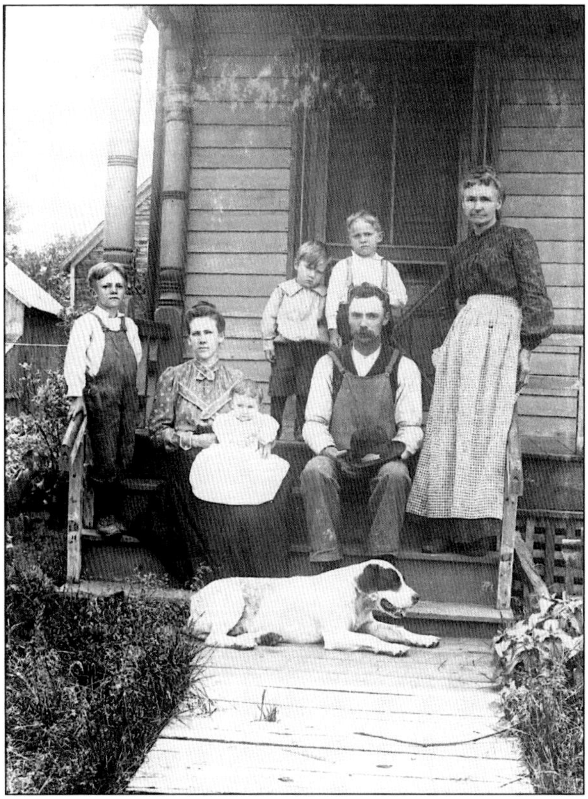

WAUGH FAMILY. Frank Waugh and his wife Elmatie are pictured on the front porch of their home in 1903 surrounded by their family. From left to right they are Edward, baby Edna, Glen and Bill Waugh, and standing at the right, Stacy Johnson, Matie's mother. Frank was a painter, trained fire horses, and operated a dray business in Chesterton. After his death in 1909, Matie supported her young family by doing housework and by working at the Chesterton china factory.

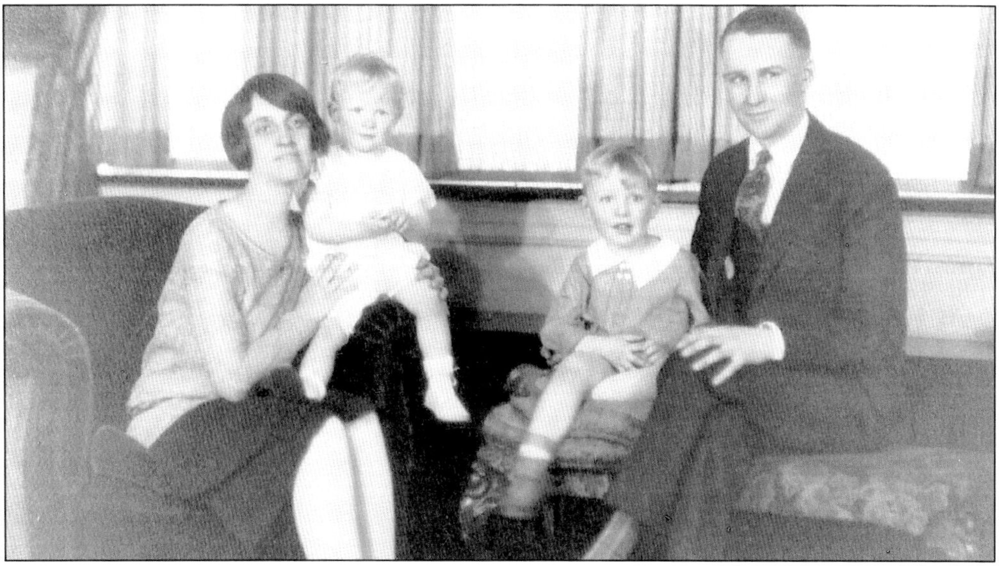

JOHNSON FAMILY, CHESTERTON. Eloise Jeffrey Johnson, daughter of Charles Jeffrey, children John and Charles, and her husband J. Oliver Johnson are pictured in their home in this 1923 photograph. Mr. Johnson was senior vice president of Chesterton State Bank. The family lived in a house on the southeast corner of Morgan Avenue and Wilson Street in Morgan Park, a wedding present from Mr. Jeffrey.

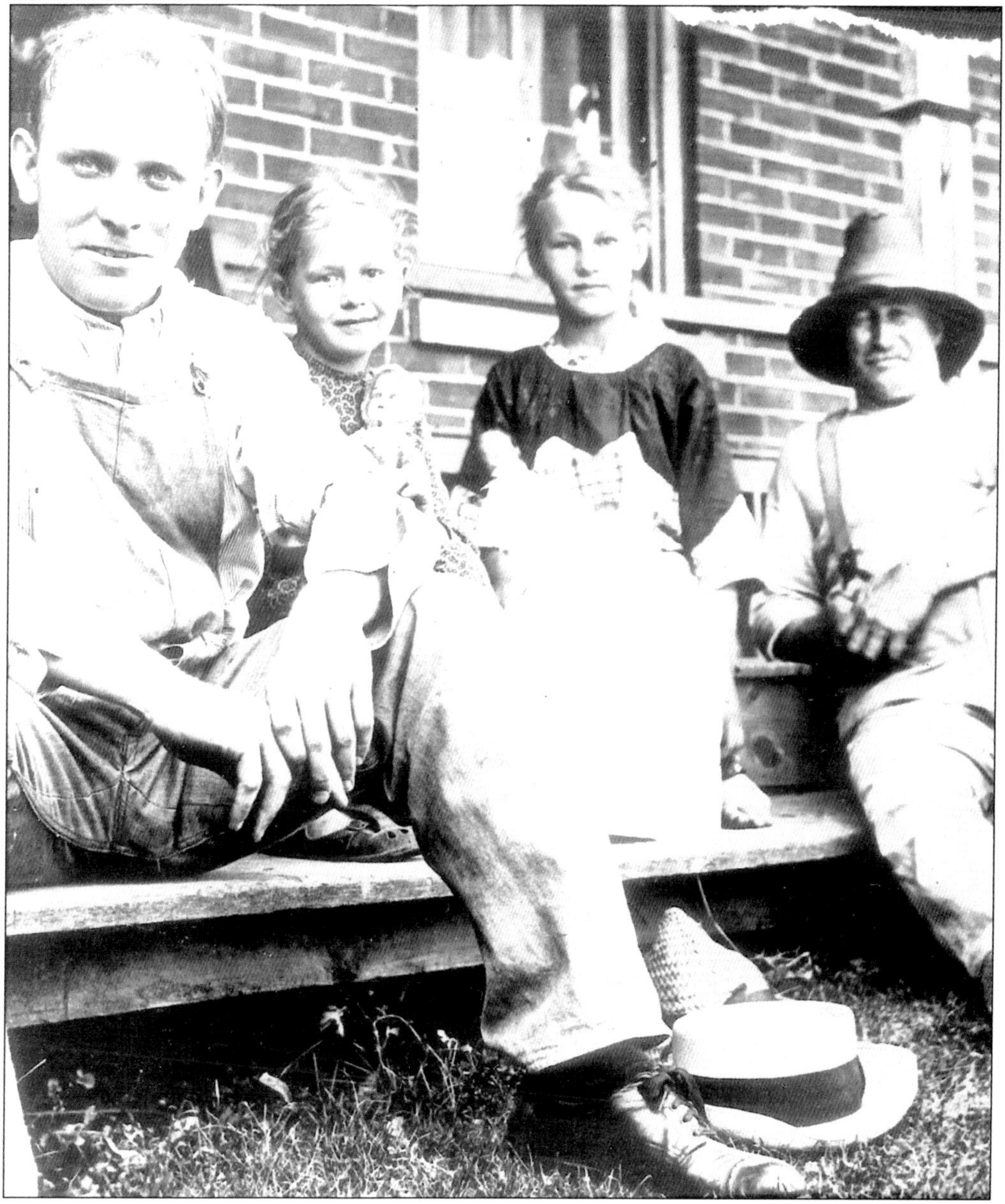

Chellberg Family, Porter. C.L. Chellberg, son of the original Chellbergs who settled in Baillytown, relaxes on the porch of the Chellberg family farmhouse. Pictured on his right are his young daughters Naomi and Ruth and an unidentified man in this *c.* 1910 photograph. (Courtesy Indiana Dunes National Lakeshore, NPS.)

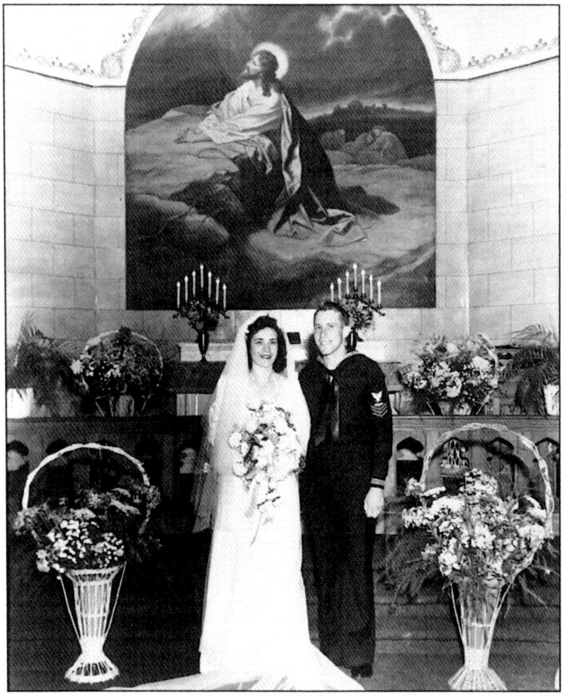

ERICKSON WEDDING, 1945. On July 26, 1945, Anna Anderson of Burdick married R. Walter Erickson of Chesterton at Bethlehem Lutheran Church in Chesterton. Mr. Erickson joined the Navy in 1942 as a seaman and was home on leave from Georgia where he was receiving pilot training in the Naval Air Corps. Following the war, Mr. Erickson returned to Chesterton. (Reggie Pomeroy photograph.)

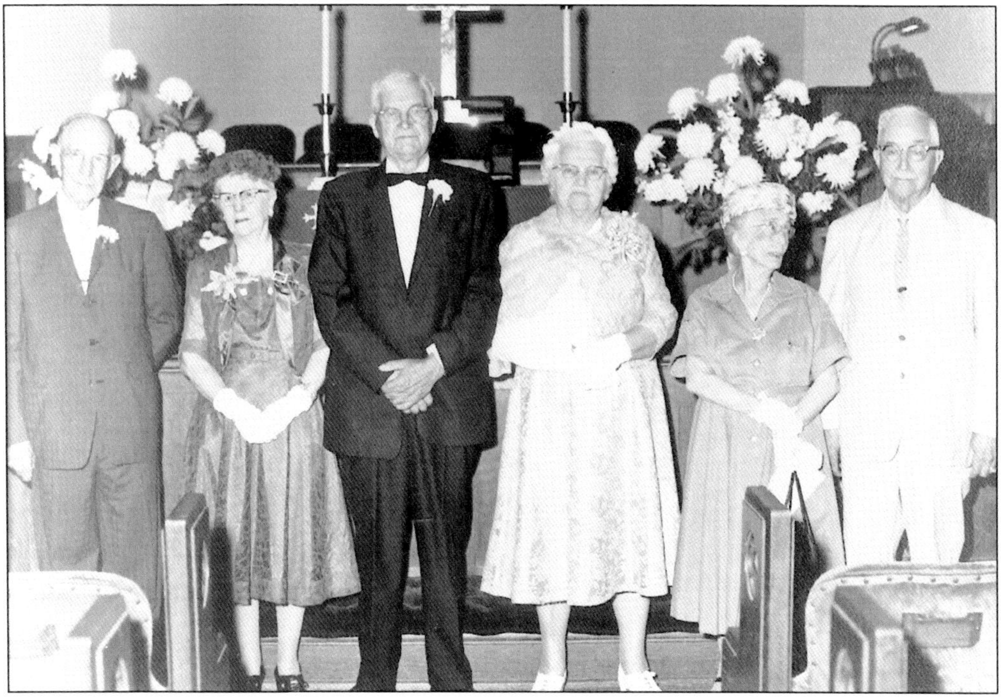

ANNIVERSARY CELEBRATION, 1961. Three prominent Chesterton couples celebrated their 60th wedding anniversaries and were honored at a ceremony at the First United Methodist Church on June 25, 1961. Pictured (left to right) are Harry R. and Anna Morgan Smith, Mr. and Mrs. John R. Nordstrom, and Mary Bell and Edward L. Morgan.

Nine

RECREATION

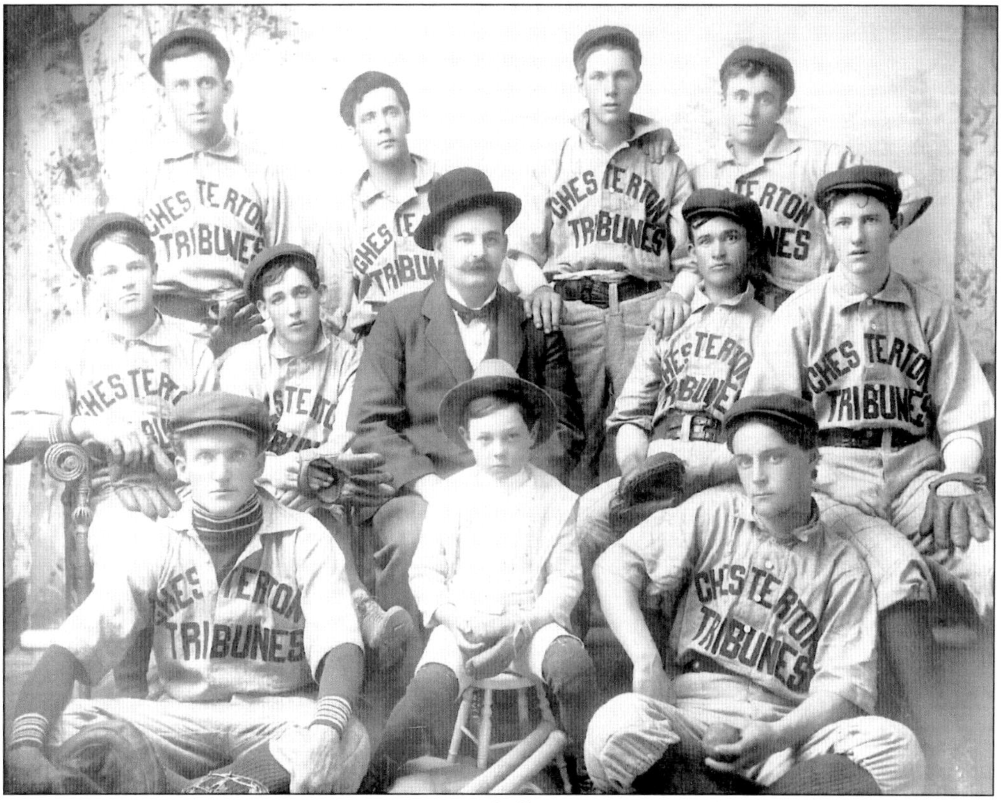

CHESTERTON TRIBUNES BASEBALL TEAM. Baseball was a very popular sport at the turn of the century. The local team was sponsored by the *Chesterton Tribune*, which provided detailed reports of the team's progress in each weekly edition. The Tribunes played teams from cities and towns throughout Northwest Indiana in many closely followed, highly competitive games.

Citizens of Westchester Township have long enjoyed social activities of many kinds. Sports, music, and many other recreational activities have been popular with locals for over 100 years. This chapter highlights some of the recreational opportunities, past and present, enjoyed by area residents.

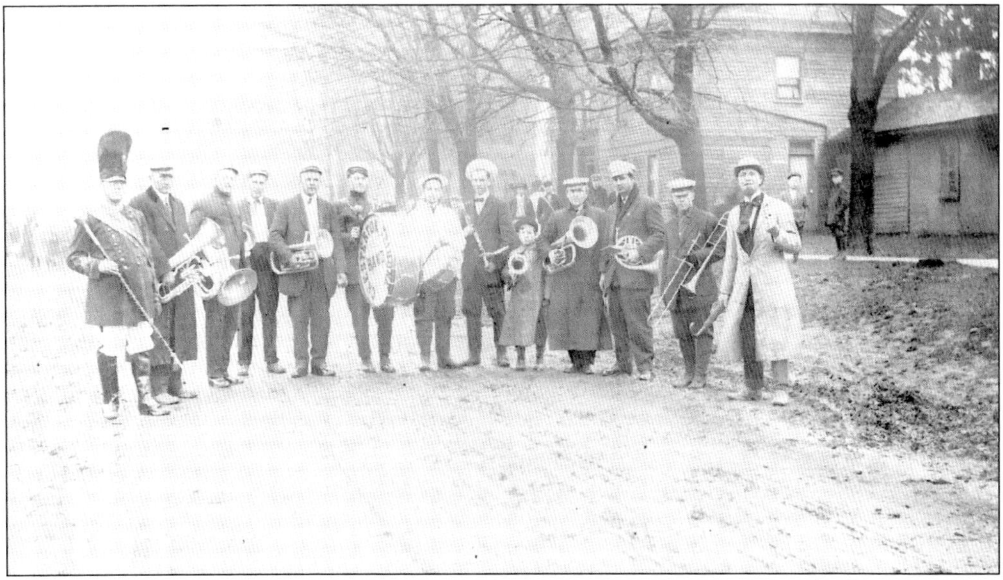

Chesterton Tribune Cornet Band. Pictured in 1914, on Indiana Avenue, looking west from Calumet Road, are (left to right) Charles L. Jeffrey, drum major, A.J. Bowser, founder of the band, F.E. Johnson, August Reglein, John Dille, Earl Wise, Edwin (Bud) Johnson, Fred Hyde, Wesley Swanson, Albert T. Swanson, John Eckhert, Earl Murray, and Dr. C.O. Wiltfong. The band was organized in 1904 and performed locally in weekly concerts in the park, at parades, and for the Men's Aid Society.

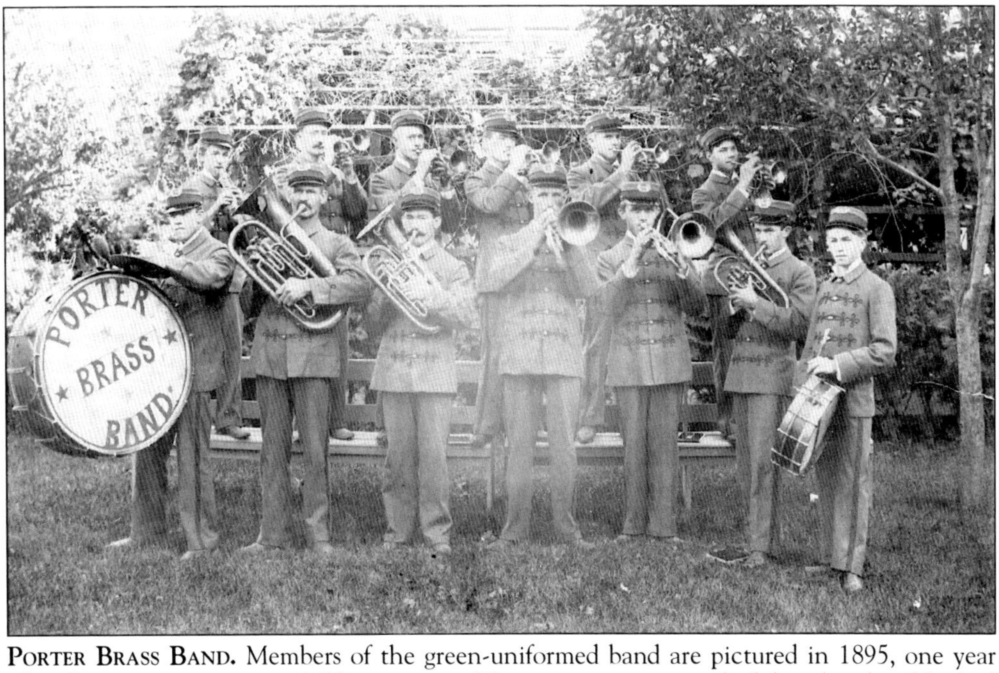

Porter Brass Band. Members of the green-uniformed band are pictured in 1895, one year after the group was organized. The citizens of Porter were very proud of their band and looked forward to the band's Saturday night concerts in the summer. The band also entertained at various social functions.

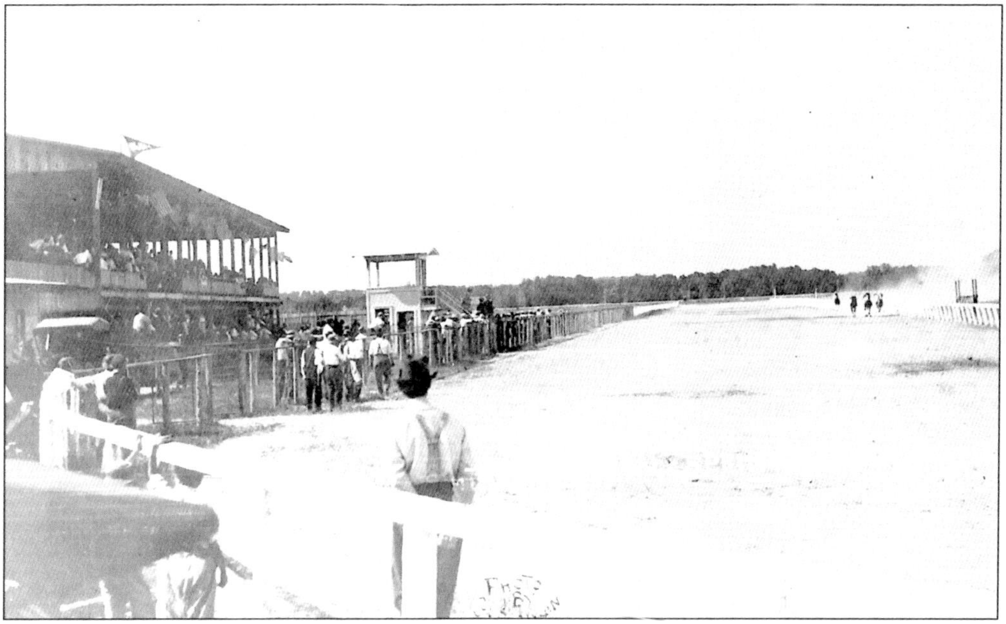

Mineral Springs Race Track, Porter. Horse-racing had a brief but colorful history in the area. In 1912, 3,500 fans attended the opening day races at the Mineral Springs Jockey Club. It was suspected that gambling was taking place, and in 1913 a company of state militia closed the track. The land, located along Highway 20 and the present I-94, was divided into lots and sold as sites for summer cottages and is presently the location of Worthington Steel in Porter.

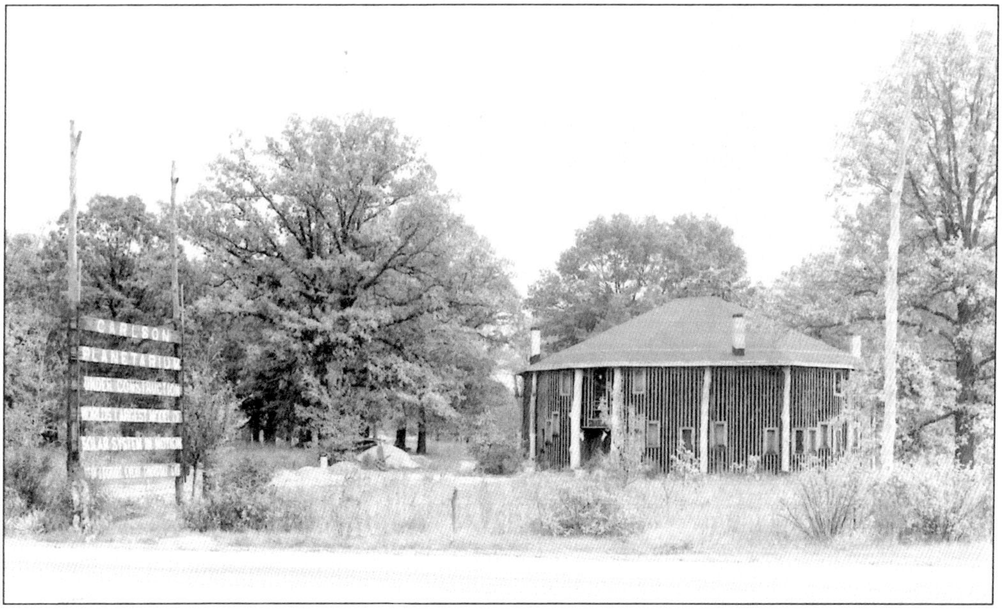

Carlson Planetarium, Porter. Organized by Rev. Dr. Erick Herman Carlson, the retired pastor of Augsburg Lutheran Church, the planetarium was located at the corner of Highway 20 and Mineral Springs Road in Porter. In operation during the 1930s and '40s, the 16-sided wooden structure was 60 feet in diameter and 32 feet high, and could accommodate up to 200 people.

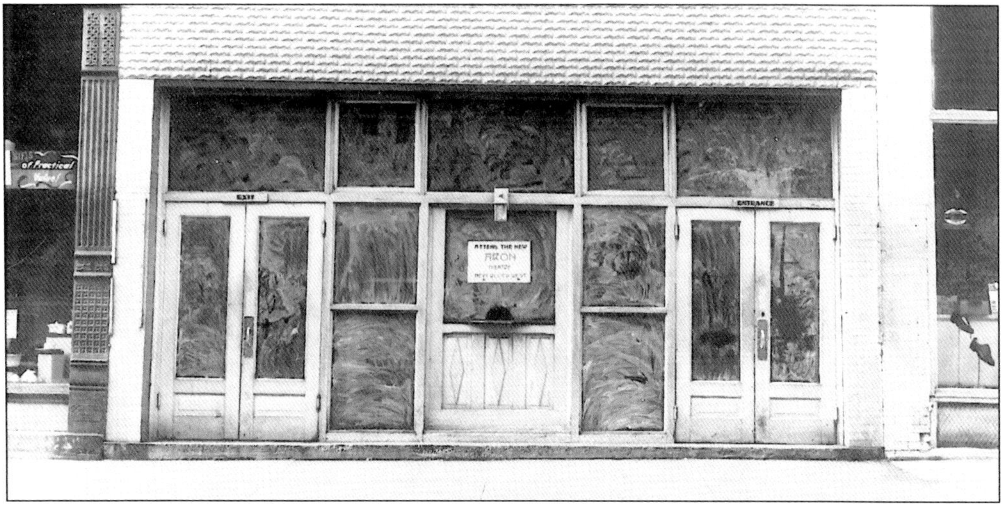

Palace Theatre, Chesterton. A trip to the local movie theater was a greatly anticipated event in the 1920s and 1930s. First-run Hollywood movies were shown at the Palace, owned and operated by H.L. Cooper. The theater, which opened in 1928 at 117 Broadway in Chesterton, began showing talking pictures in May 1930.

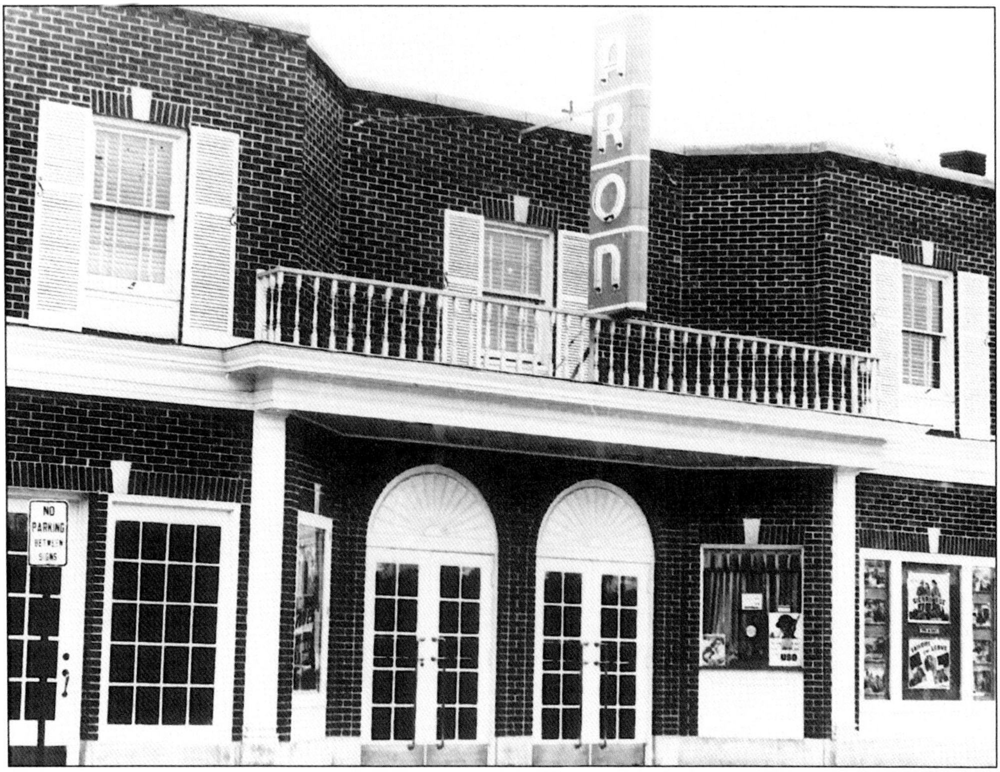

Aron Theatre, Chesterton. Construction of a larger, 440-seat movie theater one block west of the Palace was completed in 1942. Named for Mr. Cooper's wife, Nora, the Aron guaranteed "that every first-run picture will play this theatre exactly as shown in the Loop!" The theater closed in 1962, due to competition from large movie houses. The building was remodeled and enlarged for the Ben Franklin store owned by the Baur family.

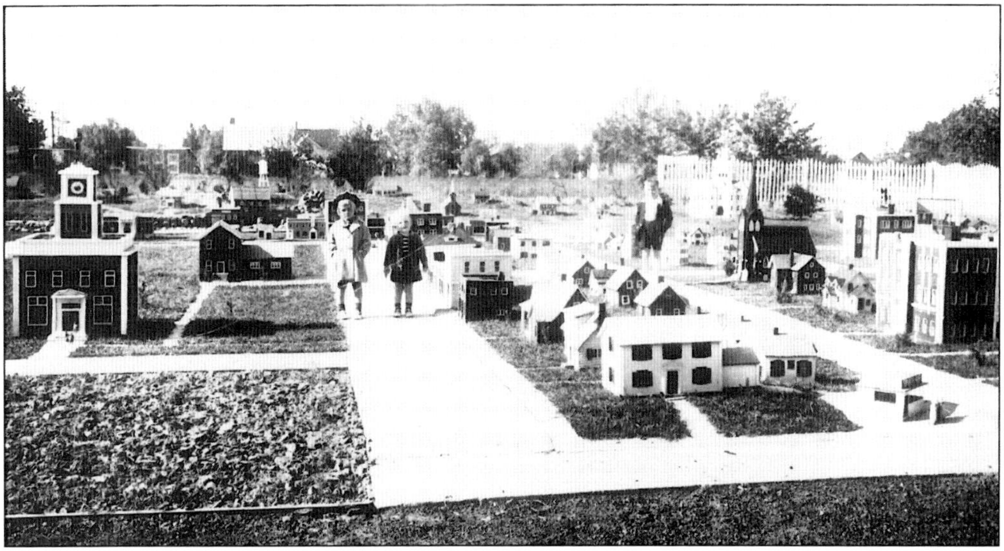

Littleville, Chesterton. William Murray designed and built the tiny town near his home, north of Porter Avenue, between 11th and 12th Streets. Littleville grew to include more than 100 miniature buildings and was a major tourist attraction in the 1930s, drawing as many as 50,000 visitors a year. Murray closed Littleville in 1942 as part of a wartime gas conservation effort. All that remains at the original site is the castle structure.

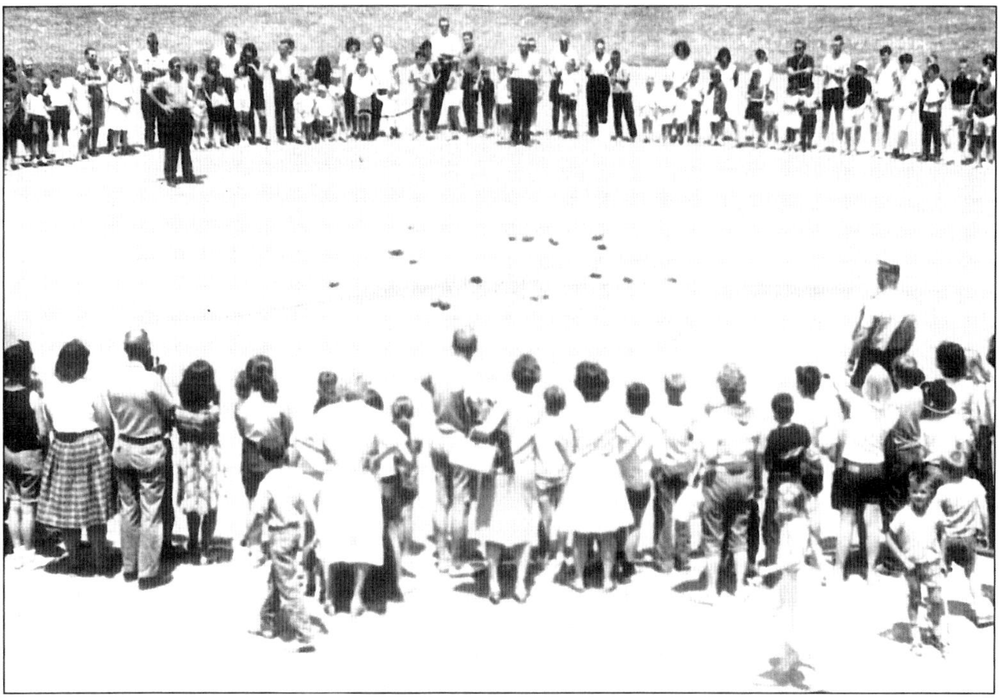

Turtle Races, Chesterton. The Lions Club Turtle Derby was an annual event in the 1950s. Local boys and girls searched area creeks and ponds for the fastest turtles to enter in the competition. Turtles started the race from the center of a ring of concentric circles and "raced" toward the outer edge. Turtle races are still periodically held in the summer.

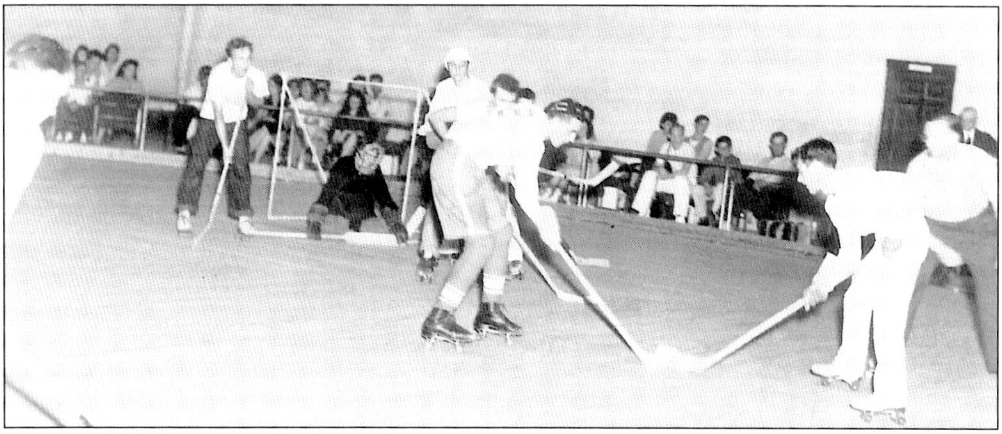

ROLLER SKATING HOCKEY, CHESTERTON. John C. Saidla popularized roller skating in this area in the 1940s and '50s, operating rinks on the second floor of the former China Factory building, and in the west half of what is now the Ben Franklin store, before opening a rink in his building at Ninth and Indiana Avenues in Chesterton. Roller skating parties, hockey games, and even a wedding on roller skates were held at the rinks.

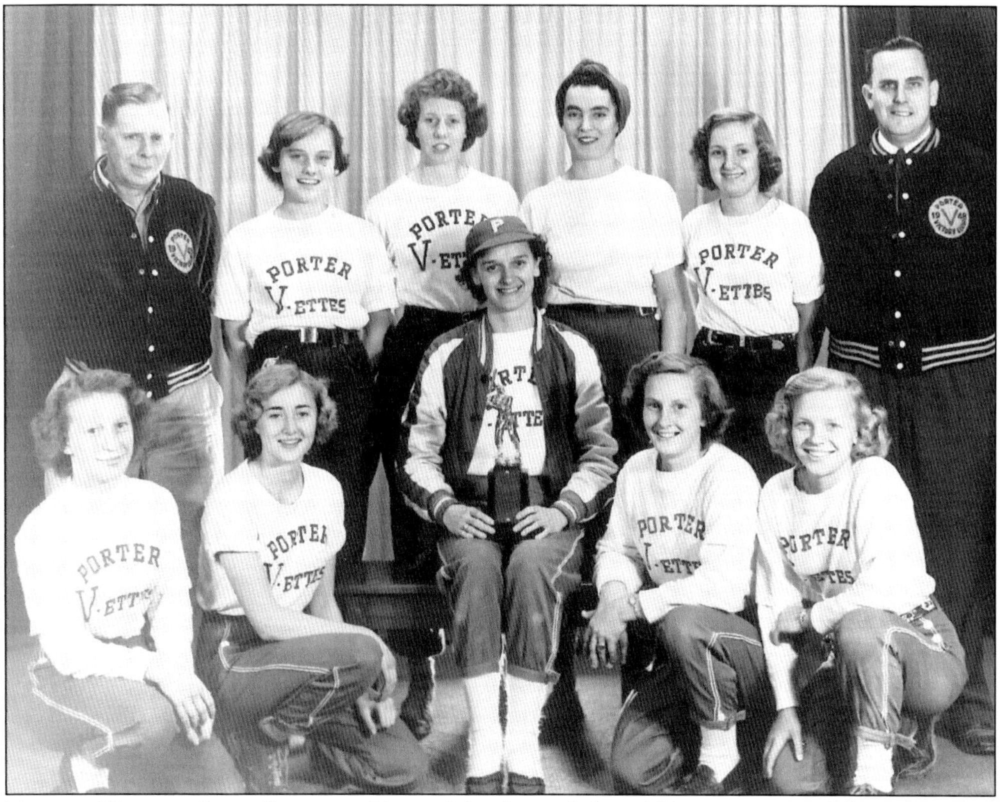

PORTER V'ETTES GIRLS SOFTBALL TEAM. Members of the 1950 team pictured here from left to right are (front row) Naomi Tavernier, Shirley Michael, Betty Wiesmann, Annabelle Flitter, and Cricky Peer; (second row) Don De Haven, business manager, Joan Miller, Patsy Marvel, Alice Pomeroy, Jean Boi, and Wesley R. Erickson, manager. The V'ettes played in the Valparaiso Park League and won many local tournaments.

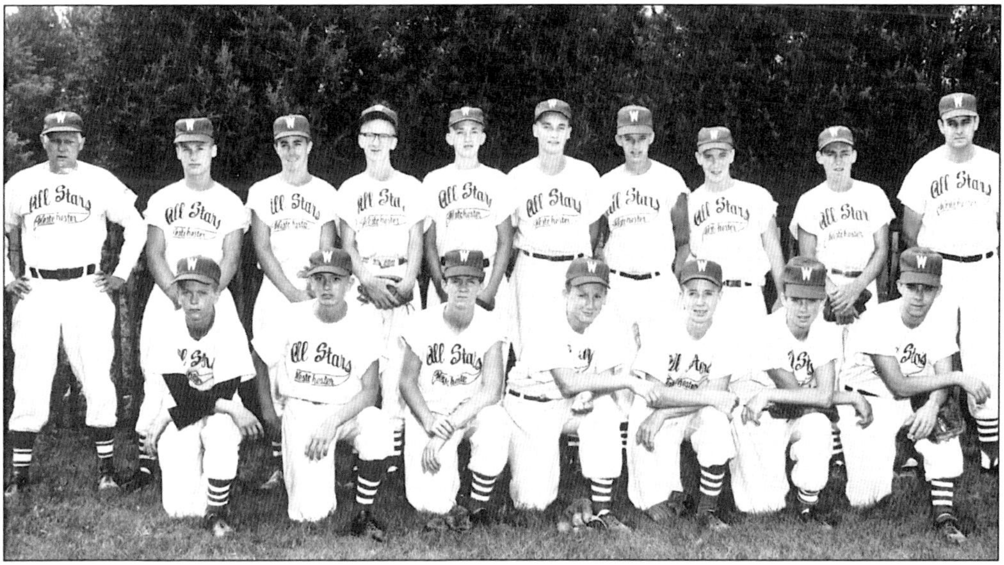

WESTCHESTER BABE RUTH LEAGUE ALL-STARS, 1957. Posing prior to the District Tournament held in Chesterton in August 1957 arc, from left to right, (bottom row) Dick Parker, Jim Thoesen, Norman McCorkel, Larry Westergren, Claude Furnish, Dick Didelot, and Rudy Van Loon; (top row) Ted Wlodarski (coach), Kenny Hoffman, John Dresh, Tom Saltzman, Ken Fraley, Les Babcock, Tim Bagby, Bill Loper, Dwight Ameling, and Jack Brigman (coach).

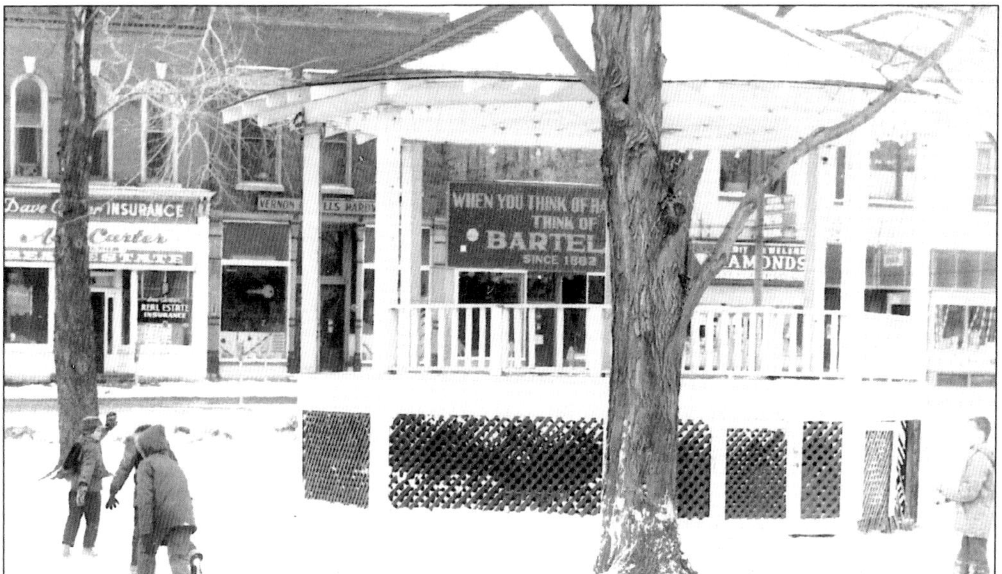

CHESTERTON BANDSTAND. This Chesterton landmark, located in Thomas Centennial Park, was constructed in 1924. One of the few remaining original bandstands in Indiana, it is noteworthy for its octagonal shape and high peaked roof, unlike most bandstands of its time, which were square. The structure originally had wooden latticework at the base, as seen in the above photograph. In 1975 the bandstand was moved about 100 feet west and placed on concrete blocks.

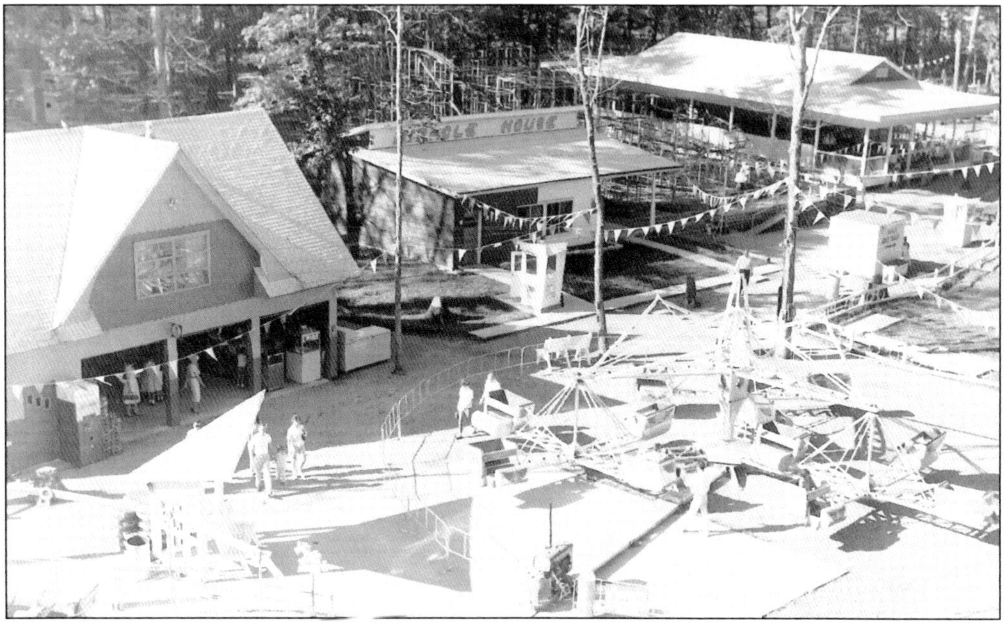

ENCHANTED FOREST AMUSEMENT PARK, PORTER. Many local families enjoyed a day of fun at this popular amusement park, located at Highway 20 and Waverly Road in Porter. It operated from the 1950s until 1991.

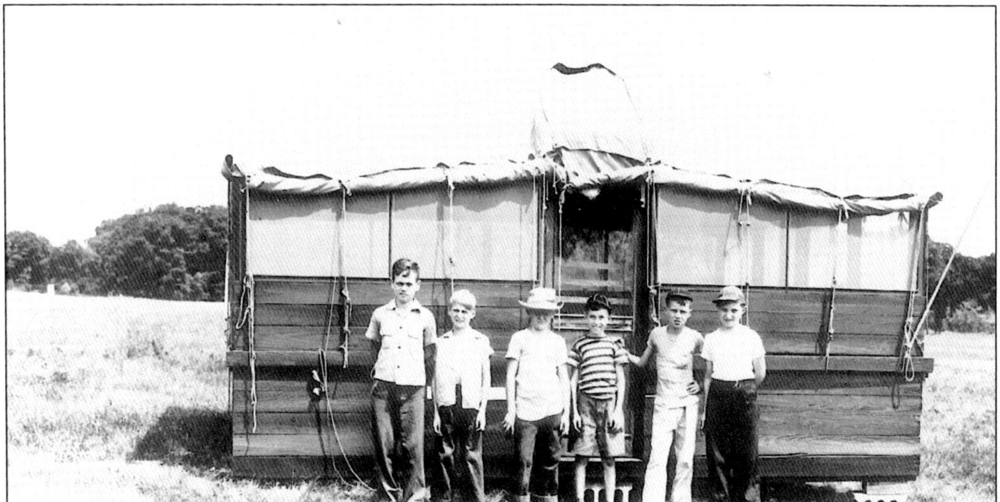

GOODFELLOW CLUB YOUTH CAMP, PORTER. Young campers pose in front of their army-type tent. By the 1960s, tents were replaced by cabins at the camp, located on 70 acres of land on Howe Road in Porter. U.S. Steel operated the camp, which was open to children of employees, each summer until 1975. In 1977 the camp was purchased by the Indiana Dunes National Lakeshore and, after extensive renovations and construction, reopened in 1998 as an environmental learning center. (Courtesy Indiana Dunes National Lakeshore, NPS.)

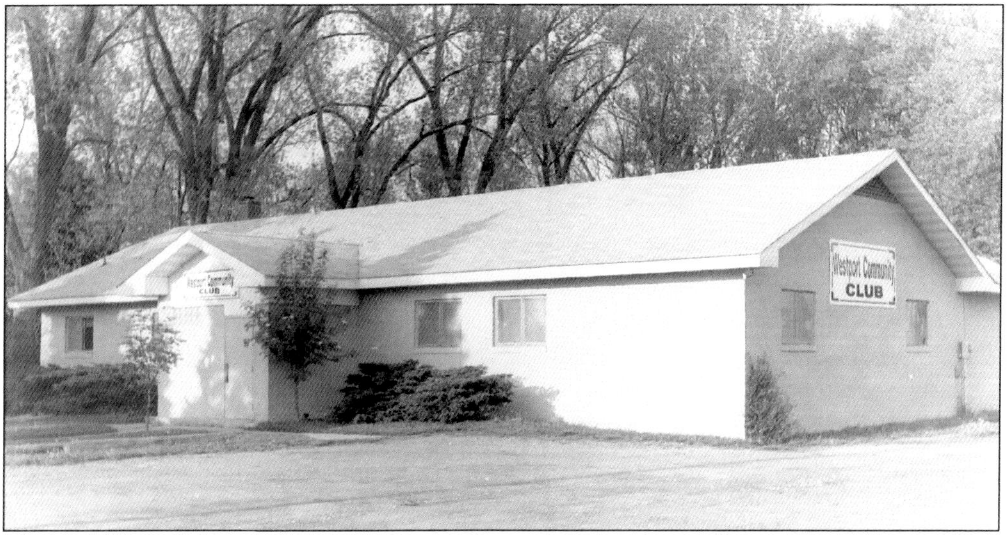

Westport Community Club, Burns Harbor. The community club has been the focal point of the close-knit community since its completion in 1954, and is the site of many social gatherings, including dinners, dances, and organizational meetings. With the financial support of Bethlehem Steel, the area's largest taxpayer, Westport residents voted for incorporation in 1966, rather than face annexation and higher taxes from Portage. The small community took the name Burns Harbor when incorporated in 1967, as there was already an Indiana town named Westport.

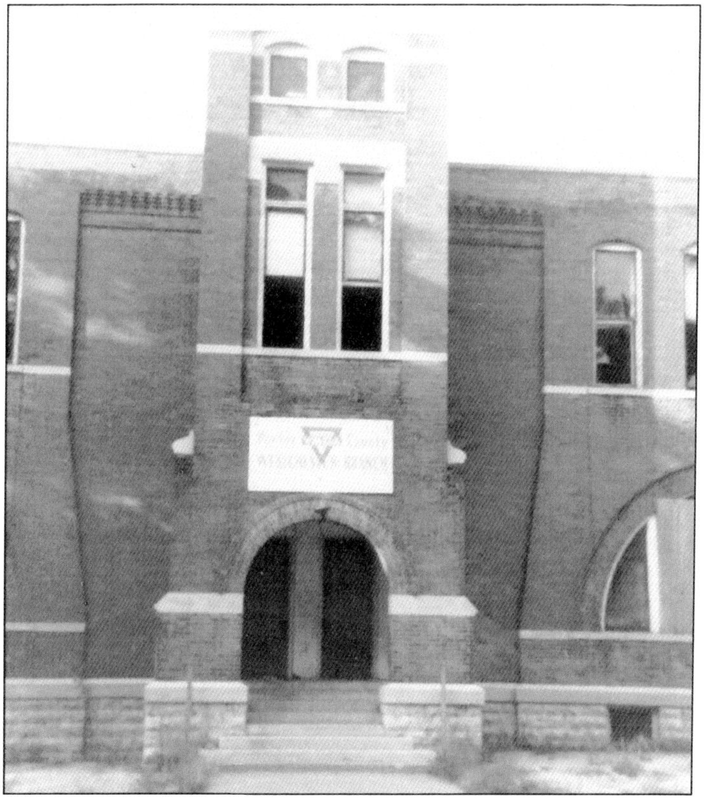

Westchester YMCA, Chesterton. The local YMCA was established in 1966 in the former Chesterton Grade School (Thomas School) pictured here. A donation of land on the east side of Morgan Park by the Smith family allowed the "Y" to build a larger facility, which opened in 1972. In 1977 the organization became the Duneland Area YMCA and continued to expand with the addition of a larger gym in 1981.

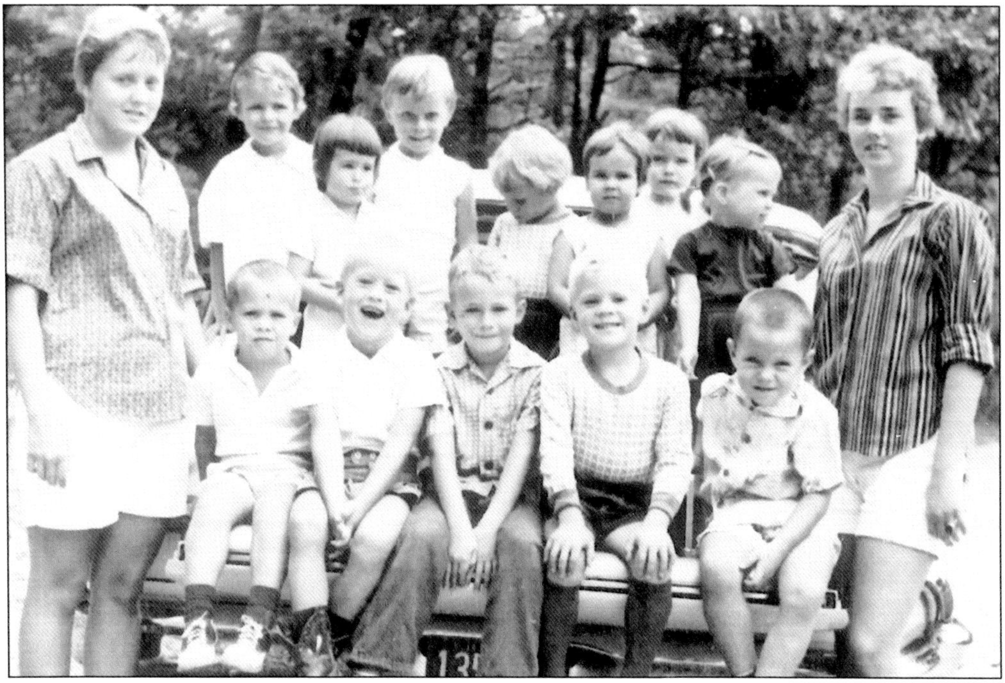

DUNE ACRES PLAY GROUP. Young residents attended an early educational and socialization program held at the Dune Acres fire station. Shown here, in a picture from the summer of 1959, from left to right are (bottom row) Tim Savore, David Wulfing, Ivan Edwards, David Wenniger, and John Barlow; (top row) Debbie Bennett, Lee Daley, Laura Snyder, Dawn Daley, Nina Wenniger, Shawn Rudy, Ellen Barlow, Pam Tittle, and Carolyn Lewis.

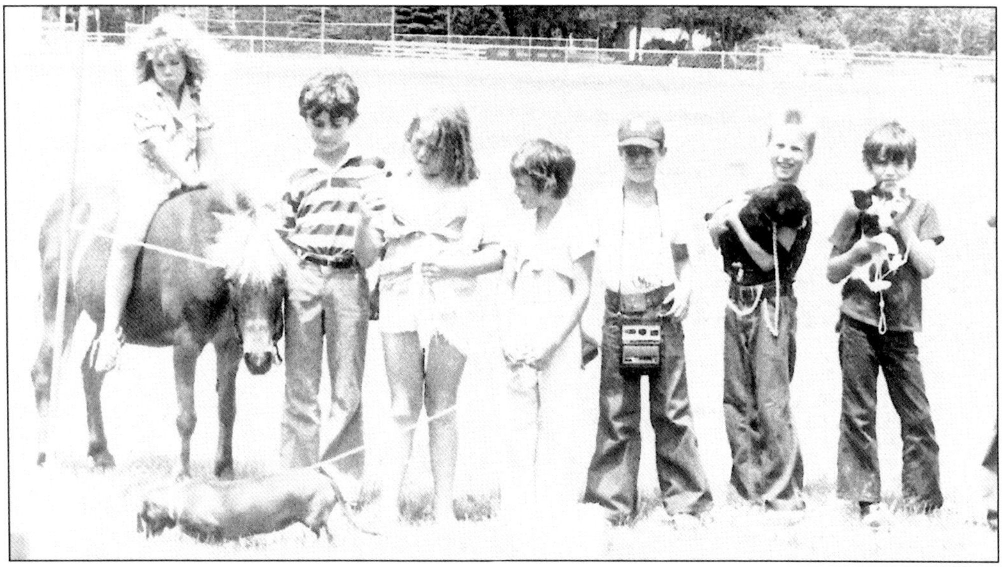

BURNS HARBOR PET PARADE. The winners of the July 1979 Pet Day contest included (left to right): Carrie Seamon, Jeff Cannon, Debbie Cannon, Samantha Schwei, Louis Schwei, Jeff Coan, and Ricky Jarosak. Other popular activities during the summer park program, which began in 1974, included bike day, Olympic day, bubblegum day, sports, arts and crafts, and swimming at Lakeland Park. (Courtesy Burns Harbor Park Dept.)

Ten

SCHOOLS

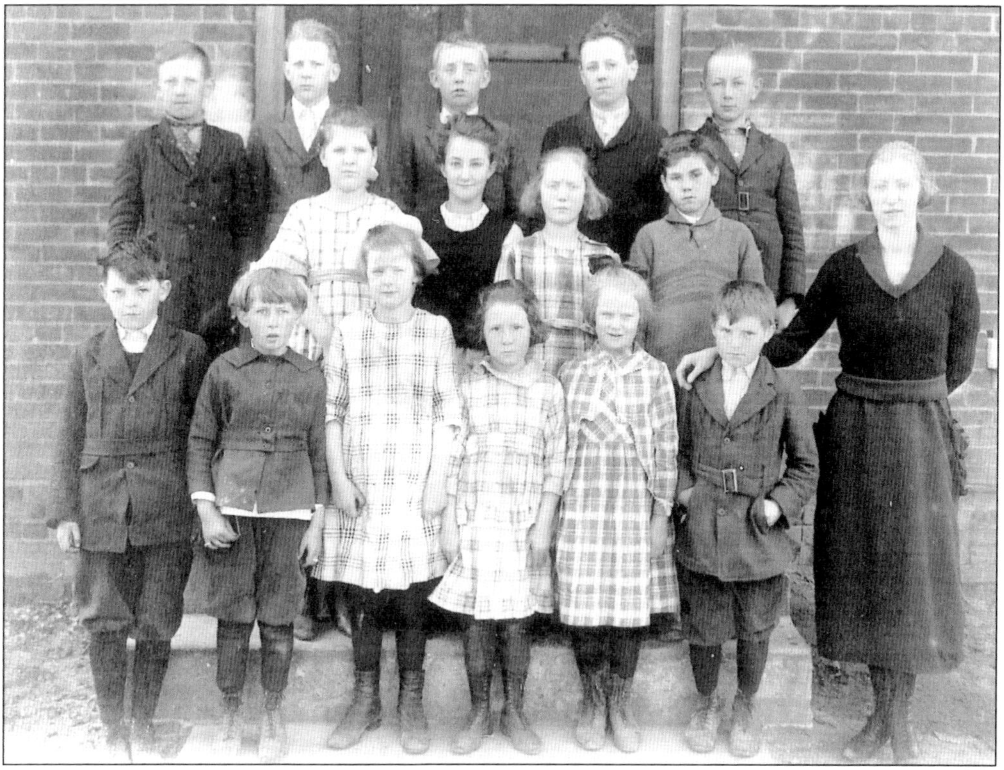

BAILLYTOWN SCHOOL, 1921. Margaret Larson stands in front of Baillytown School with some of her students in 1921. In the late 19th and early 20th centuries, before paved roads and reliable transportation were common, eight small schoolhouses dotted Westchester Township to serve outlying areas. In an effort to cut costs and centralize and standardize education, most one-room schools were closed in the 1920s. Students were then bused to Chesterton and Porter schools.

Yost, Bailly and Brummitt Elementary Schools, Westchester Middle School, and additions to the high school were all part of an ambitious building program undertaken from the 1950s to early 1970s to meet the demands of a growing school-age population. Further consolidation led to the formation of the Duneland School Corporation in 1969, encompassing the school systems of Westchester, Liberty, and Jackson Townships.

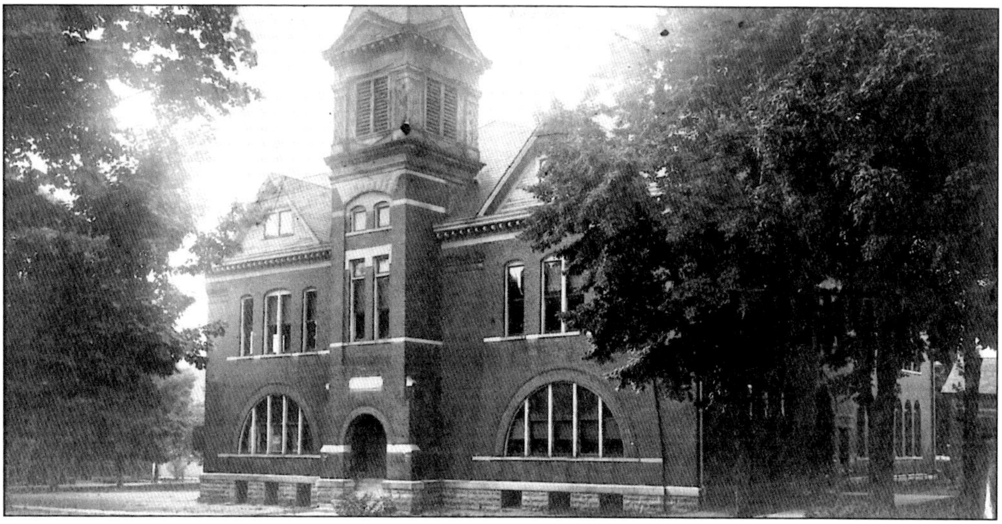

CHESTERTON GRADE SCHOOL. The first in-town school was established at Second and Indiana Avenues in the 1860s. The above building, also known as Thomas School, was an elementary school and high school until 1923. It is shown here before a fire destroyed the tower in 1924. It served as an elementary school until 1966, when Bailly Elementary was built. In 1973, the building was torn down. Thomas Library now occupies this site.

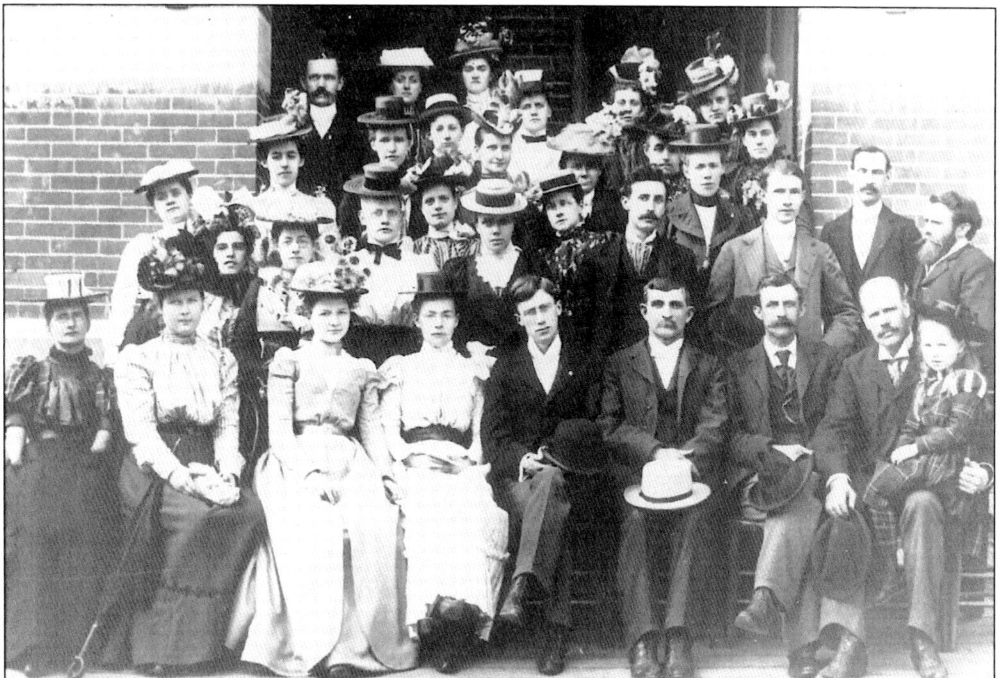

TEACHERS' INSTITUTE, 1899. Local teachers and administrators gathered in front of Chesterton Grade School for the teachers' training program in 1899. Among those pictured are Porter School teacher Mary Bradt (front row, far left); Newton E. Yost, Porter School principal (front row, sixth from left); and to the right of Yost are Charles Haslett, trustee; Spencer H. Roe, superintendent; and his daughter Clara. Also pictured in the third row, to the far left are local schoolteachers Agnes Morgan and Matilda Swanson.

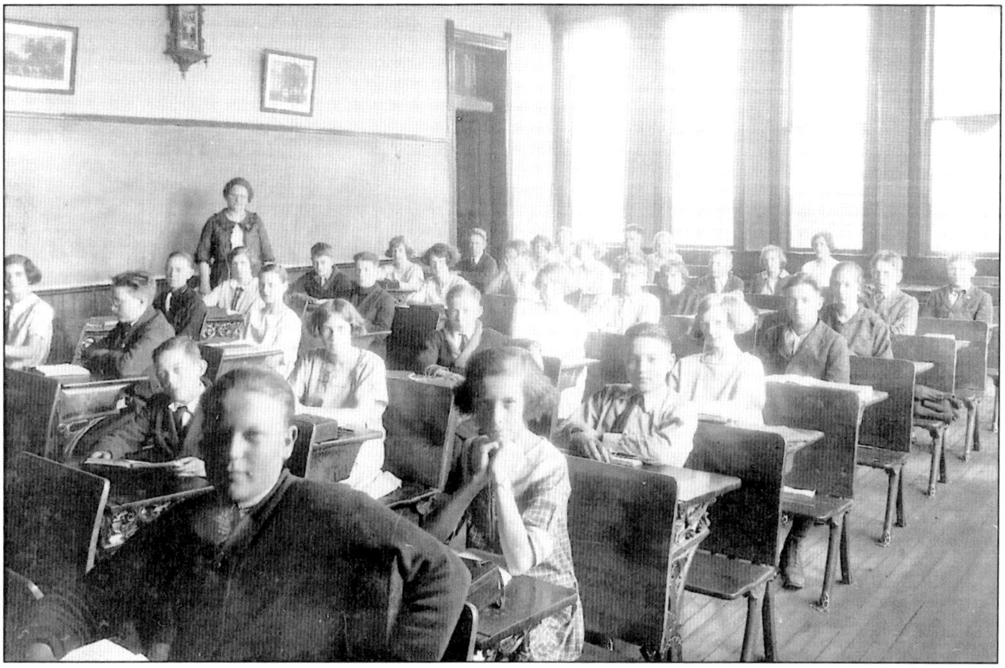

SEVENTH GRADE STUDENTS, CHESTERTON, 1923. Students in the seventh grade at Chesterton Grade School are pictured in their classroom in 1923. Upon the completion of the high school on Morgan Avenue later that year, grades seven through 12 moved to the new building. Westchester Junior High School opened in 1966 for sixth through ninth grade students. Several years later, Westchester became a middle school, and ninth graders moved to the high school.

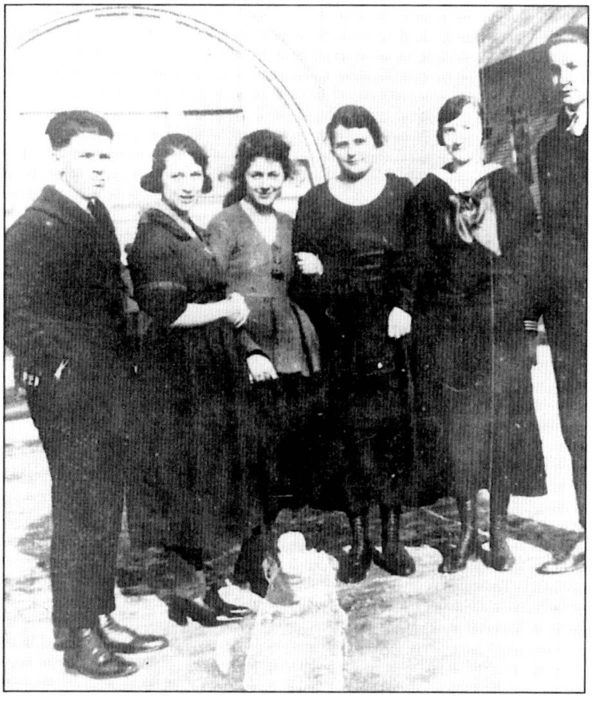

1921 GRADUATES, CHESTERTON HIGH SCHOOL. Happy graduates posing in front of the school on Indiana Avenue are (left to right): Dallas Summers, Esther Gunder, Dorothy Hopkins, Edith Johnson, Mabel LaHayne, and Harlan Bedenkop. Chesterton High School was first commissioned in 1898. Classes were held on the second floor of the Chesterton Grade School until 1923 when the high school building on Morgan Avenue was completed.

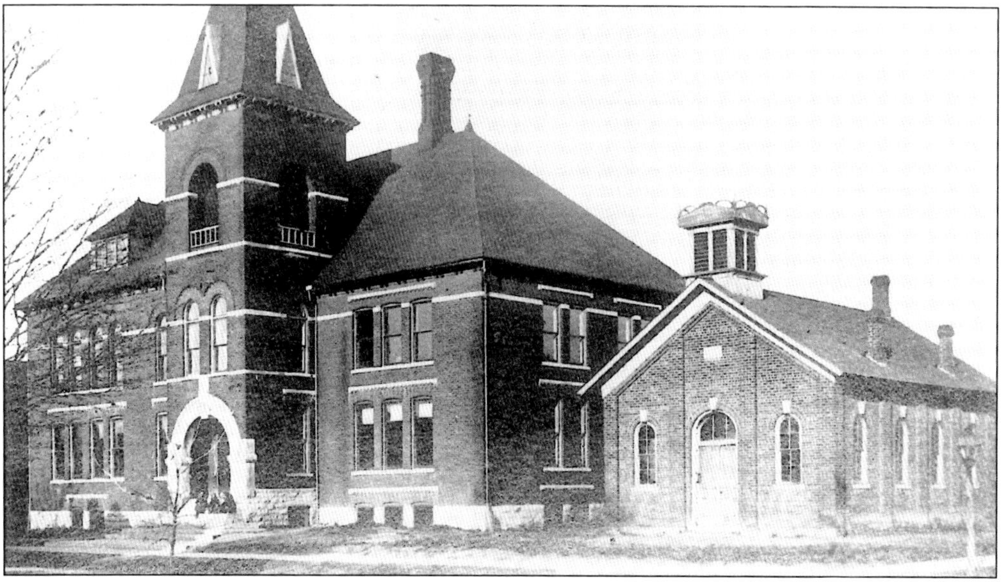

Porter Grade School. Porter's first school was located at the northwest corner of Franklin and Francis Streets on land donated by the Hageman family. The larger, six-room brick schoolhouse to the left was built in 1895 to replace the smaller structure built c. 1870. The grade school, also known as Hageman School, operated until the 1950s when Yost Elementary opened nearby. The building was torn down in 1973 and is now the site of Hageman Library.

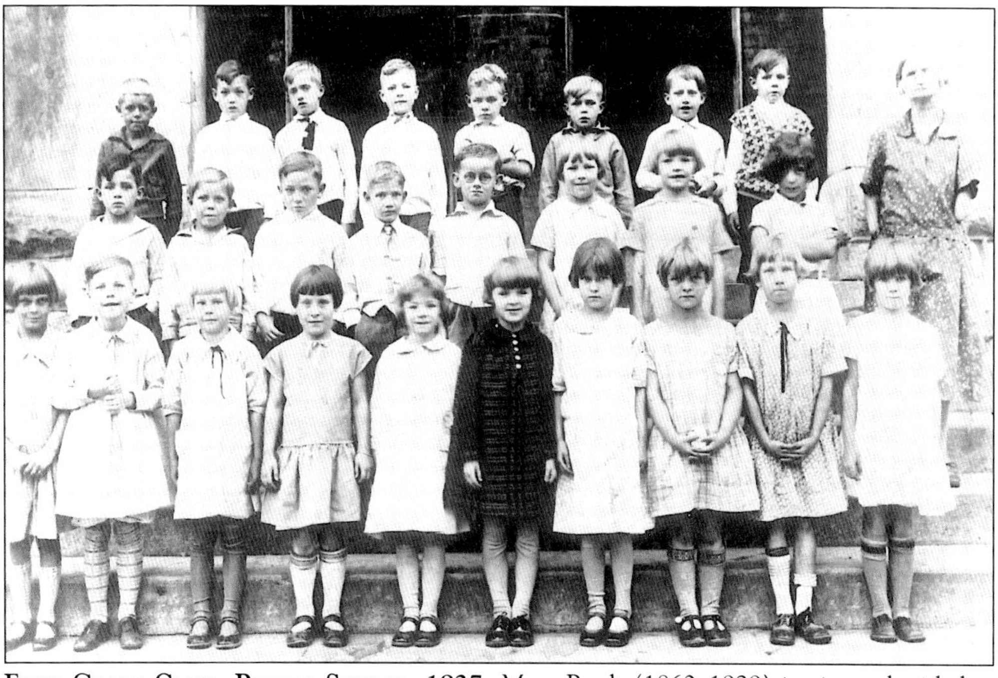

First Grade Class, Porter School, 1927. Mary Bradt (1860–1929) is pictured with her class in front of Porter School in 1927. Miss Bradt was an effective and well-regarded teacher who instructed three generations of Porter schoolchildren. She was noted for her excellent penmanship in spite of having been born without hands or forearms.

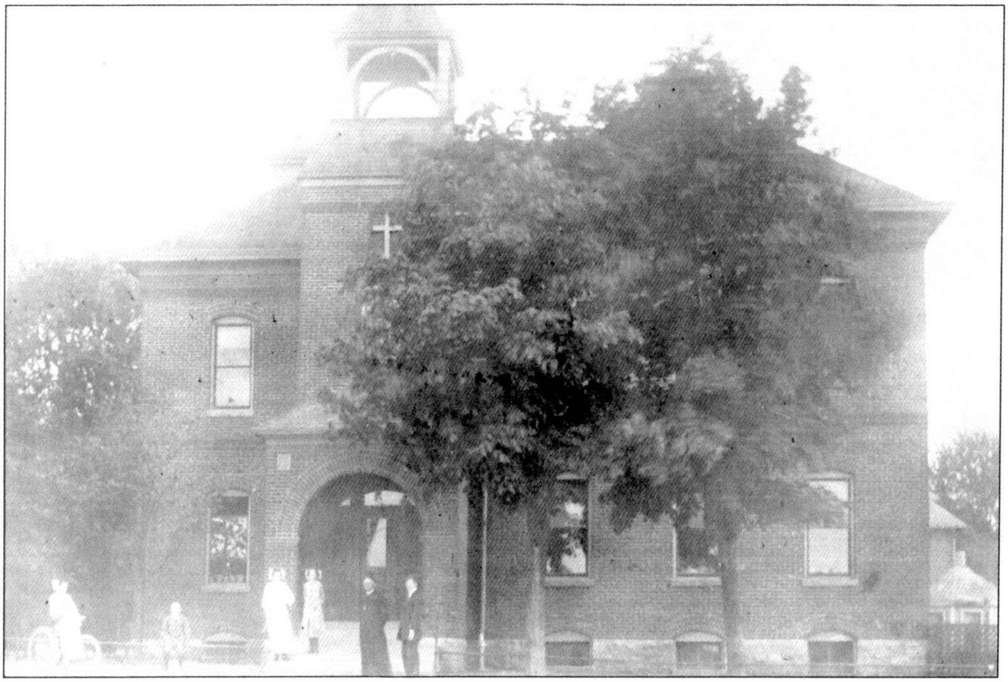

ST. PATRICK SCHOOL. Located at the corner of Broadway and Third Streets in Chesterton, the brick Catholic school opened in 1898 and replaced a smaller school established by Father Kroll in a church annex. The School Sisters of Notre Dame operated the Catholic school until 1973. A new school on N. Calumet Road in 1950 continues to provide Catholic education for preschool through eighth grade. The building seen here was demolished in 1978.

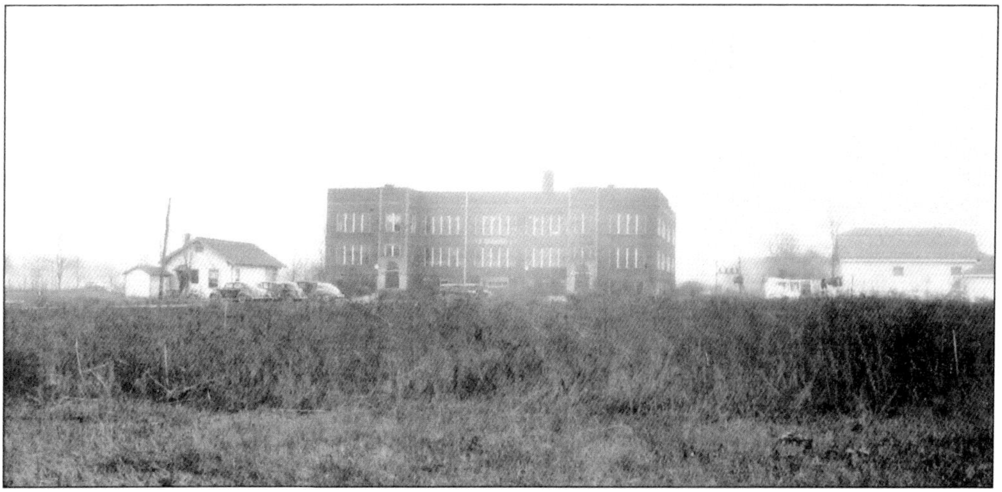

CHESTERTON HIGH SCHOOL. Taken in the 1940s, this picture shows the building at Morgan Avenue and Sixth Street surrounded by open land. Completed in 1923, the high school added a new wing and Central Elementary in the 1950s and Goldsborough Gym in 1960. The original brick building was torn down in 1970 to make way for a new auditorium, pool, and additional classrooms. The small building to the left in the above photograph was a popular after-school snack shop.

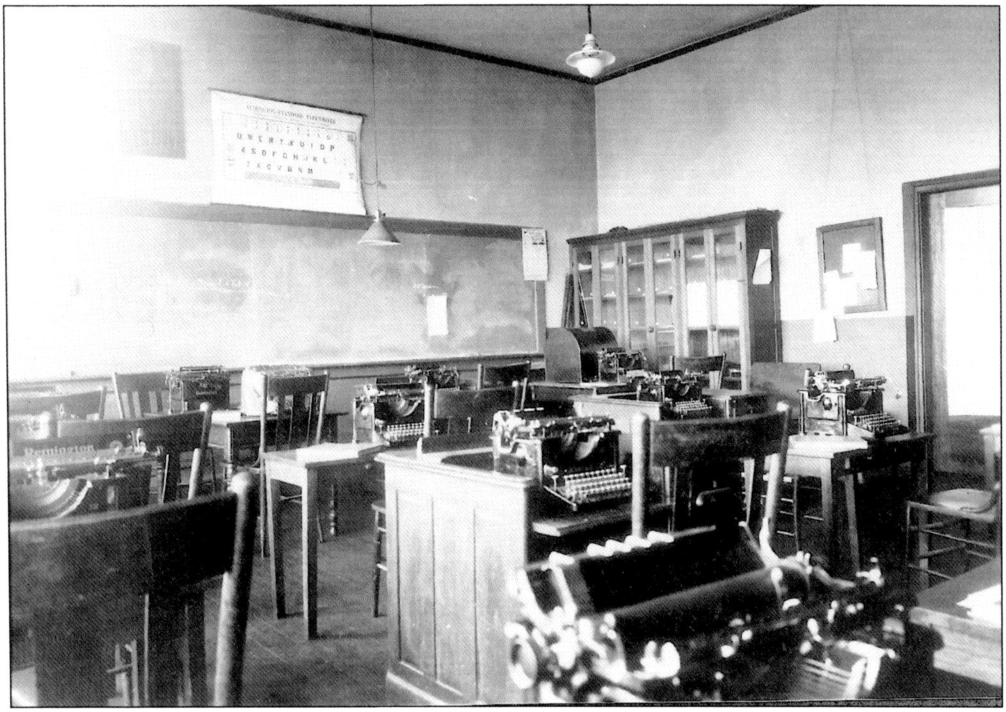

Typing Room. Mabel E. Young trained young women in shorthand, typing, and secretarial skills in this room. The 1930 high school yearbook, the *Duneland Echo*, noted that "the commercial course is proving to be more popular each year and the number of students enrolling in the course is increasing."

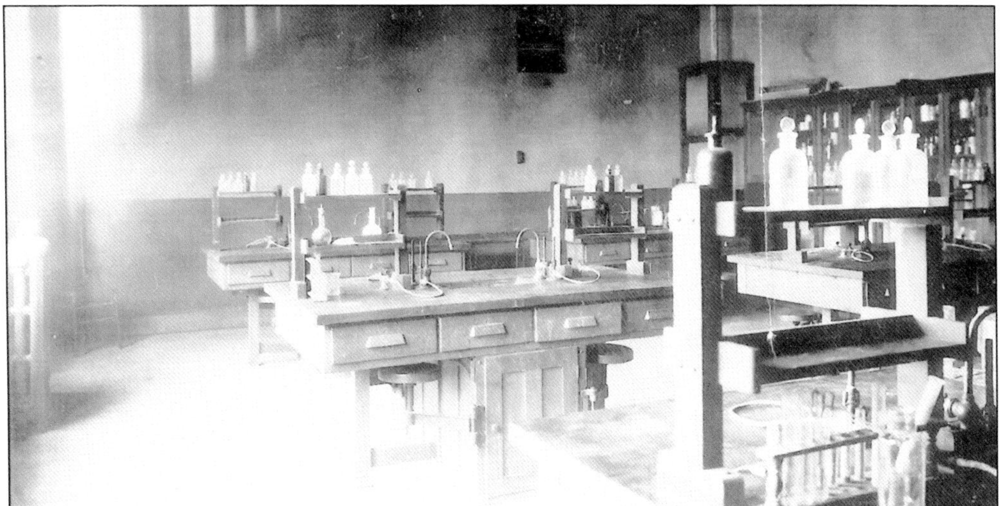

Chemistry Laboratory. Mr. Harvey instructed both male and female juniors in the school's lab on Tuesdays and Thursdays. Other days were devoted to classroom instruction. The equipment was considered "state-of-the-art" in 1930, only seven years after the building was constructed.

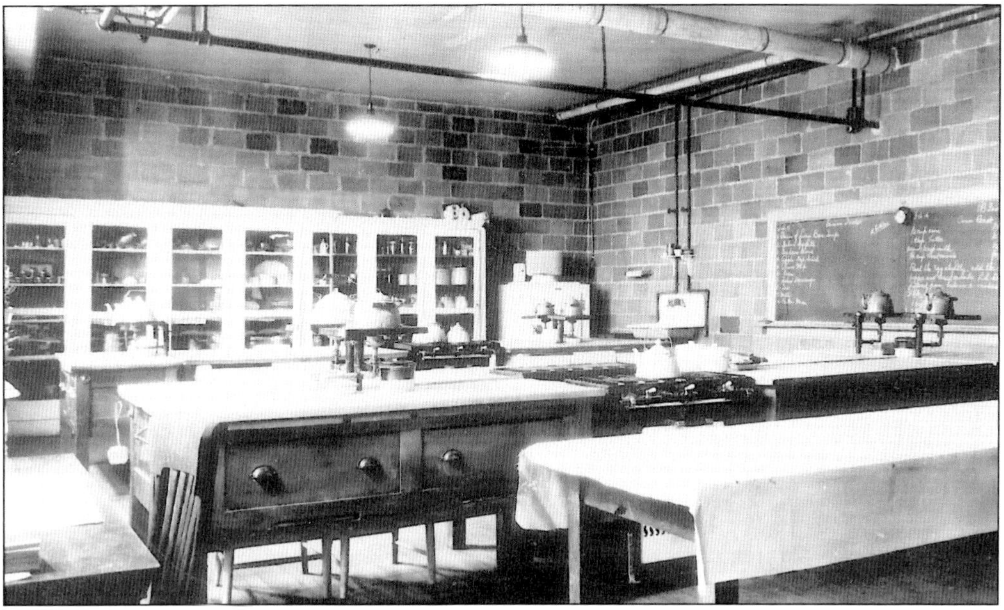

Home Economics Department. Senior girls were taught both "Foods and Cookery" and "Clothing and Textiles" during nine 45-minute periods each week in the high school's modern cooking and sewing facilities. Instructions in canning, preserving, preparation, and serving of school lunches as well as producing plain, practical garments were included.

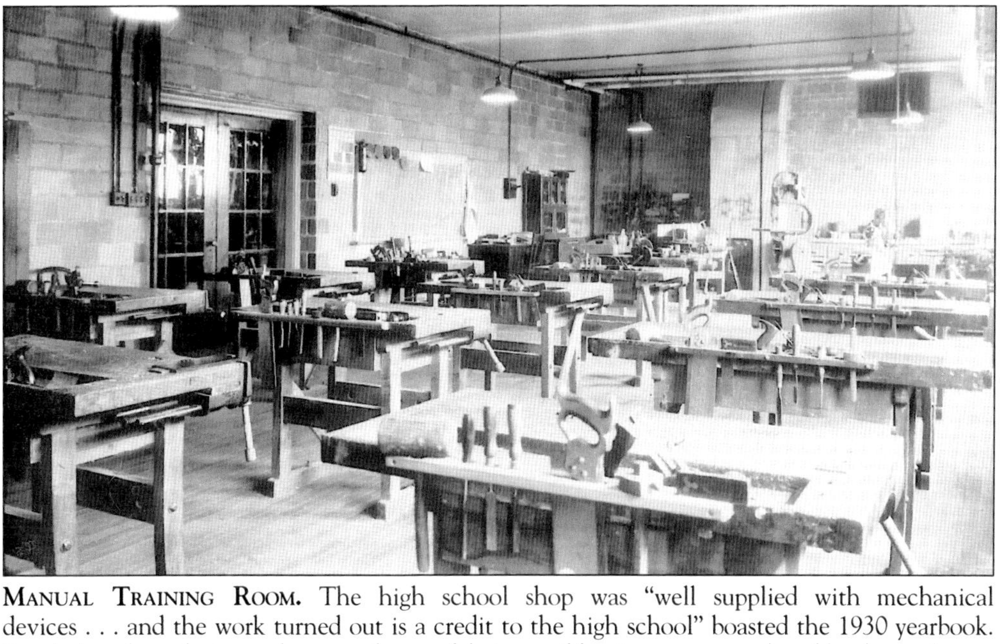

Manual Training Room. The high school shop was "well supplied with mechanical devices . . . and the work turned out is a credit to the high school" boasted the 1930 yearbook. Stools, benches, chairs, and many other useful pieces of furniture were produced by the students.

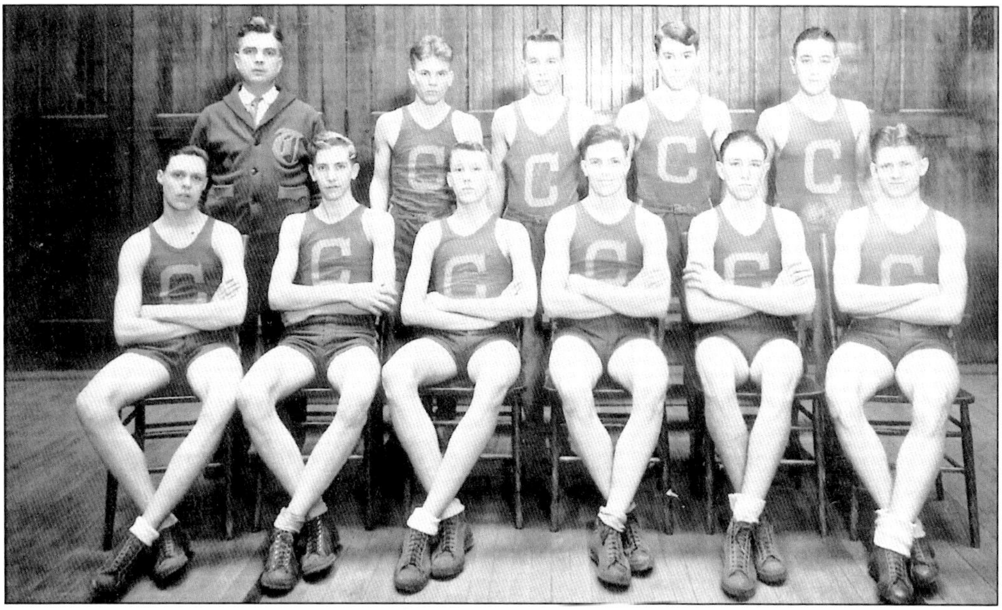

CHS Basketball Team, 1931. Basketball has long been a popular sport in Indiana, and Westchester Township is no exception. Boys' basketball began at the turn of the century; girls' teams were organized beginning in 1923. Members in the above photograph from left to right are the following: (seated) Fred Edmonds, Douglas Anderson, Donald Slont, Herbert Link, Edward Holevinsky, and Roy Holm; (standing) Coach Jones, Donald Flint, Myron Blackman, Myrl Parker, and Oscar Rosetti.

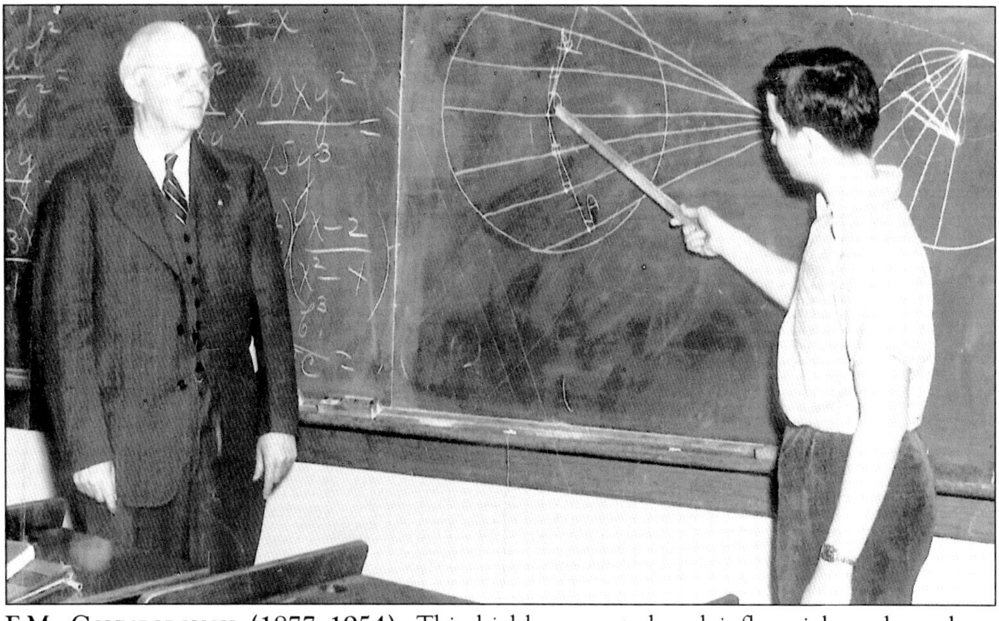

F.M. Goldsborough (1877–1954). This highly respected and influential teacher whose career spanned almost half a century is shown in his classroom at Chesterton High School. Mr. Goldsborough came to Chesterton in 1905 to teach English and Latin and served as principal of the high school from 1910 to 1941. He taught science and mathematics until his death, which was caused by a heart attack while teaching class.

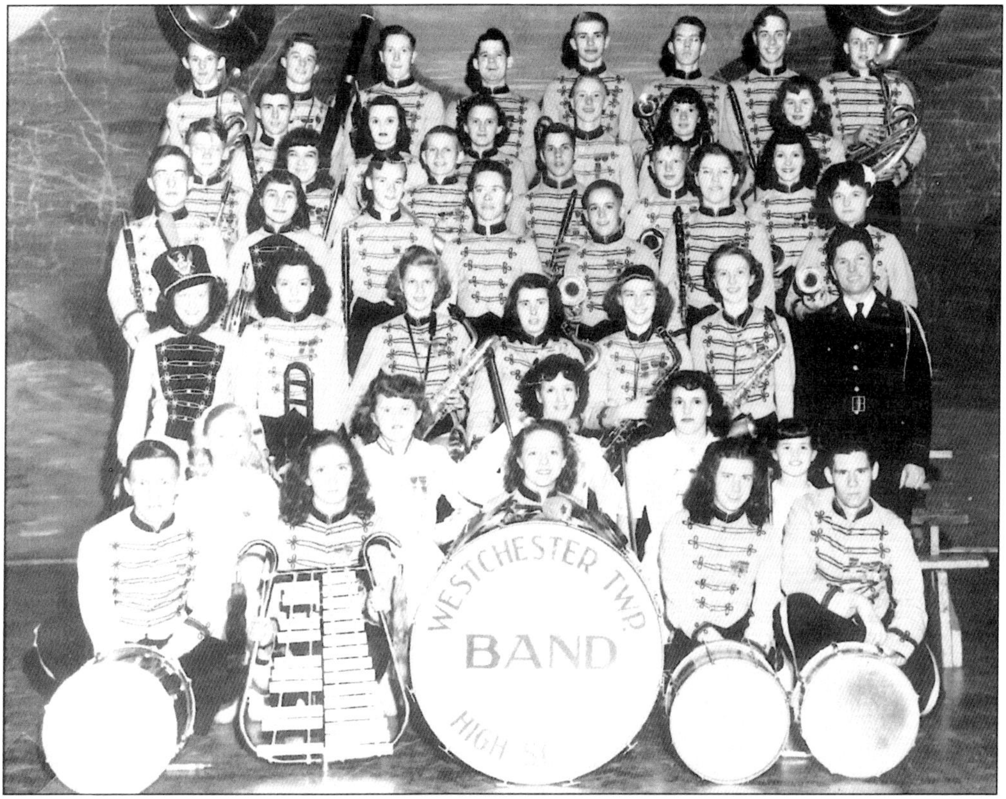

HIGH SCHOOL BAND, 1944. There is a longstanding tradition of excellent school bands in Westchester Township. The 1944–45 high school band, seen above, was directed by Glenn L. Tom (third row to the far right).

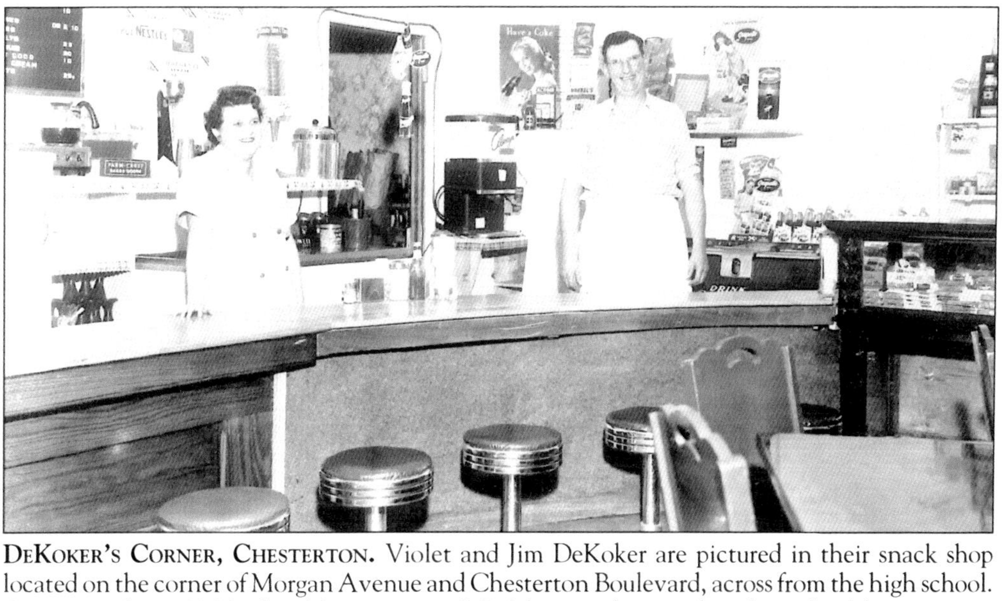

DEKOKER'S CORNER, CHESTERTON. Violet and Jim DeKoker are pictured in their snack shop located on the corner of Morgan Avenue and Chesterton Boulevard, across from the high school. Constructed in 1926 by local businessman L.P. Matson, the popular after-school hangout was also known as the Nibble Nook and the Sugar Bowl.

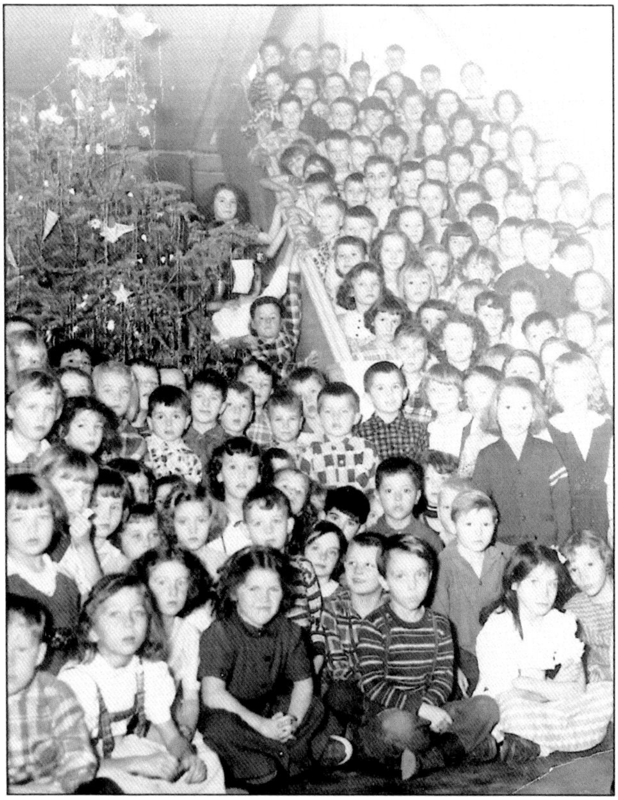

CHRISTMAS AT PORTER SCHOOL, 1952. This holiday scene was taken on the stairs of the Porter Grade School and was printed in the Christmas edition of the *Chesterton Tribune* in 1952. The Christmas tree was donated to the school by Pillman's Grocery in Porter, and the decorations were made by the school's custodian, Mr. Bluschke.

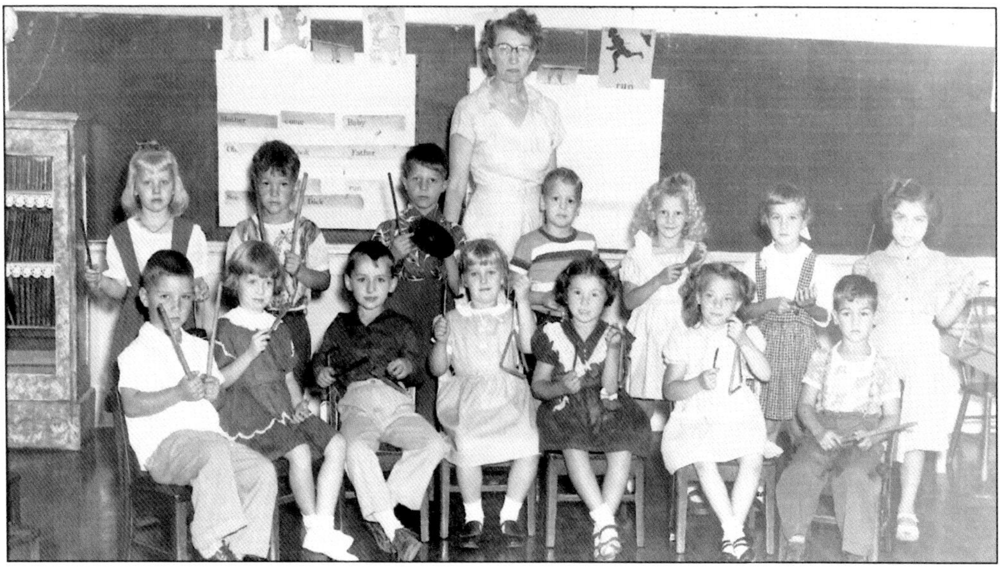

SUMMER KINDERGARTEN CLASS, CHESTERTON, 1952. Margaret Larson is pictured above with her summer kindergartners in 1952. Miss Larson held a summer program each year throughout the 1950s, before kindergarten was added to the school curriculum in the early 1960s. Cooperative community kindergarten programs also operated in several locations, including the Lions Club building. In 1966, Miss Larson founded Augsburg Pre-kindergarten, a program that continues to provide preschool education for three, four, and five year olds.

Eleven

TRANSPORTATION

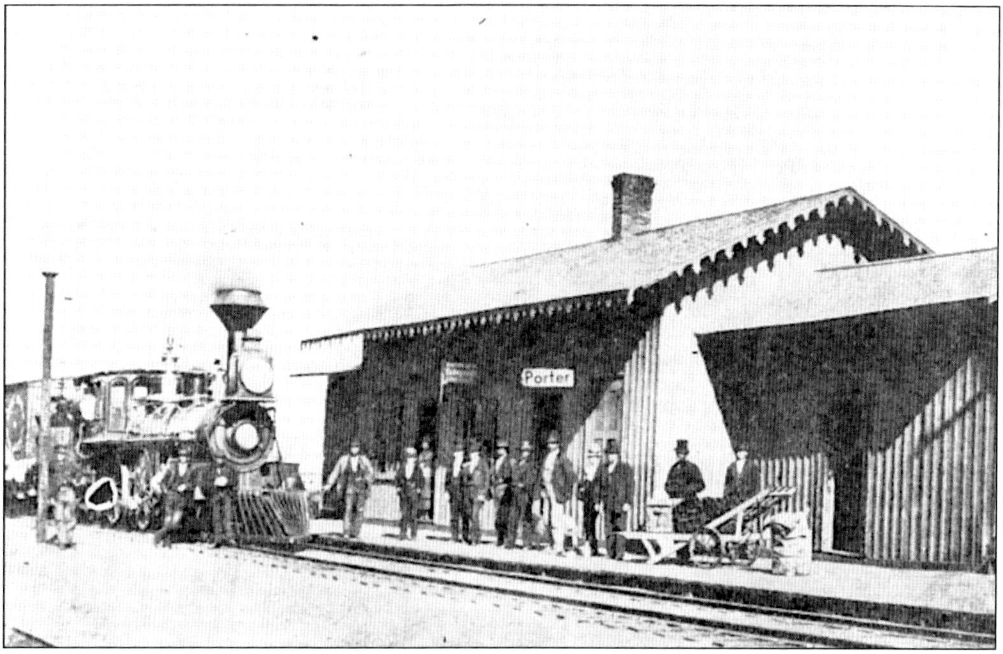

MICHIGAN CENTRAL DEPOT, PORTER. The Michigan Central built the region's first train station in Old Porter in 1852. In the above photograph, an early wood-burning steam engine with a pre-1880 smokestack is seen arriving at the station. The first goods to be shipped by rail in the county were sent to Old Porter on a construction train from Michigan City in 1851. By most accounts the Michigan Central won the race to Chicago, arriving there on May 21, 1852, beating its rival, the Lake Shore and Michigan Southern, by one day.

The coming of railroads to the area forecast the survival of the small towns of Westchester Township. Trains provided farmers with improved access to larger markets for their produce, spurred industrial growth, and encouraged people to settle in the township.

After the turn of the century, new modes of transportation such as the automobile and the Gary Inter-urban, contributed to the growth of the community and to the convenience of local citizens. Improved roads and new highways, such as Route 12, Route 20, I-94, and the Indiana Tollway gradually led to a great increase in automobile traffic in and through the township. Many local citizens continue to use the Chicago South Shore and South Bend Railroad, which has provided convenient transportation to residents since 1908.

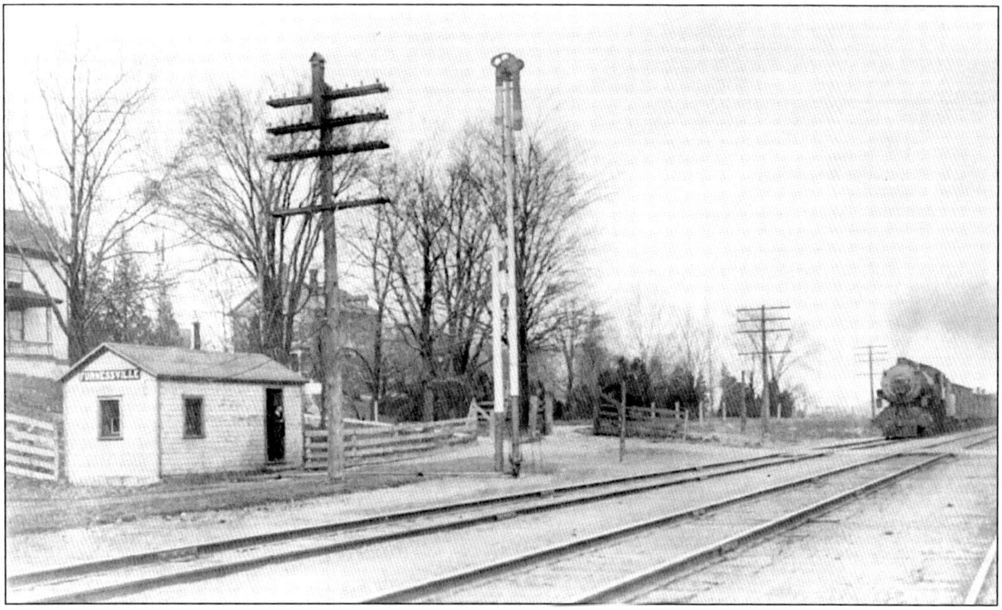

FURNESSVILLE STATION. E.L. Furness was the first agent of the Michigan Central Railroad at Furnessville. In the early years Furness, with his partners H.R. McDonald and T.E. Morgan, formed a lumber company selling wood to the railroads for fuel, finished boards to contractors, and eventually cleared land for settlers. In later years farmers shipped a variety of produce, but especially milk and strawberries, to Chicago from the Furnessville station.

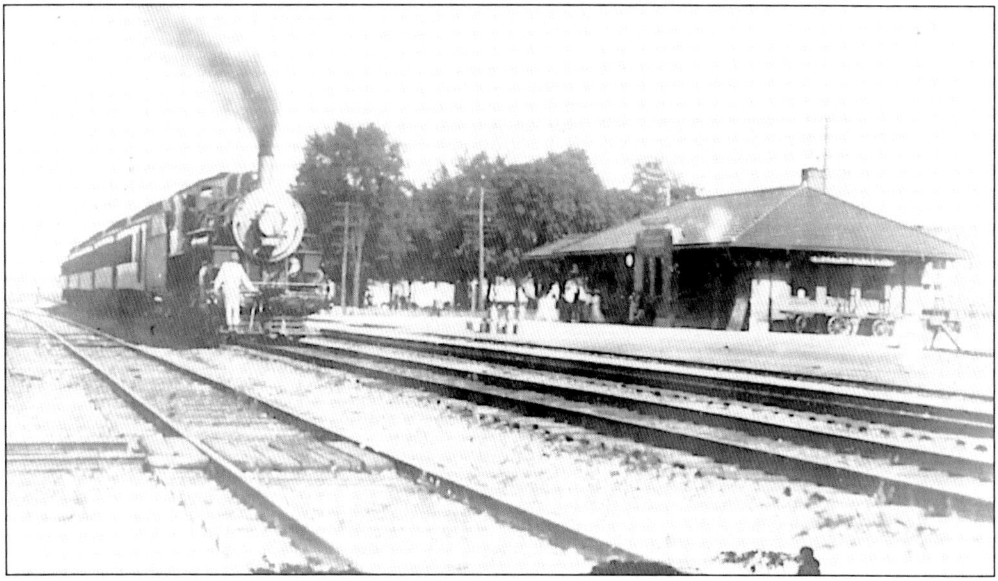

LAKE SHORE AND MICHIGAN SOUTHERN DEPOT, CHESTERTON. The Lake Shore and Michigan Southern Railroad built a wooden depot in Chesterton in 1852, just north of Third Street, south of the railroad tracks on land originally owned by the Thomas family. The railroad established a woodlot to the east of the station on land that later became Railroad Park, and then Thomas Centennial Park. Seen above is the brick passenger depot built in 1914 after the original depot burned.

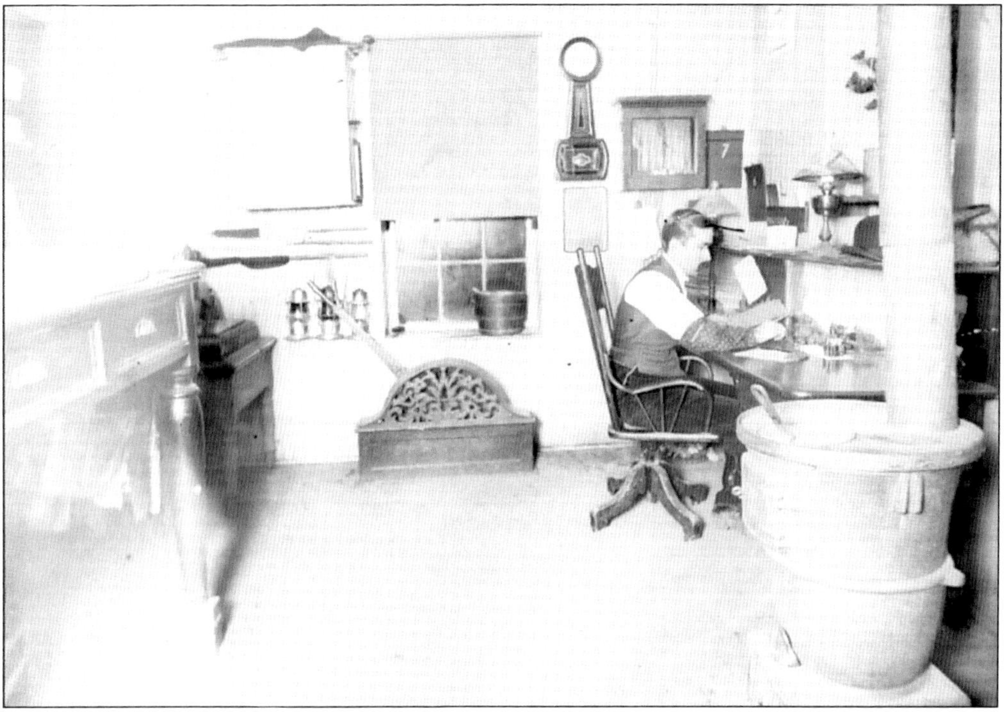

Ralph Peebles, 1852 Chesterton Depot. Ralph Peebles, station agent and telegraph operator for the Michigan Southern's Chesterton station, is seen above c. 1890 in the interior of the original wooden depot. The building housed grain storage facilities, a freight room, passenger waiting room, and telegraph office. The original depot burned in 1913, but was rebuilt in brick a year later, along with a brick freight station. The last commuter train stopped in Chesterton in 1964.

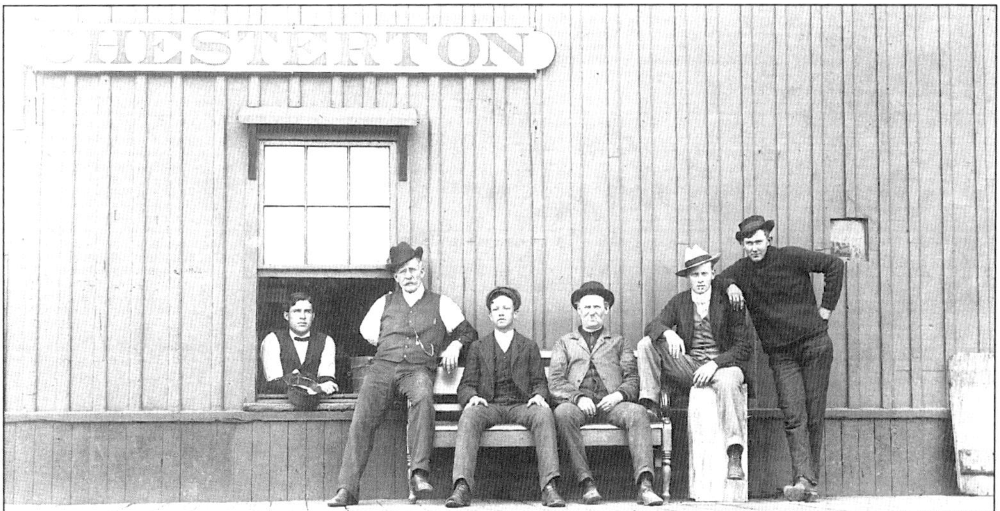

1852 Chesterton Depot. Lounging on the platform outside the original wooden Michigan Southern depot around the turn of the century were (left to right): L. Wicter, John Thompson, William A. Wood, Mr. Place, and Albert Fosberg. The stationmaster leaning out the window is thought to be Ralph Peebles.

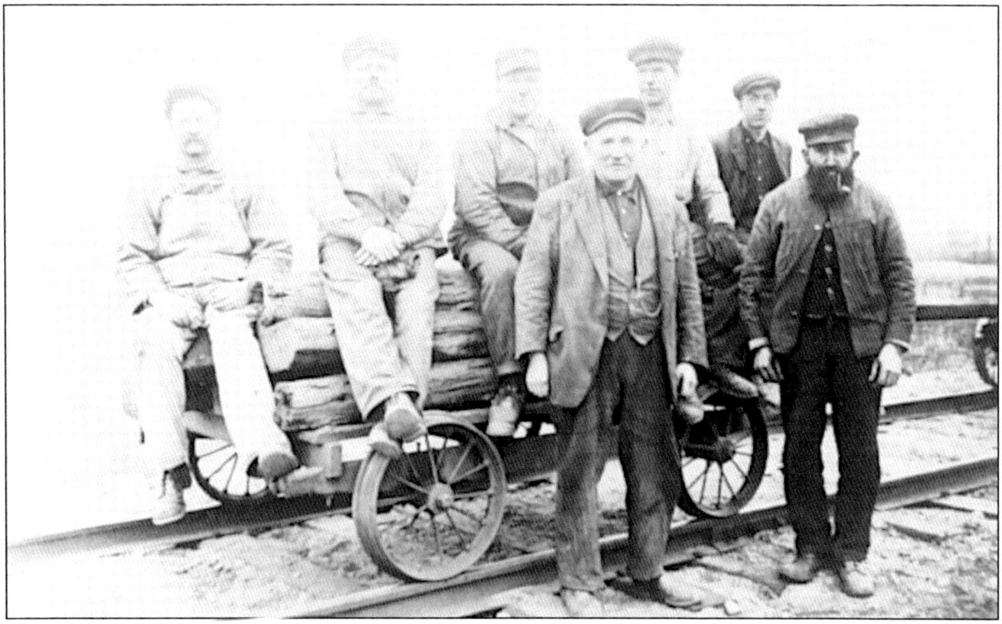

Michigan Central Section Crew, Porter. The railroads attracted many people to the area, particularly the Irish. They came first to build the railroads, then stayed on to maintain the roadbed and replace the soft iron rails. Railroad workers also established local businesses and farms. The Michigan Central crew, seen above in Porter, includes Pete Gustafson on the extreme left, the grandfather of Adeline Janowski, a lifelong resident of the area.

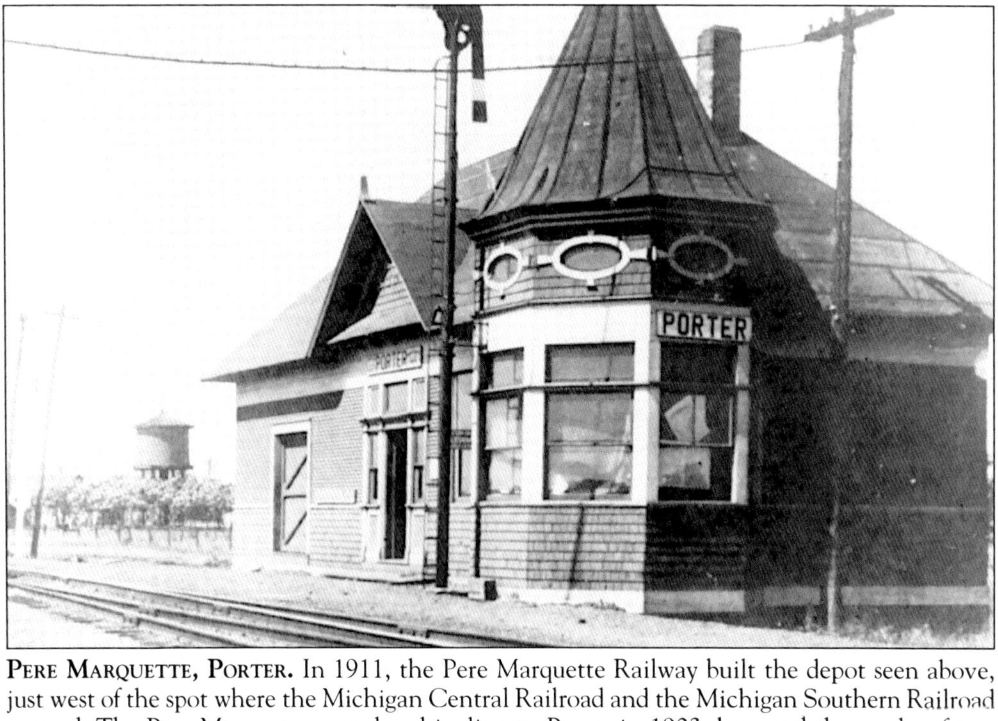

Pere Marquette, Porter. In 1911, the Pere Marquette Railway built the depot seen above, just west of the spot where the Michigan Central Railroad and the Michigan Southern Railroad crossed. The Pere Marquette completed its line to Porter in 1903, but used the tracks of two other railroads to enter Chicago.

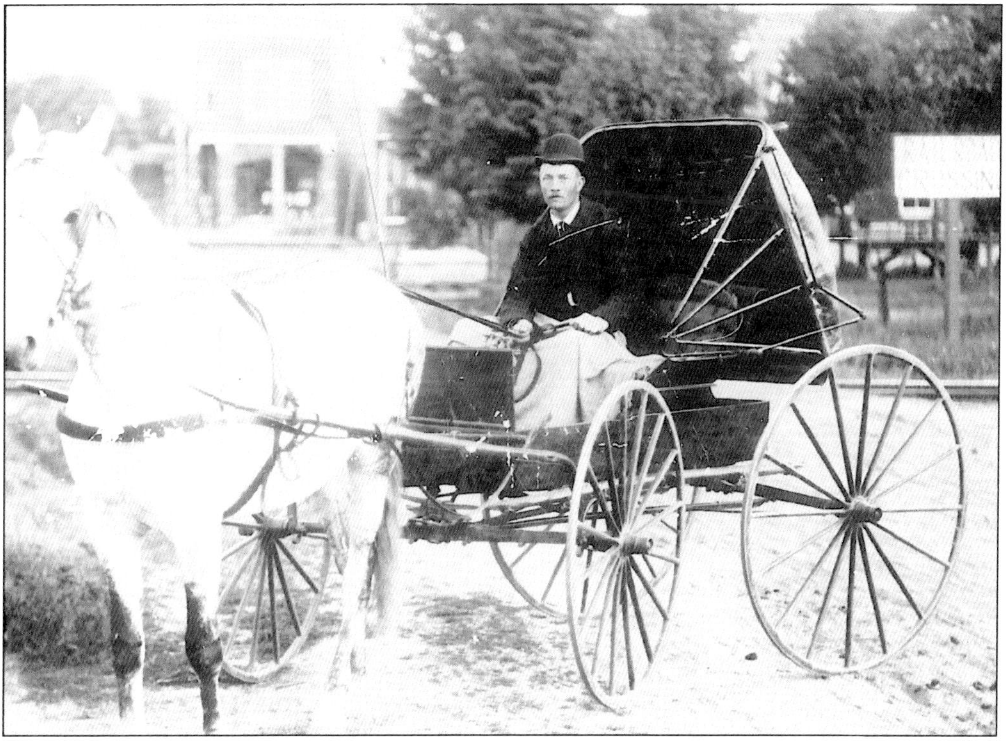

Dr. Wiltfong in Carriage, Chesterton. Before the advent of automobiles, horse-drawn carriages and wagons were the primary means of personal transportation. Dr. Charles Wiltfong is seen here as a young man in his turn-of-the-century single seat side bar runabout just north of the tracks on Calumet. Dr. Wiltfong served as family physician to the Chesterton community from *c.* 1901 until his tragic death in 1930 at the age of 54.

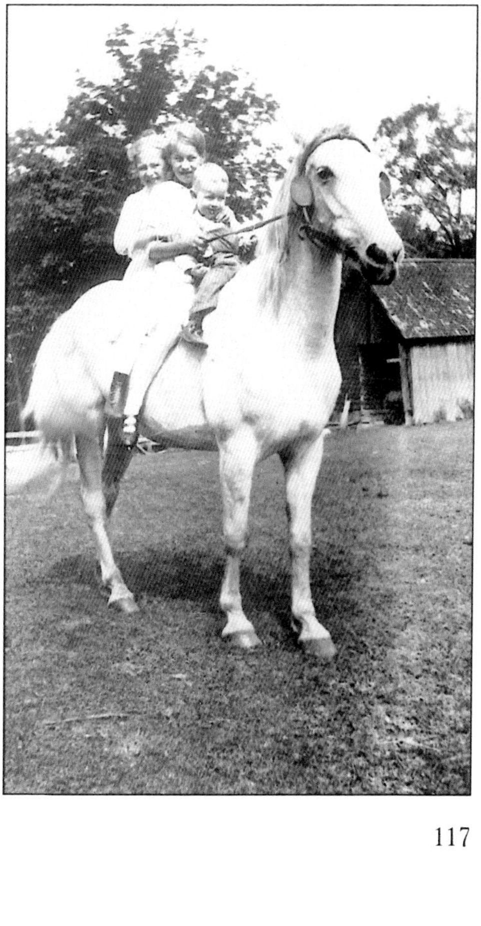

Chellberg Children, Porter. Before the coming of the automobile, people of all ages learned to ride at an early age. Seen here are the children of C.L. and Mina Chellberg. From left to right are Naomi, Ruth, and Carl, who grew up on the Chellberg farm in what was then Baillytown. (Courtesy Indiana Dunes National Lakeshore, NPS.)

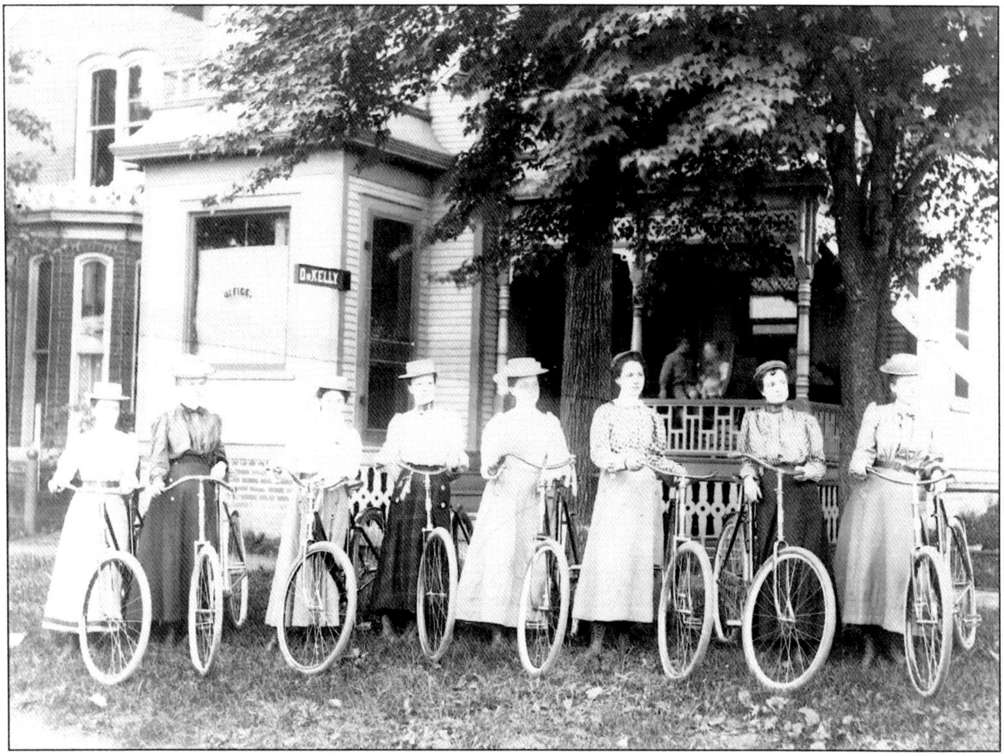

Cycling Group, Chesterton. The bicycle was a popular mode of personal transportation at the turn of the century. This group of friends posed in front of Dr. Kelly's house on Broadway about 1900. From left to right they are Christine Flynn, Cora Peterson, Agnes Morgan, Mrs. Klineman, June Quick, Bertha Anderson, Grace Osborn, and Leavanchia Bradley, who was the great-aunt of life-long Chesterton resident Howard Johnson.

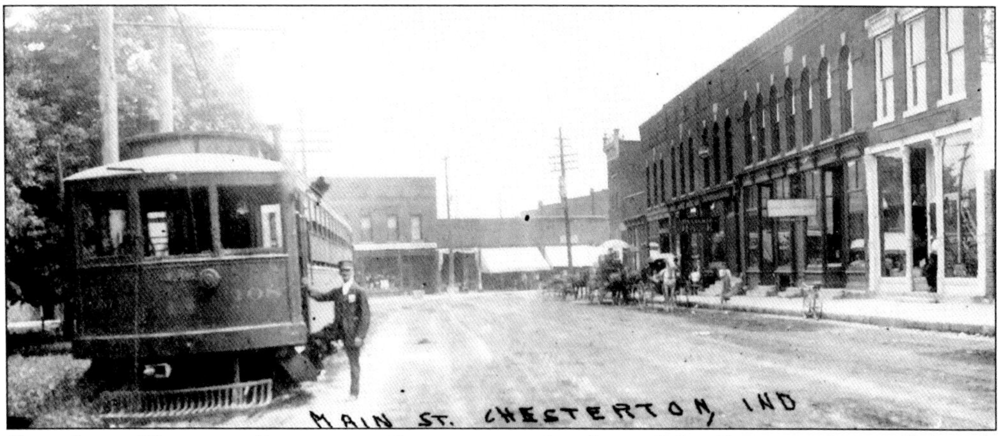

Gary Inter-Urban on Broadway, Chesterton. Conductor John Slont stands proudly beside car 108 of the Valparaiso and Northern line of the Gary Inter-urban that connected Chesterton with LaPorte, Valparaiso and Gary, and was a one-time rival to the South Shore Railroad. Used for passengers, as well as to ship area farmers' produce, the Inter-urban provided transportation for Westchester Township from 1911 to 1922. Due to the popularity of the automobile, the Gary Inter-urban discontinued operations, and by 1928 the entire rail had been removed from downtown Chesterton.

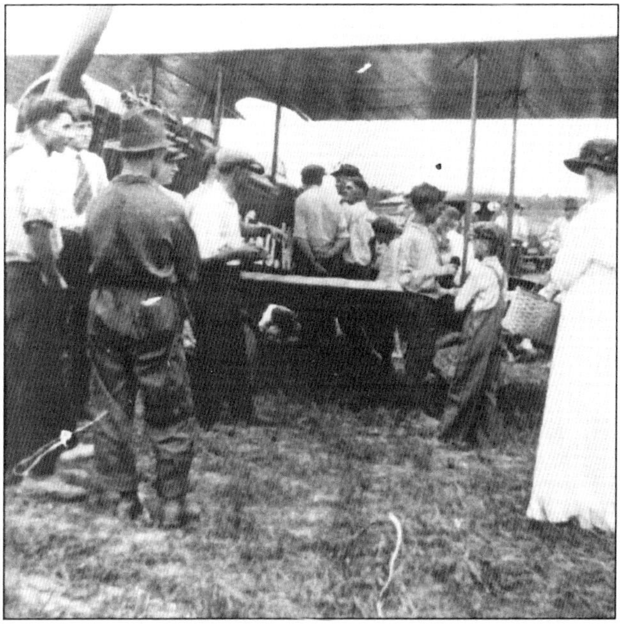

Emergency Airplane Landing, Chesterton. The *Chesterton Tribune* of July 10, 1919, reported that "Chesterton was all agog when two airplanes alighted" in a hay field for an emergency refueling stop on their way back to Chicago from Toledo. In the 1920s Chesterton had its own "flying field," at the southwest corner of Fifth Street and Porter Avenue. Area residents took flying lessons and $3 airplane rides and watched as stunt-flying barnstormers performed.

Bobsled Ride, Dune Acres. The above 1933 photograph of a winter bobsled ride was taken on Crest Drive in Dune Acres. On the dune behind the group can be seen the town's Clubhouse on the left and its Guesthouse on the right. Hugh Studebaker is on the far left, Carl Chellberg below the Guesthouse. The children are Dorothy and Henry Studebaker. Mary and Naomi Studebaker and Ruth Chellberg are standing in the back of the sled.

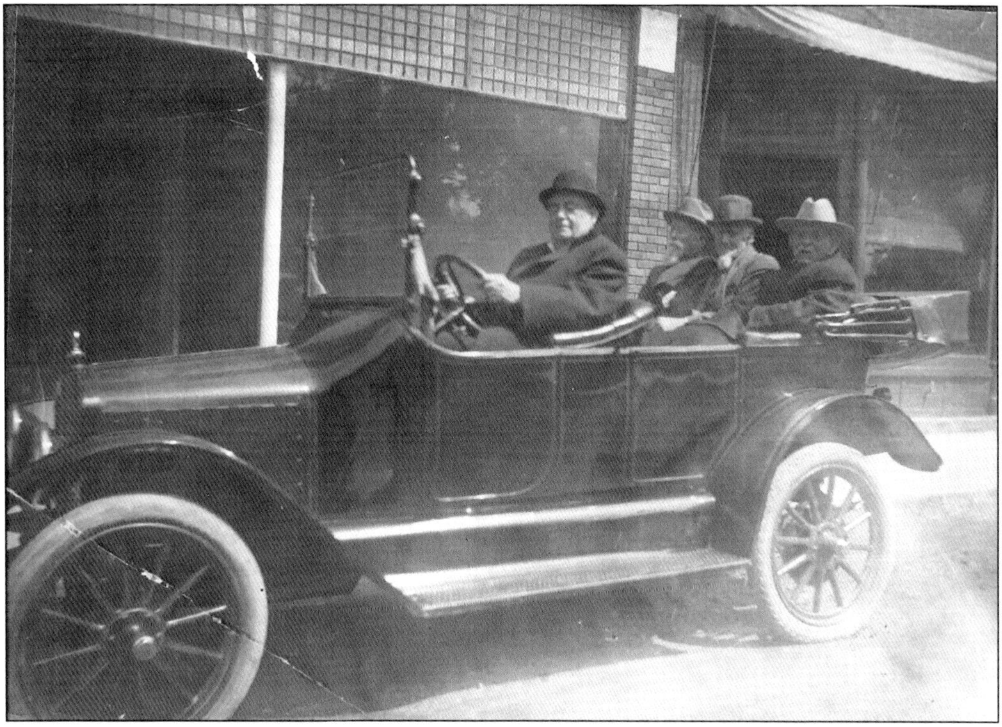

SUNDAY VISIT, 1915. The *Chesterton Tribune* reported that the four men in the above photograph "made the pilgrimage to Furnessville, Sunday, May 9, 1915 to pay their respects to Octogenarian E.L. Furness." The car, parked on Broadway, is thought to be a Studebaker. H.L. Cooper Sr. is driving the car with Theodore Schultz, John Johnson, and George Shaner in the back seat.

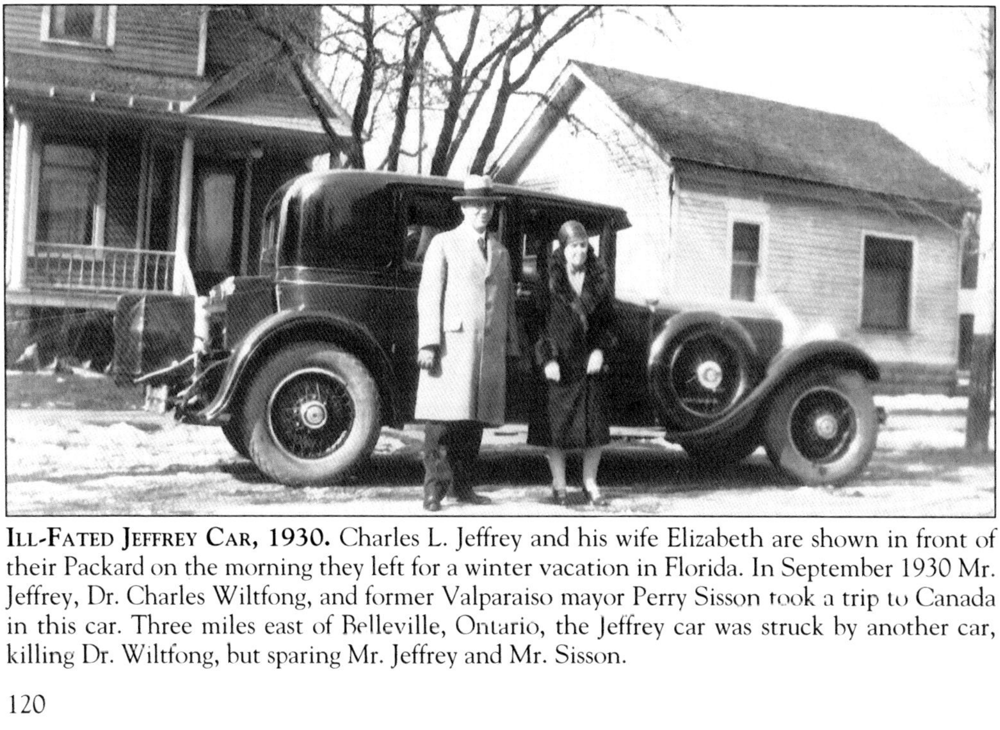

ILL-FATED JEFFREY CAR, 1930. Charles L. Jeffrey and his wife Elizabeth are shown in front of their Packard on the morning they left for a winter vacation in Florida. In September 1930 Mr. Jeffrey, Dr. Charles Wiltfong, and former Valparaiso mayor Perry Sisson took a trip to Canada in this car. Three miles east of Belleville, Ontario, the Jeffrey car was struck by another car, killing Dr. Wiltfong, but sparing Mr. Jeffrey and Mr. Sisson.

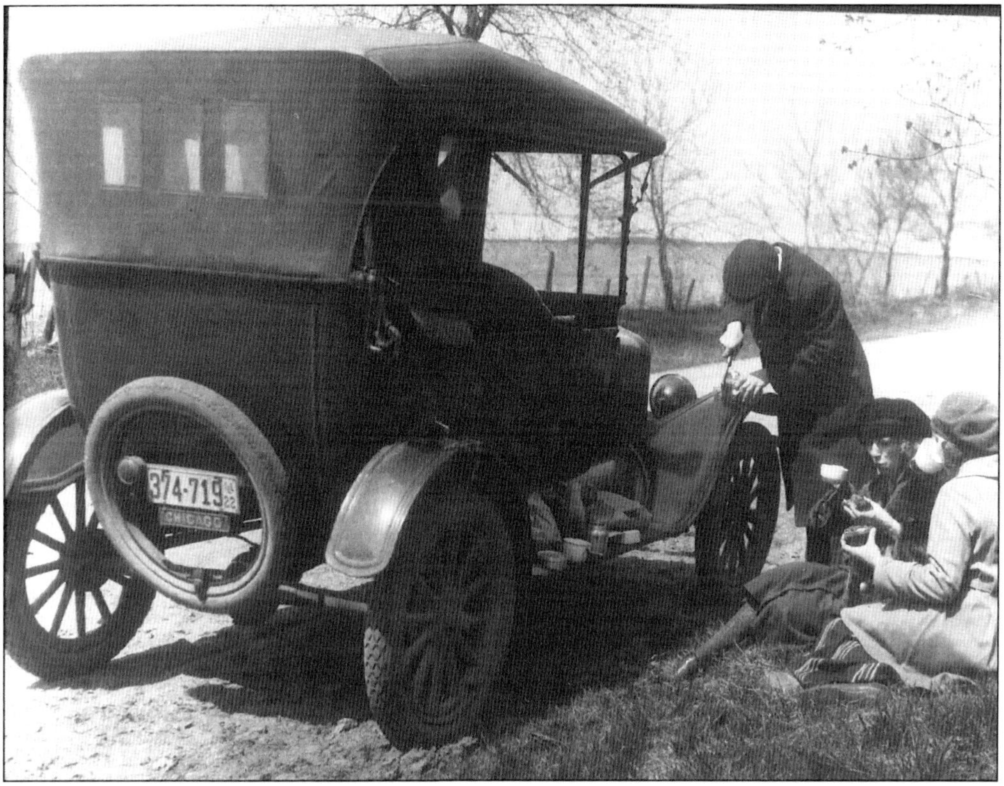

ARTHUR ANDERSON, PHOTOGRAPHER. The above photograph and the three that follow were all taken by local photographer Arthur Anderson in 1922. At the time Anderson was living in Chicago, but traveled throughout the region to photograph scenes of nature and early automobile touring and camping. In the above photograph the woman on the right, thought to be Mrs. Anderson, is seen enjoying a running board picnic with friends. (Arthur Anderson photograph.)

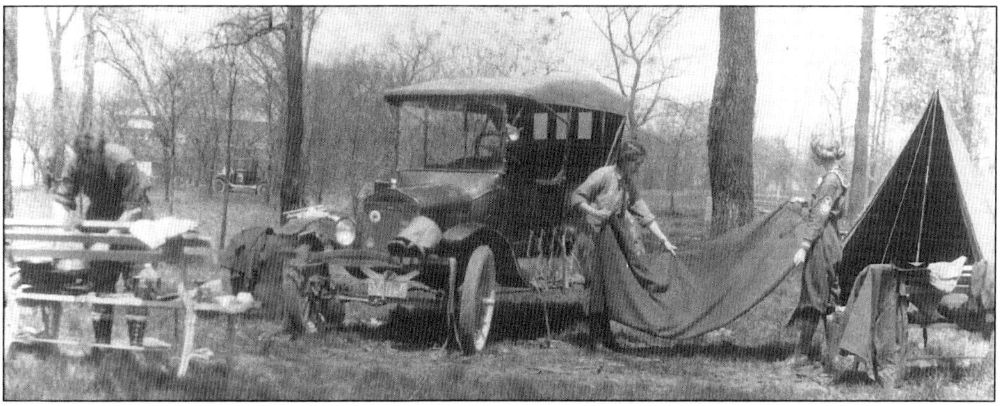

MODEL-T FORD, 1921. As cars became more affordable in the teens and '20s, people of all ages took to the road in Model-Ts like the 1921 Ford touring car seen in the above two photographs. In spite of bad roads and infrequent gas pumps, early motorists found camping a pleasurable alternative to traditional hotel accommodations. Note the Chicago Motor Club emblem on the front of the car. (Arthur Anderson photograph.)

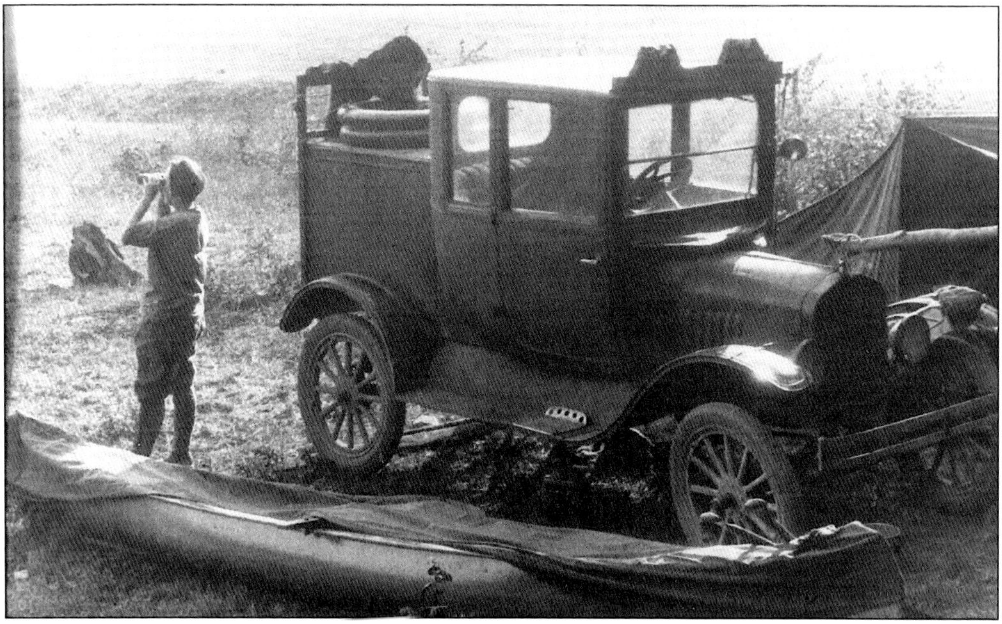

Model-T Coupe, c. 1922. This camping scene shows what is thought to be the Anderson's *c.* 1922 Model-T coupe. The two-seater is equipped with a storage compartment and a canoe rack, as the Andersons were avid canoeists. Anderson and his wife, Ruth, who met as members of the Prairie Club, married at dawn in a Furnessville blowout in June 1922. (Arthur Anderson photograph.)

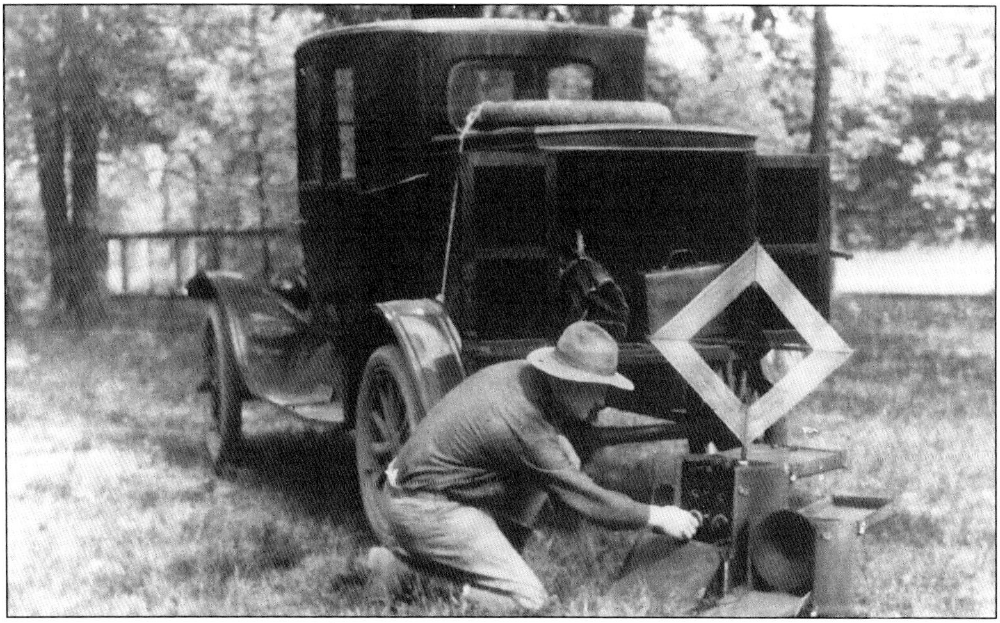

Early Portable Radio. In addition to photography, Arthur Anderson was also very interested in radio technology. In the above photograph he is seen adjusting what appears to be a homemade radio of the time. Powered by either a series of dry cells or a storage battery, it featured a square antenna made of copper wire and a small loudspeaker, an advance over earlier sets that used earphones. (Arthur Anderson photograph.)

WAUGH BROTHERS GARAGE, CHESTERTON. Edward and William Waugh are seen outside their automobile garage about 1920. Located at the corner of Grant and Calumet and built by Henry Gotens, it also housed the Chesterton Hall, the site of many town meetings and dances. According to family tradition, Ed once repaired a truck driven by one of Al Capone's gangsters during Prohibition, and was paid with an Elgin pocket-watch, which is still in the possession of a descendant.

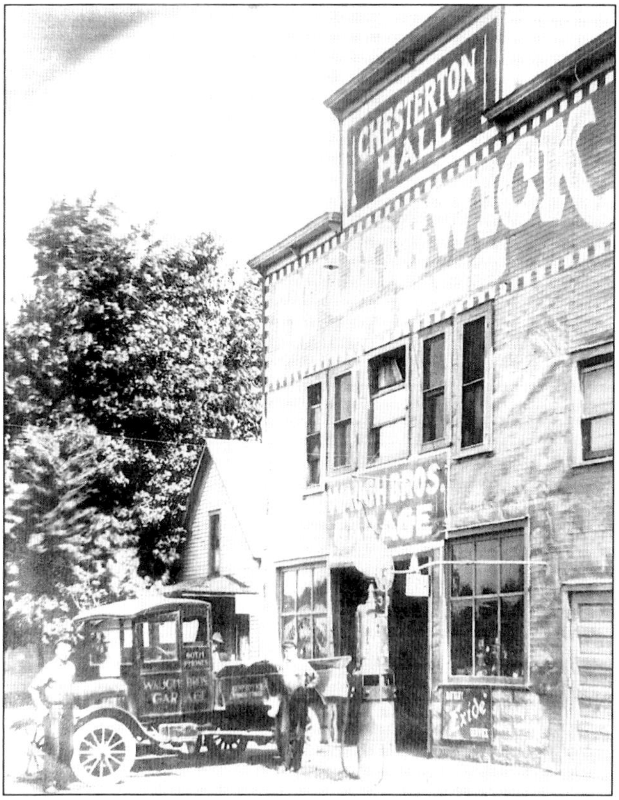

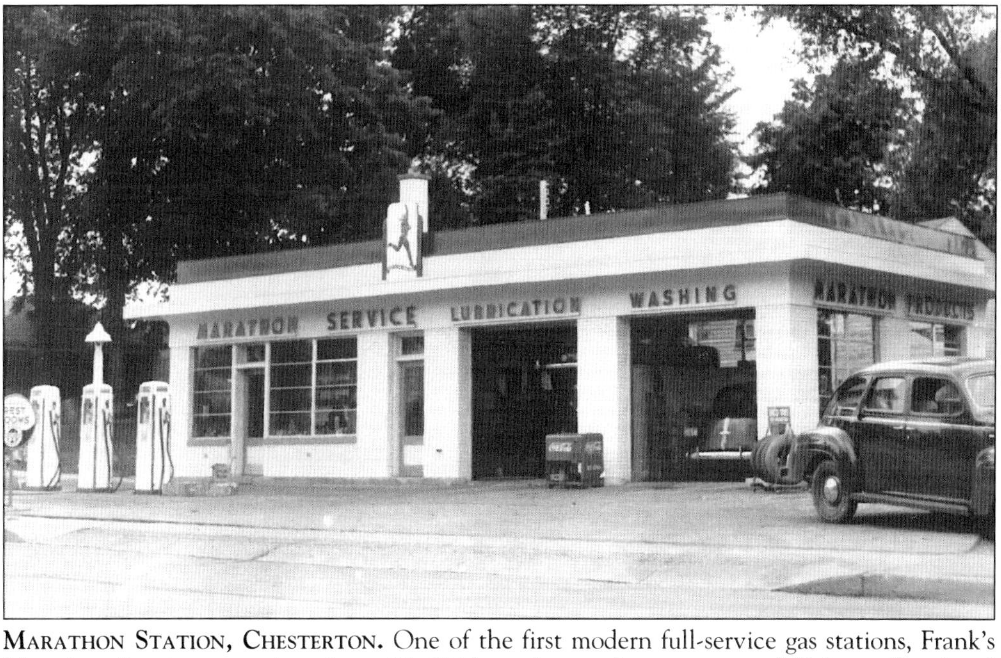

MARATHON STATION, CHESTERTON. One of the first modern full-service gas stations, Frank's Marathon Service opened on June 13, 1941, at the northwest corner of Calumet Road and West Indiana Avenue, on the site now occupied by the Westchester Library Service Center. Note the vintage Coca-Cola cooler in front of the station.

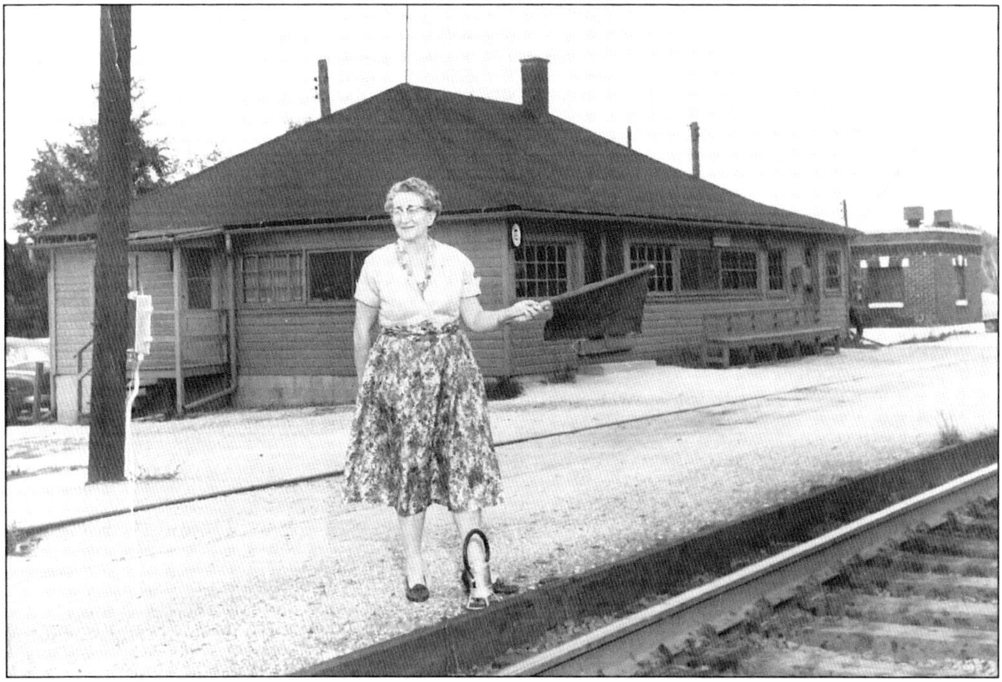

Ruth Leach, Tremont South Shore Station. Ruth Leach served as agent for the Tremont South Shore Station from the 1920s to the early 1960s when the Tremont Station was closed and demolished. She and her husband, Charles, raised their two sons in an apartment in the rear of the station. She is shown with the flag and lantern, which she used to signal to trains for unscheduled stops at Tremont. (Courtesy *Post-Tribune*.)

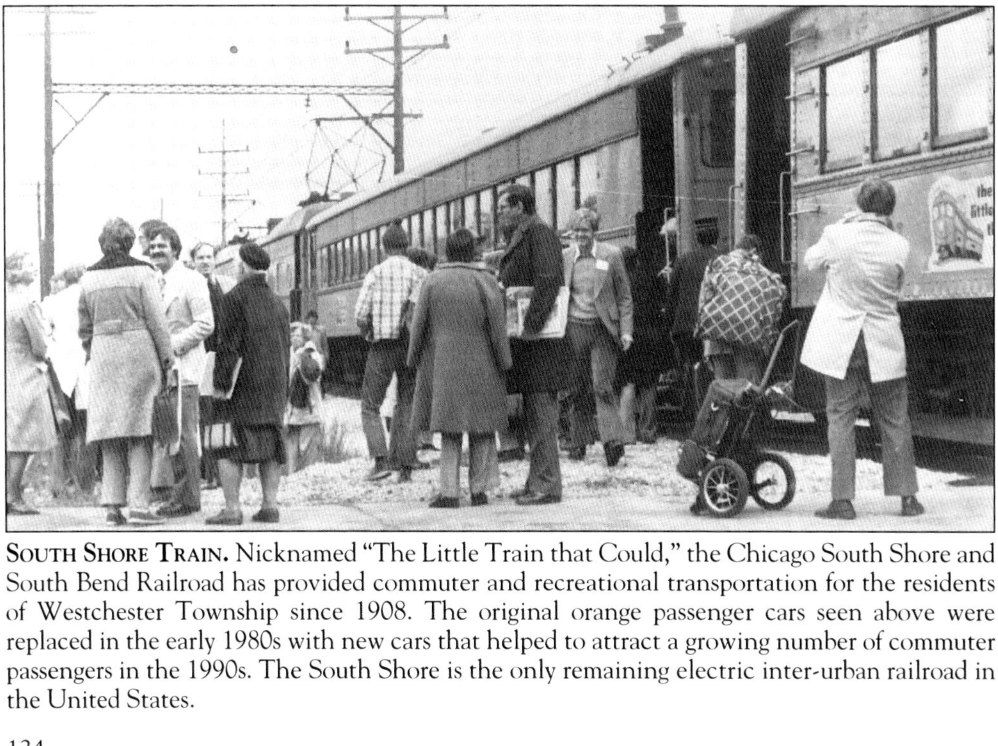

South Shore Train. Nicknamed "The Little Train that Could," the Chicago South Shore and South Bend Railroad has provided commuter and recreational transportation for the residents of Westchester Township since 1908. The original orange passenger cars seen above were replaced in the early 1980s with new cars that helped to attract a growing number of commuter passengers in the 1990s. The South Shore is the only remaining electric inter-urban railroad in the United States.

Photograph Contributors

We would like to thank the individuals and institutions who loaned or donated their photographs for this book. We apologize for any omissions from the following list.

Bethlehem Lutheran Church
Genoa Borg
Charlotte Brechner
Burns Harbor Park Department
Mary I. Byrne
The Calumet Archives at Indiana University Northwest
Carol Cherepko
Libby Conn
Chesterton-Porter Rotary Club
The *Chesterton Tribune*
The Chicago Historical Society
Marjory Crawford
Candy Davison
Jeannette DeKoker
The Dune Acres Historical Commission
R. Walter Erickson
Jeanne Gland
Ed Gustafson
Lillian E. Hall
Woods Halley
The Hokanson Family
Hugh and Eva Hopkins
Indiana Dunes National Lakeshore
Adeline Janowski
Elzene Johnson
Howard Johnson
John Johnson
Beulah Smith Kimberlin
Evelyn Komenas
Margaret Larson
Liberty Bible Church
Fran Meyer
Patricia L. Mitchell
Irene Nelson
Pauline Poparad
Porter County Parks and Recreation Dept.
The *Post Tribune*
The Prairie Club Archives
Saint Mary-of-the-Woods College
Mildred E. Sibbrell
Debi Smith Simanski
Tom Smith
A. Henry Studebaker
I. Jo. Summers
Don Swoverland
The Tittle Family
Nancy Vaillancourt
The Whalers Family
Ray Wesley
Betty Wisemann
Harry Wistrand

INDEX